The Politics of Prudence

Russell Kirk

REGNERY GATEWAY
Washington, D.C.

Regnery Gateway™ is a trademark of Salem Communications
Holding Corporation
Regnery® is a registered trademark and its colophon is a trademark
of Salem Communications Holding Corporation

Cataloging-in-Publication data on file with the Library of Congress

ISBN: 978-1-68451-531-8
eISBN: 978-1-68451-634-6

Published in the United States by
Regnery Gateway, an Imprint of
Regnery Publishing
A Division of Salem Media Group
Washington, D.C.
www.Regnery.com

Manufactured in the United States of America

10 9 8 7 6 5 4 3 2 1

Books are available in quantity for promotional or premium use.
For information on discounts and terms, please visit our website:
www.Regnery.com

To my four daughters—Monica, Cecilia, Felicia, and Andrea—now embarking hopefully upon the turbulent sea of modern discontents. May they steer clear of Scylla and Charybdis! Emulating Yeats, I set strong ghosts to watch over them.

Contents

Acknowledgements

Chapters I through XVII and the Epilogue of this book are founded upon lectures delivered to the Heritage Foundation, in Washington, on various occasions over the past five years. Chapter XVIII originated as a lecture to the Shavano Institute of Hillsdale College. Miss Kristen Sifert, Miss Eileen Balajadia, Mr. Matthew Davis, and Mr. Alan Cornett—all Fellows of the Marguerite Eyer Wilbur Foundation—much assisted me in preparation of the index to this volume.

Acknowledgments

[text illegible]

Introduction to the 2023 Edition

Michael P. Federici

O riginally published in 1993, about a year before his death, *The Politics of Prudence* is a collection of seventeen lectures given by Russell Kirk to the Heritage Foundation in Washington, D.C., one lecture delivered at Hillsdale College, and an epilogue. The purposes of the lectures, which were delivered over a period of five years, are, first, to define conservatism by contrasting it to ideology, including ideological conceptions of conservative thinking such as libertarianism, neoconservatism, and populism; second, to identify important thinkers, books, principles, and events that embody and reflect conservative thinking, culture, and politics; and, third, to speculate about the future of conservatism as the American heritage that Kirk described in *The Roots of American Order* and the conservative tradition that he evoked in *The Conservative Mind* faded from memory and were being replaced by ideology.

The lectures are designed for young conservatives working in one capacity or another in the capital or college students inclined toward conservative politics. After half a century at the center of the conservative intellectual movement, Kirk attempted to guide young conservatives away from ideological politics and the temptation to turn conservatism into a civil religion. He encouraged them to develop the habits of mind that were evident in generations of conservative exemplars. Conservatism, he argued, is a disposition of character rather than a collection of reified, abstract political doctrines. It is the rejection of ideology rather than the exercise of it. One might think that in 1993, after the Reagan presidency and the proliferation of conservative politics, publications, ideas, and media, those involved in conservative politics would know the characteristics and meaning of their political identity. Yet, the popularity and political success of conservatism did more to obscure its meaning than clarify it. A rush of politicians and commentators, often with significantly different political and philosophical beliefs, embraced the label "conservative" without knowing much about its intellectual roots. The result was widespread confusion, especially in the media, about the meaning of conservatism. *The Politics of Prudence* is an attempt to clarify the meaning of conservatism by associating it with the historical figures, experiences, and companion ideas that gave it intellectual and political life. The book is an exercise in conservative self-understanding and self-identity.

Kirk understood that there were competing conceptions of conservatism; what is referred to as "conservatism" in the popular media is a conglomeration of three or four variants of conservatism that both converge and diverge. He draws clear lines of demarcation between traditional, libertarian, neoconservative, and populist schools of thinking while advocating for a Burkean conservatism rooted in the classical and Judeo-Christian traditions. This type of conservatism formed its political identity in opposition to the French Revolution and the rise of radical and revolutionary ideological movements that centralize power as the means to escape the limits of the human condition. The inclination to preserve the wisdom of the ages, the accumulated experience and insights of past generations, when it is under assault from the forces of political, social, and intellectual radicalism is at the core of the conservative disposition. Kirk's enumeration of conservative thinkers, books, and events includes ancient statesmen like Cicero and Marcus Aurelius; British authors and statesmen such as Edmund Burke, Benjamin Disraeli, Sir Walter Scott, and Samuel Johnson; communist dissidents Alexander Solzhenitsyn and Pope John Paul II; and American figures such as John Randolph of Roanoke, Orestes Brownson, Nathaniel Hawthorne, James Fenimore Cooper, and Irving Babbitt. These figures are unified by resistance to radical change, adherence to the politics of prudence, and commitment to a moral order that obligates both city and soul and that makes politics the art of the possible.

Before comparing and contrasting variants of conservatism, Kirk explains why it is not an ideology. While ideology assumes a high level of certainty, if not possession of absolute truth, conservatism accepts the limits of human reason, virtue, and politics. Human understanding is clouded by passion, self-deception, self-interest, and moral imperfection. Consequently, humility restrains the conservative from ideological pronouncements about the end of history, gnostic[1] claims of justice, or political schemes to perfect human nature and society. Politics, Kirk repeats throughout his lectures, is the art of the possible. It requires prudential judgment that is derived from adherence to historical experience embodied in tradition, custom, and convention.

Conservatives aim to preserve and apply the wisdom of the ages, not change the constitution of being; they do not attempt to escape from the limits of the human condition but use them to distinguish between realistic and utopian expectations. Conservative politics is inspired by modesty, not conceit. Ideology is immodest and utopian at its extremes; it claims to know how to implement final solutions to age-old problems, to end war, tyranny, poverty, inequality, and injustice generally. The conservative, Kirk notes, understands that the human condition limits the extent to which justice can be realized on earth. The politics of prudence assumes that imperfection is a

---

1 Gnostics claim to possess absolute knowledge that reveals the hidden secrets of history and the structure of reality. This secret knowledge, gnosis, is only known to the leader of a political, quasi-religious, or intellectual movement and a small group of devoted followers. Gnostics assume that gnosis can be used to change, if not perfect, human nature and human society. For a detailed analysis of modern gnosticism, see Eric Voegelin, *Science, Politics and Gnosticism* (Chicago: Regnery Gateway, 1968).

permanent part of human character and human society. We grope toward a tolerable order that accepts imperfection, the devil we know, while avoiding greater evils, the devil we do not know. Preservation of civilization, as imperfect as it is, is the conservative's work. Kirk reminds us of Edmund Burke's insight that preservation requires change. Conservatives are not anti-quarians, mindlessly preserving tradition without regard for the exigencies of particular circumstances or the need to re-form. Inspired by moral imagination, they attempt to reconcile permanence and change, avoiding radical and revolutionary change that ignores the limits of reality and makes a bad situation worse. Prudent reform depends on reconciliation of cir-cumstances, the limits of politics, and what Aristotle calls the good. While the work of reform may occur in the domain of politics, statesmen prepare for it through the cultivation of a quality of imagination and character that occurs in families, schools, churches, and communities. Culture, not politics or political power, is the first concern of the conservative.

Kirk's insistence that politics is the art of the possible relates to his first and foundational principle that a transcendent moral order obligates and limits human beings in private and public life. How do we know what is possible in given circumstances? How do humans come to know the obligations and limits of the moral order? Historical experience is a guide to what is possible, but more than historical knowledge is required to prudently apply that knowledge to existing circumstances. Circumstances change, and with them the possible changes as well. Discovering the possible requires attunement to the moral order, and the moral imagination to both perceive life as it is (as opposed to the impossible dream) and to conceive of what is possible and prudent at a given time and place. Statesmanship requires creativity and conformity to the order of being. A prudent politics requires use of sail, anchor, and sextant. In short, the conservative disposition requires that historical experience be used to orient the statesman to what is possible and prudent in politics. Because prudent statesmanship is not as simple as imitating the past, it requires imagination to reconstitute old truths in new circumstances, what Kirk refers to as the reconciliation of permanence and change. In foreign affairs, for example, the statesman must avoid the rigidity of ideological politics that is interventionist or isolationist. Rather, prudent statesmanship should be what it needs to be in the circumstances, sometimes requiring intervention and sometimes restraint from intervention. What is consistent in conservative statesmanship is following the path of prudence.

Law and policy should not require what the moral order deems impossible. Experience is a guide in discovering the limits of politics and the possible. Ideology dictates that policy and law reify abstract rights, that liberties, for example, be absolute and immune from the exigencies of time, circumstance, place, and the limits of human nature. Ideology claims a monopoly of virtue and truth. It sees no need for compromise, and it recognizes little or nothing of value in the claims and interests of opponents. The conservative, Kirk asserts, is in the "habit of dining with the opposition."

Among Kirk's conservative principles is variety. Ideology is monistic. It tends to see universality and the good in stagnant, reified ways uncomplicated by circumstances. It craves uniformity even when it advocates diversity. It aims to enforce through centralized power uniform policy and thinking because it claims to possess the one solution that applies universally. Conservatism champions organic pluralism because it recognizes that universality manifests in diverse, particular ways. It favors decentralized power that enables local communities to find the true, the good, and the beautiful in their particular circumstances. The consequence is a mixture of policies across state and local communities. Kirk understood the temptation to nationalize politics, to control the reins of the federal government and impose uniform "conservative" policies on communities across the nation. Such an approach to politics violates Kirk's principle of voluntary community; it moves the country toward involuntary collectivism. To maintain prudent restraints on power, the decentralized structure of the American constitutional system created by the Framers needs to be maintained. Conservatives need to resist the temptation of a politics of conservative progressivism.

It is with these assumptions and principles in mind that Kirk rejects ideological forms of conservatism, including libertarianism, neoconservatism, and populism. Libertarians share with traditional conservatives a prejudice toward smaller, decentralized government and a modest foreign policy. Yet, many libertarians do not appreciate the challenges that stem from an imperfect human nature. They are far too confident that eliminating most constraints on individuals will maximize liberty without unintended consequences to order. Libertarians share too much philosophical ground with Jean Jacques Rousseau, who assumes that human nature is good and that conventions are the cause of injustice and evil. The conservative argues that humans will collapse into disorder when liberated from traditional constraints. Kirk crystallizes Edmund Burke's prudent view of liberty. Individuals are fit for liberty in proportion to their ability to put moral chains on their passions. The more ethically self-restrained they are, the less outer restraint they require. Yet, the balance of liberty and restraint cannot be predetermined apart from circumstances. The prudent judgment of statesmen and cultural leaders is required to find the right balance between liberty and order. Conservatives reject a priori politics, another name for ideology.

The neoconservative vision of politics contrasts with Kirk's view of conservatism. It aims to replace the American constitutional republic with a global empire intent on transforming the world into a system of democratic nation-states. To create such a global empire, power must be concentrated in the federal government and in the executive branch. In the neoconservative view, most restraints should be removed from the foreign affairs powers of the federal government, and, as was evident in George W. Bush's foreign policy, the United States should aggressively use its military to topple nondemocratic regimes and engage in nation building to convert conquered nations into viable American-style democracies. Kirk, however, argues that to build a global empire abroad is to destroy the republic at home. Organizing the world into uniform regime types defies the conservative commitment to variety. Just as state and local communities in the United States should have the autonomy to adjust their laws and policies to the particularities of their circumstances and cultures, nations should be free to create the regime types that fit their circumstances and cultures. Neoconservatives share traditional conservatives' opposition to communism and radical global ideological movements. When nations that are animated by such ideologies behave in ways that are contrary to American interests and security, the conservative response is prudent statesmanship, not the ideology of American empire. The fire of ideology should not be fought with the fire of counter-ideology.

Ideologies of all types overpromise and underdeliver because they are out of sync with human nature and historical experience. They see politics as the art of the impossible. Populism, like libertarianism and neoconservatism, is also inconsistent with traditional conservatism's sober view of politics. It attempts to replace the wisdom of the ages, embodied in tradition and convention, with the momentary will of the undeliberative and unchecked majority. The voice of the people, Kirk is quick to note, is not the voice of God. It is a mix of interests, passions, and beliefs that cannot substitute for the judgment of prudential statesmen. Kirk favors G. K. Chesterton's democracy of the dead, the Burkean community of generations dead, living, and yet to be born. The living generation does well to learn from the experiences of past generations and to consider its obligations to future generations. Continuity between generations requires the primacy of the wisdom of the ages to the wisdom of the age. Populism, by contrast, elevates the passion of the moment, as if human beings can navigate the complexities of political life without historical knowledge or example. It replaces the prudent statesman with the demagogue, who like Joe McCarthy or Huey Long incites popular passions for short-term political gain.

The appearance of a new edition of Russell Kirk's *The Politics of Prudence* is an indication that it remains relevant to current conservatives. In fact, the state of American politics suggests that conservatives would do well to heed Kirk's wisdom and warnings about American culture and politics. Since the original publication of the book, conservatives have too often succumbed to the temptation to think of themselves as advocates of a national ideology that should be imposed on the nation by laws and courts following election victories. They are losing touch with the principles articulated by Kirk in this book, that politics is the art of the possible and the art of compromise, that culture prepares the way for politics, and that the imperfectability of human beings limits the possibilities of politics, especially in foreign affairs. The conservative identity crisis that engendered *The Politics of Prudence* has deepened. Recalling to memory the historical and theoretical meaning of conservatism is a first step in the recovery of prudent political conservatism. Learning to orient the conduct of politics to the principles, wisdom, and spirit of the conservative mind and imagination is the second step to a renewed political conservatism. When conservatives sound less like advocates of a fixed ideology and more like prudent statesmen, Kirk's influence, and the aim of the book—enlargement of the first principles of conservatism and awakening the conservative imagination—will be evident.

Introduction to the 2004 Edition

Mark C. Henrie

I t is a commonplace that the defining characteristic of that characteristically modern literary form, the novel, is a concern for the revelation of the ordinary man's inner life. Hence the frequent use, beginning early in the novel's history, of the device of diaries or letters (for example, in Richardson's *Clarissa* or Defoe's *Robinson Crusoe*), culminating eventually in the stream-of-consciousness style of Joyce. This internal focus of attention stands in contrast to the classical concern of the epic with the external deeds of the *extraordinary* man.

The modern psyche hungers to identify itself with a *protagonist*, and ashamedly eschews the implicit judgment against the prosaic rendered by the exemplary life of the *hero.* The modern self seeks to have its undemanding gestures of sentimentality confirmed as natural, even praiseworthy, and expects to see even bourgeois virtue revealed as hypocritical inauthenticity. In its critical mood, the modern self seeks to rummage beneath the public deeds of conventionally heroic figures to discover below the "real," all-too-human, private man. Thereby, the modern self finds reassurance in its own mediocrity and moral failure. The tell-all biography is a special delectation for moderns.

In *The Sword of Imagination* (1995), his autobiography and his last book, the late Russell Kirk (1918-1994) completed a lifetime of chastening the unruly passions and interests of modern men. In that book, a reader in search of confessional display and melancholy introspection is quickly confounded, as the dean of the conservative intellectual movement in America recounts a life of much incident, both public and private, a life, as he calls it, of "literary conflict." And yet, as written, it remains a life in which the figure of Kirk stands at a distance, just beyond our grasp in his decorous equanimity. It is a life of formal reserve, propriety in the midst of domestic happiness; and it is a life that ends in quiet gratitude for the graces which are acknowledged to be such, unmerited. So little does Kirk's memoir meet our modern expectation of the form that we are perplexed: why go to the trouble to write a memoir, only to hide ones "authentic" self behind a mask of eighteenth-century pious platitudes?

Most extraordinarily, a modern reader is confounded by Kirk's decision to write his memoirs in the *third person*, thereby definitively frustrating the hunger for novelistic self-disclosure. Surely—one can hear the irritated objection—this is simply impossible, this is affectation gone too far. To some critics, this last stylistic choice constituted a kind of proof that Kirk could be dismissed as no thinker, but only a poseur practicing an elaborate form of the "Tory harrumph." The style of Kirk's prose—the meandering sentences, the unattributed references to Bunyan, the promiscuous use of aphorisms and epigrams, the disengagement from details, the sheer, untroubled confidence of the historical and theoretical assertions—is certainly a provocation to the contemporary academic mind. His ornate prose is often a stumbling block even for those who come to Kirk's writings with an open mind. But rather than dismissing the message because of the medium, perhaps it would be wiser to consider Kirk's provoking style in a different light—as a prompting to *inquiry.*

For there remains a larger "Kirk problem" to be resolved, a decade after his death; it is a problem about categorization. What exactly was the nature of Kirk's project? What *kind* of thinker and writer was he? *The Conservative Mind* (1953), Kirk's major achievement and the book that gave the modern American conservative movement its very name, is at one level a work of historical scholarship. But as it purports to be a history of normative political theories, a normative dimension cannot be ignored. And when we examine the rest of Kirk's large corpus, we find familiar essays, reminiscences, literary criticism, local histories and grand histories, character sketches—even ghost stories and textbooks—and in this book, a collection of lectures, all but one first delivered at the Heritage Foundation, one of Washington's premier public policy think tanks. With little variation, the style is always the same. What was Kirk attempting to effect with his idiosyncratic writing? To what was he responding? How might his writings constitute a response?

Even if we restrict ourselves to Kirk's scholarship, ought we to consider *The Conservative Mind* as a work of political theory? If so, it is political theory of an eccentric sort. The book begins with an encapsulation of "conservative thought" in six canons. But these appear to be yoked by no logical necessity, and none of them has more than an indirect relationship to political forms and institutions. The canons have none of the reductive clarity of the terms in which one can consider the development of, say, liberalism: parliamentary representation, the protection of rights, the priority of property, etc. As Kirk moves through his account, it is even evident that various of his conservative minds violate one or another of the canons.

Ought we instead to consider *The Conservative Mind* as a work of intellectual history? Again, it would be a very odd contribution to that literature. Kirk troubles himself not at all with demonstrating chains of intellectual influence, content with adducing something like a family resemblance among the thinkers he discusses. The negative work of careful discrimination, so necessary for intellectual history, appears only sporadically. The particularities of historical circumstances tend to fall away as Kirk works up a conservative archetype in that extended "essay in definition."

Rather than as either a political theorist or as an intellectual historian, Kirk considered himself to be a "man of letters," going so far as to have this inscribed on his tombstone in Mecosta, Michigan. This is a term which has nearly disappeared from current usage. While there is now a cottage industry of journalists decrying the depletion of our stock of "public intellectuals," the "man of letters" is so distant from contemporary experience that we can scarcely conjure any image of the type. The man of letters is a writer: but what kind of writer? In its imprecision and deliberate archaism, the term seems merely to keep Kirk at a distance. But it also invites us further into the question of how Kirk understood his work—and how we can understand it as well. The place to begin is *The Conservative Mind*, which was first published half a century ago.

■ ■ ■

The intellectual milieu in which Kirk's thick book appeared has been frequently recounted, notably in George Nash's definitive study, *The Conservative Intellectual Movement in America Since 1945*.[1] In 1950, the Columbia literary critic Lionel Trilling had written that in the United States of his day, "liberalism is not only the dominant but even the sole intellectual tradition." By 1955, the Harvard political theorist Louis Hartz would trump Trilling, contending that, in fact, there never had been nor could be anything but a Lockean liberal tradition in America, because America had been bourgeois from the beginning. Hartz's maxim was, *no feudalism, no socialism,* but a necessary corollary—unstated, because so patently obvious—was: *no true conservatism either.* Daniel Bell's 1962 book, *The End of Ideology*—consisting of chapters written during the 1950s—captured well the spirit of this period. It was the *first*

---

1 Wilmington, DE: ISI Books, 1996. First published 1976.

"end of history," with America's elites unable to imagine anything but the never-ending advance of various "syntheses" of
liberal and socialist progressivisms.

Kirk's book struck a perfectly discordant note. In *The
Conservative Mind*'s first paragraph, he contends that his age
is one not of liberal triumph, but rather one of both liberal
and radical disintegration. The yoking together in his indictment of liberalism and radicalism—and thus, of both Locke
and Rousseau—is significant.[2] In 1950s America, the most
recent challenge to the leftward "progress" of American society had been the opposition of certain elements of the capitalist classes to the New Deal. Their defense of an older form of
"classical liberalism" in the face of the emerging welfare state
had become equated in the American mind with "conservatism." But Kirk was striking out on a quite different path, rejecting the view that the historically available alternatives in
America ranged only from a more classical to a latter-day
liberalism. Most tendentiously, Kirk would identify even the
moderate cocktail of liberalism and the welfare state—which

---

2 It is also significant that in *The Conservative Mind*, Karl Marx is almost everywhere
a marginal presence. There are many who would consider the American
conservative movement to be a Cold War artifact. But the themes of "Cold War
conservatism"—the critique of the planned economy and collectivism, the
championing of "freedom" and "individualism"—are almost wholly absent from
Kirk's foundational work. Revolutionary Bolshevism is not among the book's
dominant themes, but the French Revolution and the industrial revolution are,
and they are frequently considered in a common light. Of all American
conservatives, it was the followers of Kirk who were least theoretically disoriented
by the astonishing collapse of communism in 1989-1991.

to Bell signaled the end of ideology—as itself a form of ideology. This was a portentous claim.

In the immediate aftermath of the Second World War, and prompted in no small part by the work of Hannah Arendt, many Western intellectuals of the Left and Right had come to appreciate the danger of *totalitarianism*, a form of ideological extremism that undertook to transform human nature through politics—with the disastrous results we now understand so well. But liberalism's great boast had always been that it founded itself upon, and best adequated to, human nature—once that nature was shorn of illusions and superstition. To the liberal mind, one might even say that if ideology is defined as a project to achieve a utopian intellectual abstraction, then liberalism is the opposite of an ideology.

To Kirk, however, steeped in history, the enormities of the eighteenth-century French Revolution were as near to hand as those of the Bolshevik and National Socialist Revolutions of the twentieth century. Kirk saw that a claim to be founded systematically upon certain "facts" of human nature was no unique property of liberalism but was shared by all ideologies. Socialism could claim to be a truer adequation than liberalism to the natural equality of human beings, and National Socialism to natural inequality. Communism understood itself as a kind of "natural science" of the movements of human history. Each proceeded by a rationalist reduction of real human beings to the ideological "construction" of an abstract human nature, together with the institutions appropriate to that abstraction. Kirk's response was the remarkable claim that *conservatism* was the true "negation of ideology" and, thus, the genuine (and largely unexplored) alternative in the modern age.

If the modern world is a largely liberal "construction" rather than a liberal "revelation (and liberation) of nature," then a conservative must proceed by way of excavation and recovery. And if this liberal construction represents a "leap" out of a putatively superceded world of "tradition," then there is a burden to demonstrate that an alternative conservative tradition persists as a historical availability. That is what Kirk was attempting in *The Conservative Mind*, a book which represents itself, in the first instance, as a scholarly recovery of the "underside" of the history of modern social and political thought. Kirk would give voice to those who participated in the "great dissent" from the modern project—but in particular, to those whose sense of political responsibility prevented their own fall into a mere counter-ideology of reaction. At the opposite pole from ideological politics stands *the politics of prudence*.

In seeking to grasp the substance of a political or social idea, it is useful to examine that which is negated. Who are the subjects of actively disdainful treatment in *The Conservative Mind*? There are, first of all, the rationalists of the French Enlightenment: Condorcet, Turgot, Voltaire, their English disciple Tom Paine, and at least half of Jefferson. There are the utilitarians: Bentham and both Mills. There is Comte, in a category of his own. And there are the naturalistic romantics: Emerson, and above all, everywhere, Rousseau. All are understood as partisans of *innovation*. Against these, Kirk assembles his conservative tradition, beginning with the Burke of the *Reflections* and proceeding through John Adams, John Randolph and John C. Calhoun, Sir Walter Scott and Samuel Taylor Coleridge, Macaulay and Tocqueville, Disraeli and Newman, and so on (after a rather dispiriting set of figures around the turn of the twentieth century) to Irving Babbitt, Paul Elmer More, and George Santayana—later, to T. S. Eliot. These represent the "party of order," the defenders of "tradition"—itself understood as the full truth about man which is trimmed away in ideological abstraction. A politics of prudence does justice to those truths which are known uniquely in tradition.

As can readily be seen from even this partial recounting, Kirk's genealogy was not only an act of recovery, or rehabilitation, of a set of marginalized conservative minds. He was also engaged in reinterpreting or (re)claiming certain well regarded thinkers who, it would seem, might just as plausibly be claimed for "the other side"—such as Macaulay, or Newman, or Coleridge. Kirk would bring to light certain dimensions of their thought that had been deliberately obscured in the "standard account" of the progress of modern thought. Where others might dismiss the conservative elements of their thought as forgivable lapses and fasten instead upon more progressive views deemed to be "central," Kirk's evaluation of the ambiguous evidence was exactly the reverse. Simply by bringing forward the conservative thoughts of minds that might have been "half-liberal," Kirk was confronting his readers with the deepest biases of the intellectual history of his day.

Now, during the past half century the progress of *Wissenschaft* in the American universities has piled monograph upon monograph about virtually every major and minor figure in European and American history, including those found in *The Conservative Mind*. We have also experienced "the revival of political philosophy" in several important "schools," bringing into existence a particularly sophisticated generation of readers in this field. And one frequently finds a skeptical prejudice against Kirk, since he did not hold a regular university appointment or participate in the routines of academic life. As a result, a number of pointed questions have been raised about Kirk's scholarly account of the conservative tradition, and these questions are often pressed in the manner of an indictment. For example, it is sometimes observed that Burke was a lifelong Whig rather than a Tory: can he therefore be considered a conservative in the robust sense that Kirk attributes to him? Does not John Adams's rejection of the canon and the feudal law demonstrate his fundamental lack of sympathy for the kinds of institutions for which Burke (and Kirk) had such solicitude? Conversely, was the Enlightenment really as dogmatic as Kirk claims? Are there not "conservative" strains among the *lumières*, and even in Rousseau? More generally, has Kirk really *recovered* a tradition? Or has he invented one?

Kirk's book actually compares quite favorably with the level of American scholarship of its period, a fact of which Kirk's most dismissive critics seem ignorant. And it remains a valuable corrective to misleading tendencies in even the best current scholarship. For example, in the deepest questions of political philosophy Americans in recent decades have typically oriented themselves with reference to German thinkers, an artifact of the Germanization of the American mind after the 1930s. But before the twentieth century, the Anglo-American world had only the slightest contact with German thought. Kirk's orientation with respect to French thinkers is surely a more defensible point of departure for understanding our history aright. Moreover, some of Kirk's apparently eccentric historical judgments, though now contrary to conventional wisdom, still show promise of one day gaining currency: for example, his view that Alexander Hamilton was an essentially backward-looking mercantilist, whereas John Adams, deep in his study of the ancients, had a surer grasp of the future problematics of American political economy.

Almost always, when Kirk's interpretations differ from "what we now know" it can be demonstrated that Kirk is aware of the excluded alternative; he has simply come to a different judgment. This is true, most significantly, in his treatment of Burke's Whiggery. Many students of political theory now tend to see Burke more as a statesman than as a philosopher, and if a (mere) statesman, then necessarily a statesmen operating within the political horizon "legislated" by a true philosopher. Locke was the great Whig philosopher, and he was the founder of modern liberal democracy. Thus, it is a mistake to discover in Burke, a Whig, any fundamental revolt against the modern world. Kirk, however, does not share the contemporary opinion about the supremacy of the philosophers: in fact, he clearly held that the *poets* are the true legislators of the world, identifying the better part of the twentieth century as "the age of Eliot." But Kirk also takes pains to show that despite his Whig political commitments, Burke in the *Reflections* "disavowed a great part of the principles of Locke." Conservatism after Burke owes "almost nothing" to Locke. These are strong, and carefully considered, claims.

Similarly, students of political theory who are wedded to the notion of the supremacy of the philosophers and who cannot find an adequately rigorous system in Burke have sought for a philosophical founder for modern conservatism elsewhere, thus implicitly questioning a central pillar of Kirk's achievement. Most frequently, attempts are made to find such a "true" founder in Hume or Hegel, both "respectable" philosophers. Kirk rejects them both, however, describing them as conservatives only "by chance." There is ample evidence in *The Conservative Mind* of Kirk's deliberation on sophisticated questions of historical and theoretical interpretation, but unlike most academic writing, this intellectual work is subdued in the text rather than highlighted. If we are to learn from Kirk, we must learn a different way of reading.

Kirk's claim concerning Burke's repudiation of Lockean principles brings to light another question, however. What can it mean for a thinker to reject Locke's principles while defending essentially Whig, or "Lockean," political institutions, as Burke apparently does? This question relates to a further objection to Kirk's presentation of the conservative tradition. Are not the thinkers that Kirk treats in his book primarily engaged in some form of social and cultural *critique*? Do they not, with only rare exception, fail to proffer any set of institutions which might stand as a concrete alternative to the "constructed" world of liberalism? When they do make arguments about institutions, Kirk's conservative minds seem to disagree as often as they agree, and Kirk in any event never organizes his discussion around constitutional issues. Lacking any evident institutional program, in what sense can Kirk's conservatism be understood as a form of *political* thought? We have returned to our original question. What kind of thinker was Kirk? What was he attempting to accomplish in his writing?

. . .

In a sense, we have also returned to the question of the style and the form of Kirk's writing. In *The Conservative Mind*, after a couple of cursory paragraphs to introduce his theme, we find Kirk digressing to tell a story, or rather to paint a personal vignette. He pauses to remark on Number 12, Arran Quay, in Dublin, the birthplace of Edmund Burke. Kirk, a would-be pilgrim, laments that the house was subsequently demolished in the name of progress—in its place stood a shabby government office building—so little did even the "conservative" Irish think to commemorate their great men. Here, Kirk evokes solicitude for a concrete heritage; he prompts and affirms a sentiment to conserve in opposition to the defining spirit of the age, innovative self-assurance; he sardonically deprecates the modern follies of the children of men. Before he has barely begun, he has already "wandered" far from scholarship. But such repeated digressions appear intrinsic to the structure of the book, and so, must be intrinsic to Kirk's purposes.

Despite his formal reserve, Kirk is everywhere a real presence in even his most scholarly writings, almost a "character" in the "story," and this presence became ever more prominent as he progressed in his career. The unexpectedly personal quality of Kirk's otherwise archaically formal prose has, it appears, never been given due consideration. Yet it is no exaggeration to say that it is the "figure" of Kirk, the "sage of Mecosta" speaking in his texts, that remains most vivid, most alive, to us today. Long after this or that judgment about a particular thinker is forgotten, long after the disciplined advance of academic inquiry has obscured the original insight of the arguments, what is remembered—and keenly so—is the elevated, dispassionate tone, the gothic refusal to streamline prose to meet the purported needs of "efficient" communication, the structure of a peculiar kind of Tory romantic sentiment that "would have given any number of neo-classical pediments for one poor battered gargoyle." What continues to insinuate is a certain sensibility, which is associated in Kirk's mind with the Burkean phrase, "the moral imagination." By the end of the 1950s, Kirk had himself become the icon of the conservative mind, but that mind seems to have concentrated itself in an effort to speak, usually quite indirectly, to the heart.

There is perhaps a precedent for writing of this kind, in the least likely of places: the works of Jean-Jacques Rousseau. The academic political theorists have lately taught us to appreciate the subtlety and penetration of Rousseau's philosophical arguments concerning the state of nature and the general will, republican virtue, and civil religion—the basic elements of Rousseau's explicitly political thought. But such sympathetic judgments are a quite recent development. Among his contemporaries, *The Social Contract* was thought to be Rousseau's least successful effort. Even the *philosophes* found his political writings to be little more than visionary fantasies. Nevertheless, Rousseau was a literary phenomenon. His *Confessions* and the *Emile* were international bestsellers of scandalously wide appeal. In both books Rousseau is himself a "character." And beyond the particular arguments, what was most memorable in these works (and most talked about in the salons) was "Jean-Jacques" himself, the sometime "Citizen of Geneva," now embodying a novel "virtue": the compassionate love of humanity.

As Clifford Orwin has nicely formulated it, whereas Machiavelli worked to construct "new modes and orders" in politics, Rousseau sought instead to insinuate "new moods and feelings" in the most private of spheres.[3] "He aimed at a revolution from within, not one of reason, but of those reasons of the heart that the reason does not know," Orwin writes. Rousseau would introduce a new "sensibility," one that might transform everything—while leaving "everything" relatively intact. Humanitarianism would supersede both the classical and the bourgeois virtues in the heart of moral life. Of course, this effort at sentimental education was related to a set of distinctly radical political ideas, a distinct understanding of the nature and the needs of that historical being, modern man, who inhabits the modes and orders of a bourgeois civilization. But Rousseau's

---

3 Clifford Orwin, "Moist Eyes—From Rousseau to Clinton," *The Public Interest* No. 128, Summer 1987, 4.

"work" was not to be accomplished by a political program; it was not to be accomplished simply by a philosophical break-through; it was accomplished by a tacit appeal to the deepest movements of the heart. And Rousseau remains, whether we like it or not, at once among the philosophical and the poetic legislators of our age.

Edmund Burke understood well the character of Rousseau's project when he observed that "Rousseau is a moralist or he is nothing." And much of Burke's own late work may be understood as a form of sentimental (moral) education aimed at countering the achievement of Rousseau—especially as the Rousseauan ro-mantic sensibility formed a deadly synthesis with the rationalism of the French Enlightenment.[4] This, at least, seems to be the de-cisive lesson that Kirk learned from Burke, who remains the pre-eminent model of the conservative mind.

Following Burke, Kirk was alarmed at the oppressive dis-enchantment of the world, the handiwork of the Enlighteners. Following Burke, Kirk was alarmed at the sentimental "cure" proffered by Rousseau, which acquiesced in the construction of liberalism's iron cage of rational self-interest while offering as compensation only the naturalistic idyll of indiscriminate compassion. Following Burke, Kirk appreciated the real politi-cal achievements of many modern institutions; what was prob-lematic were the ideological and sentimental meanings with

---

4 Consider, for example, the famous passage about the Queen of France in the *Reflections*. Burke was advised repeatedly to remove it, because its unfashionable sentiment tended to undermine the persuasive force of his political and economic arguments. Burke, however, insisted on including it, and two centuries later it remains the singularly most memorable passage in his entire corpus.

which those institutions were invested and by which their development was guided. Thus, if ideological reduction and sentimental gesturing were to be overcome, if man were to reclaim the nobility that was traditionally his birthright, it could only be through an education of the moral imagination. The complexity of the human good and the demanding life of virtue had to be rendered compelling by a new, and very different, appeal to the heart. "The conservative finds himself . . . a pilgrim in a realm of mystery and wonder, where duty, discipline, and sacrifice are required— and where the reward is that love which passeth all understanding."[5] It is passages such as these that mark Kirk's central legacy, the legacy of a moralist educator of the sentiments.

Viewed another way, the *critical* quality of the conservative minds in Kirk's genealogy illustrates most forcefully that conservatism is not a matter simply of preserving the status quo, whatever it may be. Conservatism's original intuition is one of *dis*content with the present age. There is thus a certain formal commonality between conservatism and radicalism, a fact to which Karl Marx paid a kind of tribute: large portions of *The Communist Manifesto* essentially paraphrase standard nineteenth-century conservative critiques of liberalism. But the conservative discontent extends also to all the "solutions" proffered in the radical tradition. The conservative seeks to recover human nature from beneath the ideological constructions. But differing sharply from Rousseau, the conservative recognizes

---

5 Russell Kirk, "Libertarians: Chirping Sectaries," *Redeeming the Time* (Wilmington, DE: ISI Books, 1996), 281.

that this nature is complex rather than simple. Man's nature is discontinuous with, and nobler than, non-human nature. But when the dark pall of Enlightenment doubt has covered everything, this conviction can only become fecund through an education of the moral imagination.

It is in this light that one must approach the six canons that Kirk articulates in the introduction to *The Conservative Mind*.[6] One of them, the fourth, concerns the relationship between property and freedom. It is the single element of Locke that survives in conservative thought, a recognition of the practical achievements of modern political institutions. The first three canons, however, are the most substantive ones, and they are virtually a catalog of the aristocratic mores that Tocqueville considered untenable in the democratic social state that marks our age. The first canon is the belief that "a divine intent rules society as well as conscience": in the post-Enlightenment age, the boast is that man is rightly *autonomous*, the proper sovereign of the world. The second is an "[a]ffection for the proliferating variety and mystery of traditional life": liberal construction results in the homogenization of all social spheres. The third is the "[c]onviction that civilized society requires orders and classes": the straightforward opposite of the democratic

---

6 In the present volume, the six canons are extended to "ten principles," since Kirk was giving a series of talks at the Heritage Foundation on various "tens"—events, books, principles, etc. The six original canons of *The Conservative Mind* also differ, on some points considerably, from the six "premises" of conservatism that Kirk presented in his introduction to *The Portable Conservative Reader* (New York: Penguin Books, 1982). The flexibility, not to say indifference, with which Kirk treated abstract political principles illustrates rather well what he meant by his claim that conservatism is the negation of ideology.

leveling impulse. Kirk was seeking to cultivate something like an "aristocratic" sensibility within modern mass society, Tocqueville's doubts notwithstanding.

The last two of Kirk's six canons concern adherence to "prescription" and skepticism toward "innovation," and they introduce the further problematic which Kirk understood himself to be confronting. They are conservative "meta-principles"—not substantive social goods but rather critical attitudes toward permanence and change. The early liberal thinkers were engaged in a great effort to build institutions in which "progress" could become self-sustaining. Later liberal thinkers such as Mill developed arguments for the beneficent nature of widespread experimental innovation. And even Tocqueville, possessed of profound doubts about democracy's effects on human dignity, could see no way to halt the progress of the modern spirit. In the end, the most disabling element of the modern age is the widespread conviction that progress is inevitable, and so conservatism is, strictly speaking, *impossible.*

. . .

F. J. C. Hearnshaw once observed that "[i]t is commonly sufficient . . . if conservatives, without saying anything, just sit and think, or even if they merely sit."[7] But this cannot be a correct assessment. In the age of progress, to sit still is to be swept "forward"—to what exactly is never quite clear. The

---

7 Quoted in *The Conservative Mind* (Washington: Regnery Publishing Co., 1953, 7th ed., 1985), 3.

fundamental modern belief that progress is "inevitable"—a belief especially pronounced in the land that was founded to be *novus ordo seclorum*—conveniently spares the partisan liberal the requirement of arguing that this or that anticipated bit of "progress" is actually, on balance, *good* for human beings. Historical "inevitability," after all, presumes for itself the hard quality of a "fact," and so stands incontestably above all the subjective squabblings over mere "values." "Facts" cannot be argued with.

Russell Kirk's prose style was an impossible anachronism. And yet in the second half of the twentieth century, he published more than thirty volumes of it, commanding a broad and devoted readership. The fact of the books belied the "fact" that only crisply efficient academic prose is "possible" in our time. The "facts" of the progressive age could be shown to be a congeries of opinion and sentiment.

Kirk's very life would be accounted equally impossible. Having grown up near Detroit, he labeled the automobile "the mechanical Jacobin" and seems never quite to have learned to drive. A visitor to the economically distressed and utterly undistinguished village of Mecosta, Michigan, would spend the evening at Kirk's fancifully gothic house singing songs around a piano or listening to tales by the fireside. On walks through the woods, Kirk might leap out from behind a tree to enact a scene from Sir Walter Scott. Are we to take these as anachronisms? As charming idiosyncrasies? As fantastical retreats from the harsh "realities" of the modern age? Or as living proofs that the impossible remains possible even today, for those with moral imagination; as glimpses of what we are missing—and need not miss; as affirmations that our "mere" nostalgia surely points the human heart toward the human good? Kirk's sentimental education of the moral imagination encompassed both words and deeds. And it is staggering to realize that Kirk's "affected" prose in fact reveals the authentic man, a man who imagined his way out of the intellectual prison of modern ideology—and beckoned others to follow.

Throughout his writings, and with a special intensity in his later years and before younger audiences, Kirk fairly preached that *life is worth living*—despite "Giant Boredom" astride in the land. This was a curious counsel to have delivered to a rising generation full of ambitious plans and projects, and some no doubt thought it a platitude. While Kirk's was frequently described as a medieval mind, this is far from a medieval theme: a schoolman would have offered a demonstration of the goodness of the created order, and there's the end of it. This insistent exhortation shows how closely Kirk had peered into the heart of modern acedia, how sensitively he had diagnosed the tendencies of the specifically modern sensibility. Burke described the liberal account of human nature in appalled terms: "On this scheme of things, a king is but a man, a queen is but a woman; a woman is but an animal; and an animal not of the highest order." The nearly irresistible modern temptation is to acquiesce in this reduction of human dignity and to compensate with frenetic Lockean activity or idyllic Rousseauan indulgence. But Kirk knew that the human heart is fit for something nobler. He sought to enable his readers to achieve the same conviction, through the cultivation of the moral imagination:

> It is not inevitable that we submit ourselves to a social life-in-death of boring uniformity and equality. It is not inevitable that we indulge all our appetites to fatigued satiety. It is not inevitable that we reduce our schooling to the lowest common denominator. It is not inevitable that obsession with creature comforts should sweep away belief in a transcendent order. It is not inevitable that the computer should supplant the poet.[8]

Is it going too far to attribute to Kirk an eccentric form of socratism? For where modern men, all about, pursue their narrow ends, certain of the historically inevitable rightness of the modern dispensation, Kirk was convinced that in our age, the *unimagined* life is not worth living for a human being. He labored to reform our sensibilities, so that we could see ourselves both for what we have become and for what we are. He labored to make available an intellectual tradition of dissent from the modern age. He labored to release our hearts from the bondage of ideology.

---

8 Russell Kirk, "The Wise Men Know What Wicked Things Are Written on the Sky," *Redeeming the Time* (Wilmington, DE: ISI Books, 1996), 308.

I

The Errors of Ideology

This small book is a defense of prudential politics, as opposed to ideological politics. The author hopes to persuade the rising generation to set their faces against political fanaticism and utopian schemes, by which the world has been much afflicted since 1914. "Politics is the art of the possible," the conservative says: he thinks of political policies as intended to preserve order, justice, and freedom.

The ideologue, on the contrary, thinks of politics as a revolutionary instrument for transforming society and even transforming human nature. In his march toward Utopia, the ideologue is merciless.

Ever since the end of the Second World War, the tendency of American public opinion has been more or less conservative. But there exists some danger that conservatives themselves might slip into a narrow ideology or quasi-ideology—even though, as H. Stuart Hughes wrote some forty years ago, "Conservatism is the negation of ideology."

This book, then, is addressed to conservatives especially. Its chapters are essays (originally lectures) examining conservative principles, people, books, and problems, and contrasting conservative views with ideological dogmas.

In this present first chapter, I distinguish between conservative beliefs and ideology. In the following four chapters, I discuss conservative principles, events of a conservative significance, conservative books, and conservative leaders—ten of each. Next, in chapters VI, VII, VIII, and IX, I describe four conservative writers of the twentieth century. In chapters X, XI, XII, and XIII, I examine four types or factions of American conservatives. After that, in chapters XIV, XV, XVI, and XVII, I take up conundrums for conservatives—questions of foreign policy, political centralization, educational standards, and the American proletariat. In my concluding chapter, I fulminate against the ideology of Democratism, *vox populi vox Dei*. Permit me to commence with an attempt to define *ideology*.

* * *

The word *ideology* was coined in Napoleonic times. Destutt de Tracy, the author of *Les eléments d'ideologie* (five volumes, 1801-15), was an abstract intellectual of the sort since grown familiar on the Left Bank of the Seine, the haunt of all budding ideologues, among them in recent decades the famous liberator of Democratic Kampuchea, Pol Pot. Tracy and his disciples intended a widespread reform of education, to be founded upon an alleged science of ideas; they drew heavily upon the psychology of Condillac and more remotely upon that of John Locke.

Rejecting religion and metaphysics, these original ideologues believed that they could discover a system of natural laws—which system, if conformed to, could become the foundation of universal harmony and contentment. Doctrines of self-interest, economic productivity, and personal liberty were bound up with these notions. Late-born children of the dying Enlightenment, the Ideologues assumed that systematized knowledge derived from sensation could perfect society through ethical and educational methods and by well-organized political direction.

Napoleon dismissed the Ideologues with the remark that the world is governed not by abstract ideas, but by imagination. John Adams called this new-fangled *ideology* "the science of idiocy". Nevertheless, during the nineteenth century ideologues sprang up as if someone, like Jason, had sown dragons' teeth that turned into armed men. These ideologues generally have been enemies to religion, tradition, custom, convention, prescription, and old constitutions.

The concept of ideology was altered considerably in the middle of the nineteenth century, by Karl Marx and his school. Ideas, Marx argued, are nothing better than expressions of class interests, as related to economic production. Ideology, the alleged science of ideas, thus becomes a systematic apology for the claims of a class—nothing more.

Or, to put this argument in Marx's own blunt and malicious terms, what has been called political philosophy is merely a mask for the economic self-seeking of oppressors—so the Marxists declared. Ruling ideas and norms constitute a delusory mask upon the face of the dominant class, shown to the exploited "as a standard of conduct, partly to varnish, partly to provide moral support for, domination." So Marx wrote to Engels.

Yet the exploited too, Marx says, develop systems of ideas to advance their revolutionary designs. So what we call Marxism is an ideology intended to achieve revolution, the triumph of the proletariat, and eventually communism. To the consistent Marxist, ideas have no value in themselves: they, like all art, are worthwhile only as a means to achieve equality of condition and economic satisfaction. While deriding the ideologies of all other persuasions, the Marxist builds with patient cunning his own ideology.

Although it has been the most powerful of ideologies, Marxism—very recently diminished in strength—has competitors: various forms of nationalism, negritude, feminism, fascism (a quasi-ideology never fully fleshed out in Italy), naziism (an ideology in embryo, Hannah Arendt wrote), syndicalism, anarchism, social democracy, and Lord knows what all. Doubtless yet more forms of ideology will be concocted during the twenty-first century.

Kenneth Minogue, in his recent book *Alien Powers: the Pure Theory of Ideology*, uses the word "to denote any doctrine which presents the hidden and saving truth about the world in the form of social analysis. It is a feature of all such doctrines to incorporate a general theory of the mistakes of everybody else." That "hidden and saving truth" is a fraud—a complex of contrived falsifying "myths", disguised as history, about the society we have inherited. Raymond Aron, in *The Opium of the Intellectuals*, analyzes the three myths that have seduced Parisian intellectuals: the myths of the Left, of the Revolution, of the Proletariat.

To summarize the analysis of ideology undertaken by such scholars as Minogue, Aron, J. L. Talmon, Thomas Molnar, Lewis Feuer, and Hans Barth, this word *ideology*, since the Second World War, usually has signified a dogmatic political theory which is an endeavor to substitute secular goals and doctrines for religious goals and doctrines; and which promises to overthrow present dominations so that the oppressed may be liberated. Ideology's promises are what Talmon calls "political messianism". The ideologue promises salvation in this world, hotly declaring that there exists no other realm of being. Eric Voegelin, Gerhart Niemeyer, and other writers, have emphasized that ideologues "immanentize the symbols of transcendence"—that is, corrupt the vision of salvation through grace in death into false promises of complete happiness in this mundane realm.

Ideology, in short, is a political formula that promises mankind an earthly paradise; but in cruel fact what ideology has created is a series of terrestrial hells. I set down below some of the vices of ideology.

1. Ideology is inverted religion, denying the Christian doctrine of salvation through grace in death, and substituting collective salvation here

on earth through violent revolution. Ideology in-
herits the fanaticism that sometimes has afflicted
religious faith, and applies that intolerant belief to
concerns secular.

2. Ideology makes political compromise impossible:
the ideologue will accept no deviation from the
Absolute Truth of his secular revelation. This narrow vision brings about civil war, extirpation of
"reactionaries", and the destruction of beneficial
functioning social institutions.

3. Ideologues vie one with another in fancied fidelity
to their Absolute Truth; and they are quick to denounce deviationists or defectors from their party
orthodoxy. Thus fierce factions are raised up
among the ideologues themselves, and they war
mercilessly and endlessly upon one another, as did
Trotskyites and Stalinists.

The evidence of ideological ruin lies all about us. How then
can it be that the allurements of ideology retain great power in
much of the world?

* * *

The answer to that question is given in part by this observation from Raymond Aron: "When the intellectual feels
no longer attached either to the community or the religion
of his forebears, he looks to progressive ideology to fill the

vacuum. The main difference between the progressivism of the disciple of Harold Laski or Bertrand Russell and the Communism of the disciple of Lenin concerns not so much the *content* as the *style* of the ideologies and the allegiance they demand."

Ideology provides sham religion and sham philosophy, comforting in its way to those who have lost or never have known genuine religious faith, and to those not sufficiently intelligent to apprehend real philosophy. The fundamental reason why we must set our faces against ideology—so wrote the wise Swiss editor Hans Barth—is that ideology is opposed to truth: it denies the possibility of truth in politics or in anything else, substituting economic motive and class interest for abiding norms. Ideology even denies human consciousness and power of choice. In Barth's words, "The disastrous effect of ideological thinking in its radical form is not only to cast doubt on the quality and structure of the mind that constitute man's distinguishing characteristic but also to undermine the foundation of his social life."

Ideology may attract the bored man of the Knowledge Class who has cut himself off from religion and community, and who desires to exercise power. Ideology may enchant young people, wretchedly schooled, who in their loneliness stand ready to cast their latent enthusiasm into any exciting and violent cause. And ideologues' promises may win a following among social groups that feel pushed to the wall—even though such recruits may not understand much of anything about the ideologues' doctrines. The early composition of the Nazi party is sufficient illustration of an ideology's power to attract disparate elements of this sort.

On the first page of this introductory chapter I suggested that some Americans, conservatively-inclined ones among them, might embrace an ideology of Democratic Capitalism, or New World Order, or International Democratism. Yet most Americans with a sneaking fondness for the word *ideology* are not seeking to sweep away violently all existing dominations and powers. What such people really mean when they call for a "democratic ideology" is a formula for a civil religion, an ideology of Americanism, or perhaps of the Free World. A trouble with this civil-religion notion is that the large majority of Americans think they already have a religion of their own, not one cobbled up by some department in Washington. If the approved civil religion, or mild ideology, should be designed, by some subtle process, to supplant the congeries of creeds at present flourishing in this land—why, such hostility toward belief in the transcendent, such contempt for the "higher religions", is precisely the most bitter article in the creed of those ideologies which have ravaged the world for the past eight decades.

Yet possibly all that is intended by enthusiasts for this proposed new anti-communist ideology is a declaration of political principles and economic concepts, to be widely promulgated, legislatively approved as a guide to public policy, and taught in public schools. If this is all, then why insist upon labelling the notion an ideology? An innocent ideology is as unlikely a contraption as Christian Diabolism; to attach the sinister tag "ideology" would be like inviting friends to a harmless Hallowe'en bonfire, but announcing the party as the new Holocaust.

If this "democratic ideology" should turn out, in practice, to be nothing worse than a national civics program for public schools, still it would require being watched jealously. Cloying praise in every classroom of the beauties of democratic capitalism would bore most pupils and provoke revulsion among the more intelligent. And it is not civics courses, primarily, that form minds and consciences of the rising generation: rather, it is the study of humane letters. I should not wish to see what remains of literary studies in the typical public school supplanted by an official propaganda about the holiness of the American Way or of the Free World Way or of the Democratic Capitalist Way.

I am not of the opinion that it would be well to pour the heady wine of a new ideology down the throats of the American young. If one summons spirits from the vasty deep, can they be conjured back again? What we need to impart is political prudence, not political belligerence. Ideology is the disease, not the cure. All ideologies, including the ideology of *vox populi vox dei*, are hostile to enduring order and justice and freedom. For ideology is the politics of passionate unreason.

. . .

Permit me, then, to set down here, in a few paragraphs, some reflections on political prudence, as opposed to ideology.

To be "prudent" means to be judicious, cautious, sagacious. Plato, and later Burke, instruct us that in the statesman, prudence is the first of the virtues. A prudent statesman is one who looks before he leaps; who takes long views; who knows that politics is the art of the possible.

A few pages ago I specified three profound errors of the ideological politician. Now I contrast with those three failings certain principles of the politics of prudence.

1. As I put it earlier, ideology is inverted religion. But the prudential politician knows that "Utopia" means "Nowhere"; that we cannot march to an earthly Zion; that human nature and human institutions are imperfectible; that aggressive "righteousness" in politics ends in slaughter. True religion is a discipline for the soul, not for the state.

2. Ideology makes political compromise impossible, I pointed out. The prudential politician, *au contraire*, is well aware that the primary purpose of the state is to keep the peace. This can be achieved only by maintaining a tolerable balance among great interests in society. Parties, interests, and social classes and groups must arrive at compromises, if bowie-knives are to be kept from throats. When ideological fanaticism rejects any compromise, the weak go to the wall. The ideological atrocities of the "Third World" in recent decades illustrate this point: the political massacres of the

Congo, Timor, Equatorial Guinea, Chad, Cambodia, Uganda, Yemen, Salvator, Afghanistan, and Somalia. Prudential politics strives for conciliation, not extirpation.

3. Ideologies are plagued by ferocious factionalism, on the principle of brotherhood—or death. Revolutions devour their children. But prudential politicians, rejecting the illusion of an Absolute Political Truth before which every citizen must abase himself, understand that political and economic structures are not mere products of theory, to be erected one day and demolished the next; rather, social institutions develop over centuries, almost as if they were organic. The radical reformer, proclaiming himself omniscient, strikes down every rival, to arrive at the Terrestrial Paradise more swiftly. Conservatives, in striking contrast, have the habit of dining with the opposition.

In the preceding sentence, I employed deliberately the word conservative as synonymous, virtually, with the expression "prudential politician". For it is the conservative leader who, setting his face against all ideologies, is guided by what Patrick Henry called "the lamp of experience". In this twentieth century, it has been the body of opinion generally called "conservative" that has defended the Permanent Things from ideologues' assaults.

Ever since the end of the Second World War, the American public has looked with increasing favor upon the term *conservative.* Public-opinion polls suggest that in politics, the majority of voters regard themselves as conservatives. Whether they well understand conservatives' political principles may be another matter.

Halfway through the second administration of President Reagan, an undergraduate of my acquaintance was conversing in Washington with a young man who had secured a political appointment in the general government. That fledgling public man commenced to talk of a "conservative ideology". The college student somewhat sharply reminded him of the sinister signification of that word "ideology". "Well, you know what I mean," the youthful politician replied, somewhat lamely.

Yet it is doubtful if the officeholder himself knew precisely what he had meant. Did he fancy that *ideology* signifies a body of well-reasoned political principles? Did he desire to discover a set of simplistic formulas by which capitalism might be extended over all the world? Or did he indeed wish to overthrow by violent action our existing social order and to substitute an artificial society nearer to his heart's desire?

We live in a time when the signification of old words, like much else, has become insecure. "Words strain,/Crack and sometimes break, under the burden," as T. S. Eliot puts it. In the beginning was the Word. But nowadays the Word is confronted by Giant Ideology, which perverts the word, spoken and written.

It is not merely the rising political talents of our age that fail to apprehend the proper employment of important words—and particularly misunderstand the usage of *ideology.*

An elderly lady writes to me in defense of yesteryear's movement called Moral Rearmament, which three decades ago claimed to provide America with an ideology. "Perhaps I am wrong, but it has always seemed to me that Ideology means the power of ideas," this correspondent states. "The world is run by ideas, good ones or bad ones. We need a great idea or ideal to replace the false ideas that dominate today. How long can we survive as a free nation when the *word freedom* has been corrupted?"

This lady's concluding point is a keen one. But I must add, "How long can we survive as a free nation when the word *ideology*, with its corrupting power, is mistaken for a guardian of ordered liberty?"

I do not mean to mock; for I encounter this confusion among people whom I know well and respect heartily. One such, a woman who is an able writer and a bold spirit, retorts that her dictionaries—Webster and Oxford—disagree with Russell Kirk's more lengthy definition of *ideology*. "If Oxford is right and ideology means 'the science of ideas', could they not be good ideas? I quite agree that many ideologies do great harm, but surely not all? In any event, I'm a congenital pragmatist," she concludes, "and semantics are not my strong point."

Nay, madam, *all* ideologies work mischief. I am fortified by a letter from an influential and seasoned conservative publicist, who applauds my excoriation of young ideologues fancying themselves to be conservatives, and of young conservatives fondly hoping to convert themselves into ideologues. This latter correspondent agrees with me that ideology is founded merely upon "ideas"—that is, upon abstractions, fancies, for the most part unrelated to personal and social reality, while conservative views are founded upon custom, convention, the long experience of the human species. He finds himself confronted, from time to time, by young people, calling themselves conservative, who have no notion of prudence, temperance, compromise, the traditions of civility, or cultural patrimony.

"The woods are full of these creatures," this gentleman writes. "The conservative 'movement' seems to have reared up a new generation of rigid ideologists. It distresses me to find them as numerous and in so many institutions. Of course, many are libertarians, not conservatives. Whatever they call themselves, they are bad for the country and our civilization. Theirs is a cold-blooded, brutal view of life."

Amen to that. Is conservatism an ideology? Only if, with Humpty Dumpty, we claim the prerogative of forcing words to mean whatever we desire them to signify, so that "It's a question of who's to be master, that's all." Let us conservatives conserve the English language, along with many other surviving good things. Let us raise up the banner of honest and accurate vocabulary. Let us venture, whatever the odds, to contend against ideologues' Newspeak.

The triumph of ideology would be the triumph of what Edmund Burke called "the antagonist world"—the world of disorder; while what the conservative seeks to conserve is the world of order that we have inherited, if in a damaged condition, from our ancestors. The conservative mind and the ideological mind stand at opposite poles. And the contest between those two mentalities may be no less strenuous in the twenty-first century than it has been during the twentieth. Possibly this book of mine may be of help to those of the rising generation who have the courage to oppose ideological zealots.

II

Ten Conservative Principles

Being neither a religion nor an ideology, the body of opinion termed *conservatism* possesses no Holy Writ and no *Das Kapital* to provide dogmata. So far as it is possible to determine what conservatives believe, the first principles of the conservative persuasion are derived from what leading conservative writers and public men have professed during the past two centuries. After some introductory remarks on this general theme, I will proceed to list ten such conservative principles.

A witty presidential candidate of recent times, Mr. Eugene McCarthy, remarked publicly in 1985 that nowadays he employs the word "liberal" as an adjective merely. That renunciation of "liberal" as a noun of politics, a partisan or ideological tag, is some measure of the triumph of the conservative mentality during the 1980s—including the triumph of the conservative side of Mr. McCarthy's own mind and character.

Perhaps it would be well, most of the time, to use this word "conservative" as an adjective chiefly. For there exists no Model Conservative, and conservatism is the negation of ideology: it is a state of mind, a type of character, a way of looking at the civil social order.

The attitude we call conservatism is sustained by a body of sentiments, rather than by a system of ideological dogmata. It is almost true that a conservative may be defined as a person who thinks himself such. The conservative movement or body of opinion can accommodate a considerable diversity of views on a good many subjects, there being no Test Act or Thirty-Nine Articles of the conservative creed.

In essence, the conservative person is simply one who finds the permanent things more pleasing than Chaos and Old Night. (Yet conservatives know, with Burke, that healthy "change is the means of our preservation.") A people's historic continuity of experience, says the conservative, offers a guide to policy far better than the abstract designs of coffee-house philosophers. But of course there is more to the conservative persuasion than this general attitude.

It is not possible to draw up a neat catalogue of conservatives' convictions; nevertheless, I offer you, summarily, ten general principles; it seems safe to say that most conservatives would subscribe to most of these maxims. In various editions of my book *The Conservative Mind* I have listed certain canons of conservative thought—the list differing somewhat from edition to edition; in my anthology *The Portable Conservative Reader* I offer variations upon this theme. Now I present to you a summary of conservative assumptions differing somewhat from my canons in those two books of mine. In fine, the diversity of ways in which conservative views may find expression is itself proof that conservatism is no fixed ideology. What particular principles conservatives emphasize during any given time will vary with the circumstances and necessities of that era. The following ten articles of belief reflect the emphases of conservatives in America nowadays.

First, the conservative believes that there exists an enduring moral order. That order is made for man, and man is made for it: human nature is a constant, and moral truths are permanent.

This word *order* signifies harmony. There are two aspects or types of order: the inner order of the soul, and the outer order of the commonwealth. Twenty-five centuries ago, Plato taught this doctrine, but even the educated nowadays find it difficult to understand. The problem of order has been a principal concern of conservatives ever since *conservative* became a term of politics.

Our twentieth-century world has experienced the hideous consequences of the collapse of belief in a moral order. Like the atrocities and disasters of Greece in the fifth century before Christ, the ruin of great nations in our century shows us the pit into which fall societies that mistake clever self-interest, or ingenious social controls, for pleasing alternatives to an oldfangled moral order.

It has been said by liberal intellectuals that the conservative believes all social questions, at heart, to be questions of private morality. Properly understood, this statement is quite true. A society in which men and women are governed by belief in an enduring moral order, by a strong sense of right and wrong, by personal convictions about justice and honor, will be a good society—whatever political machinery it may utilize; while a society in which men and women are morally adrift, ignorant of norms, and intent chiefly upon gratification of appetites, will be a bad society—no matter how many people vote and no matter how liberal its formal constitution may be. For confirmation of the latter argument, we have merely to glance at the unhappy District of Columbia.

Second, the conservative adheres to custom, convention, and continuity. It is old custom that enables people to live together peaceably; the destroyers of custom demolish more than they know or desire. It is through convention— a word much abused in our time—that we contrive to avoid perpetual disputes about rights and duties: law at base is a body of conventions. Continuity is the means of linking generation to generation; it matters as much for society as it does for the individual; without it, life is meaningless. When successful revolutionaries have effaced old customs, derided old conventions, and broken the continuity of social institutions—why, presently they discover the necessity of establishing fresh customs, conventions, and continuity; but that process is painful and slow; and the new social order that eventually emerges may be much inferior to the old order that radicals overthrew in their zeal for the Earthly Paradise.

Conservatives are champions of custom, convention, and continuity because they prefer the devil they know to the devil they don't know. Order and justice and freedom, they believe, are the artificial products of a long social experience, the result of centuries of trial and reflection and sacrifice. Thus the body social is a kind of spiritual corporation, comparable to the church; it may even be called a community of souls. Human society is no machine, to be treated mechanically. The continuity, the life-blood, of a society must not be interrupted. Burke's reminder of the necessity for prudent change is in the mind of the conservative. But necessary change, conservatives argue, ought to be gradual and discriminatory, never unfixing old interests at once.

Third, conservatives believe in what may be called the principle of prescription. Conservatives sense that modern people are dwarfs on the shoulders of giants, able to see farther than their ancestors only because of the great stature of those who have preceded us in time. Therefore conservatives very often emphasize the importance of *prescription*—that is, of things established by immemorial usage, so that the mind of man runneth not to the contrary. There exist rights of which the chief sanction is their antiquity—including rights to property, often. Similarly, our morals are prescriptive in great part. Conservatives argue that we are unlikely, we moderns, to make any brave new discoveries in morals or politics or taste. It is perilous to weigh every passing issue on the basis of private judgment and private rationality. The individual is foolish, but the species is wise, Burke declared. In politics we do well to abide by precedent and precept and even prejudice, for the great mysterious incorporation of the human race has acquired a prescriptive wisdom far greater than any man's petty private rationality.

Fourth, conservatives are guided by their principle of prudence. Burke agrees with Plato that in the statesman, prudence is chief among virtues. Any public measure ought to be judged by its probable long-run consequences, not merely by temporary advantage or popularity. Liberals and radicals, the conservative says, are imprudent: for they dash at their objectives without giving much heed to the risk of new abuses worse than the evils they hope to sweep away. As John Randolph of Roanoke put it, Providence moves slowly, but the devil always hurries. Human society being complex, remedies cannot be simple if they are to be efficacious. The conservative declares that he acts only after sufficient reflection, having weighed the consequences. Sudden and slashing reforms are as perilous as sudden and slashing surgery.

Fifth, conservatives pay attention to the principle of variety. They feel affection for the proliferating intricacy of long-established social institutions and modes of life, as distinguished from the narrowing uniformity and deadening egalitarianism of radical systems. For the preservation of a healthy diversity in any civilization, there must survive orders and classes, differences in material condition, and many sorts of inequality. The only true forms of equality are equality at the Last Judgment and equality before a just court of law; all other attempts at levelling must lead, at best, to social stagnation. Society requires honest and able leadership; and if natural and institutional differences are destroyed, presently some tyrant or host of squalid oligarchs will create new forms of inequality.

Sixth, conservatives are chastened by their principle of imperfectibility. Human nature suffers irremediably from certain grave faults, the conservatives know. Man being imperfect, no perfect social order ever can be created. Because of human restlessness, mankind would grow rebellious under any utopian domination, and would break out once more in violent discontent—or else expire of boredom. To seek for utopia is to end in disaster, the conservative says: we are not made for perfect things. All that we reasonably can expect is a tolerably ordered, just, and free society, in which some evils, maladjustments, and suffering will continue to lurk. By proper attention to prudent reform, we may preserve and improve this tolerable order. But if the old institutional and moral safeguards of a nation are neglected, then the anarchic impulse in humankind breaks loose: "the ceremony of innocence is drowned." The ideologues who promise the perfection of man and society have converted a great part of the twentieth-century world into a terrestrial hell.

Seventh, conservatives are persuaded that freedom and property are closely linked. Separate property from private possession, and Leviathan becomes master of all. Upon the foundation of private property, great civilizations are built. The more widespread is the possession of private property, the more stable and productive is a commonwealth. Economic levelling, conservatives maintain, is not economic progress. Getting and spending are not the chief aims of human existence; but a sound economic basis for the person, the family, and the commonwealth is much to be desired.

Sir Henry Maine, in his *Village Communities*, puts strongly the case for private property, as distinguished from communal property: "Nobody is at liberty to attack several property and to say at the same time that he values civilization. The history of the two cannot be disentangled." For the institution of several property—that is, private property—has been a powerful instrument for teaching men and women responsibility, for providing motives to integrity, for supporting general culture, for raising mankind above the level of mere drudgery, for affording leisure to think and freedom to act. To be able to retain the fruits of one's labor; to be able to see one's work made permanent; to be able to bequeath one's property to one's posterity; to be able to rise from the natural condition of grinding poverty to the security of enduring accomplishment; to have something that is really one's own—these are advantages difficult to deny. The conservative acknowledges that the possession of property fixes certain duties upon the possessor; he accepts those moral and legal obligations cheerfully.

Eighth, conservatives uphold voluntary community, quite as they oppose involuntary collectivism. Although Americans have been attached strongly to privacy and private rights, they also have been a people conspicuous for a successful spirit of community. In a genuine community, the decisions most directly affecting the lives of citizens are made locally and voluntarily. Some of these functions are carried out by local political bodies, others by private associations: so long as they are kept local, and are marked by the general agreement of those affected, they constitute healthy community. But when these functions pass by default or usurpation to centralized authority, then community is in serious danger. Whatever is beneficent and prudent in modern democracy is made possible through cooperative volition. If, then, in the name of an abstract Democracy, the functions of community are transferred to distant political direction—why, real government by the consent of the governed gives way to a standardizing process hostile to freedom and human dignity.

For a nation is no stronger than the numerous little communities of which it is composed. A central administration, or a corps of select managers and civil servants, however well intentioned and well trained, cannot confer justice and prosperity and tranquility upon a mass of men and women deprived of their old responsibilities. That experiment has been made before; and it has been disastrous. It is the performance of our duties in community that teaches us prudence and efficiency and charity.

Ninth, the conservative perceives the need for prudent restraints upon power and upon human passions. Politically speaking, power is the ability to do as one likes, regardless of the wills of one's fellows. A state in which an individual or a small group are able to dominate the wills of their fellows without check is a despotism, whether it is called monarchical or aristocratic or democratic. When every person claims to be a power unto himself, then society falls into anarchy. Anarchy never lasts long, being intolerable for everyone, and contrary to the ineluctable fact that some persons are more strong and more clever than their neighbors. To anarchy there succeeds tyranny or oligarchy, in which power is monopolized by a very few.

The conservative endeavors to so limit and balance political power that anarchy or tyranny may not arise. In every age, nevertheless, men and women are tempted to overthrow the limitations upon power, for the sake of some fancied temporary advantage. It is characteristic of the radical that he thinks of power as a force for good—so long as the power falls into his hands. In the name of liberty, the French and Russian revolutionaries abolished the old restraints upon power; but power cannot be abolished; it always finds its way into someone's hands. That power which the revolutionaries had thought oppressive in the hands of the old regime became many times as tyrannical in the hands of the radical new masters of the state.

Knowing human nature for a mixture of good and evil, the conservative does not put his trust in mere benevolence. Constitutional restrictions, political checks and balances, adequate enforcement of the laws, the old intricate web of restraints upon will and appetite—these the conservative approves as instruments of freedom and order. A just government maintains a healthy tension between the claims of authority and the claims of liberty.

Tenth, the thinking conservative understands that permanence and change must be recognized and reconciled in a vigorous society. The conservative is not opposed to social improvement, although he doubts whether there is any such force as a mystical Progress, with a Roman P, at work in the world. When a society is progressing in some respects, usually it is declining in other respects. The conservative knows that any healthy society is influenced by two forces, which Samuel Taylor Coleridge called its Permanence and its Progression. The Permanence of a society is formed by those enduring interests and convictions that gives us stability and continuity; without that Permanence, the fountains of the great deep are broken up, society slipping into anarchy. The Progression in a society is that spirit and that body of talents which urge us on to prudent reform and improvement; without that Progression, a people stagnate.

Therefore the intelligent conservative endeavors to reconcile the claims of Permanence and the claims of Progression. He thinks that the liberal and the radical, blind to the just claims of Permanence, would endanger the heritage bequeathed to us, in an endeavor to hurry us into some dubious Terrestrial Paradise. The conservative, in short, favors reasoned and temperate progress; he is opposed to the cult of Progress, whose votaries believe that everything new necessarily is superior to everything old.

Change is essential to the body social, the conservative reasons, just as it is essential to the human body. A body that has ceased to renew itself has begun to die. But if that body is to be vigorous, the change must occur in a regular manner, harmonizing with the form and nature of that body; otherwise change produces a monstrous growth, a cancer, which devours its host. The conservative takes care that nothing in a society should ever be wholly old, and that nothing should ever be wholly new. This is the means of the conservation of a nation, quite as it is the means of conservation of a living organism. Just how much change a society requires, and what sort of change, depend upon the circumstances of an age and a nation.

Such, then, are ten principles that have loomed large during the two centuries of modern conservative thought. Other principles of equal importance might have been discussed here: the conservative understanding of justice, for one, or the conservative view of education. But such subjects, time running on, I must leave to your private investigation.

Who affirms those ten conservative principles nowadays? In practical politics, commonly a body of general convictions is linked with a body of interests. Marxists argue, indeed, that professed political principle is a mere veil for advancement of the economic interests of a class or faction: that is, no real principle exists—merely ideology. Such is not my view: but we ought to recognize connections between political doctrines and social or economic interest-groups, when such connections exist; they may be innocent enough, or they may make headway at the expense of the general public interest. What interest or group of interests back the conservative element in American politics?

That question is not readily answered. Many rich Americans endorse liberal or radical causes; affluent suburbs frequently vote for liberal men and measures; attachment to conservative sentiments does not follow the line that Marxist analysts of politics expect to find. The owners of small properties, as a class, tend to be more conservative than do the possessors of much property (this latter often in the abstract form of stocks and bonds). One may remark that most conservatives hold religious convictions; yet the officers of mainline Protestant churches, together with church bureaucracies, frequently ally themselves with radical organizations; while some curious political affirmations have been heard recently among the Catholic hierarchy. Half a century ago, it might have been said that most college professors were conservative; that could not be said truthfully today; yet physicians, lawyers, dentists, and other professional people—or most of them—subscribe to conservative journals and generally vote for persons they take to be conservative candidates.

In short, the conservative interest appears to transcend the usual classification of most American voting-blocs according to wealth, age, ethnic origin, religion, occupation, education, and the like. If we may speak of a conservative interest, this appears to be the interest-bloc of people concerned for stability: those citizens who find the pace of change too swift, the loss of continuity and permanence too painful, the break with the American past too brutal, the damage to community dismaying, the designs of innovators imprudent and inhumane. Certain material interests are bound up with this resistance to insensate change: nobody relishes having his savings reduced to insignificance by inflation of the currency. But the moving power behind the renewed conservatism of the American public is not some scheme of personal or corporate aggrandizement; rather, it is the impulse for survival of a culture that wakes to its peril near the end of the twentieth century. We might well call militant conservatives the Party of the Permanent Things.

Perhaps no words have been more abused, both in the popular press and within the Academy, than *conservatism* and *conservative*. The *New York Times*, not without malice prepense, now and again refers to Stalinists within communist states as conservatives. Silly anarchistic tracts, under the label *libertarian*, are represented in some quarters as conservative publications—this in the United States of America, whose Constitution is described by Sir Henry Maine as the most successful conservative device in all history! Even after more than three decades of the renewal of conservative thought in this land, it remains necessary to make it clear to the public that conservatives are not merely folk content with the dominations and powers of the moment; nor anarchists in disguise who would pull down, if they could, both the political and the moral order; nor persons for whom the whole of life is the accumulation of money, like so many Midases.

Therefore it is of importance to know whereof one speaks, and not to mistake the American conservative impulse for some narrow and impractical ideology. If the trumpet give an uncertain sound, who shall go forth to battle? For intellectual development, the first necessity is to define one's terms. If we can enlarge the understanding of conservatism's first principles, we will have begun a reinvigoration of the conservative imagination.

The great line of demarcation in modern politics, Eric Voegelin used to point out, is not a division between liberals on one side and totalitarians on the other. No, on one side of that line are all those men and women who fancy that the temporal order is the only order, and that material needs are their only needs, and that they may do as they like with the human patrimony. On the other side of that line are all those people who recognize an enduring moral order in the universe, a constant human nature, and high duties toward the order spiritual and the order temporal.

Conservatives cannot offer America the fancied Terrestrial Paradise that always, in reality, has turned out to be an Earthly Hell. What they can offer is politics as the art of the possible; and an opportunity to stand up for that old lovable human nature; and conscious participation in the defense of order and justice and freedom. Unlike liberals and radicals, conservatives even indulge in prayer, let the Supreme Court say what it may.

This general description of basic assumptions by conservatives I have thrust upon you in the hope of persuading you to think upon these things at your leisure, for the Republic's sake. Conceivably I may have succeeded in rousing some tempers and some hopes. *Pax vobiscum.*

III

The Conservative Cause: Ten Events

D uring the past two centuries, conservatives often have gone forth to battle, like the Celts of the Twilight—but seldom to victory. Forty years ago, when I was finishing the book now entitled *The Conservative Mind*, I intended to call it *The Conservatives' Rout*—not *route*, but *rout*. My publisher, in 1953, dissuaded me from that, however; and indeed I might have contributed to the disaster, turning a rout into a flight, had I persisted in my gloomy title.

For the past two hundred years, nevertheless, conservative men and measures have fought rear-guard actions against the antagonists of order. Edmund Burke, whose imagination and eloquence gave men of conservative impulse some coherent understanding of the contest with the forces of disruption, wrote at the beginning of the dissolution of the old order of things that if mankind demands what cannot be, "the law is broken; nature is disobeyed; and the rebellious are outlawed, cast forth, and exiled, from this world of reason, and order, and peace, and virtue, and fruitful penitence, into the antagonist world of madness, discord, vice, confusion, and unavailing sorrow." The contest between conservatives and radicals in the modern world has been a fierce battle between the world of order, on the one hand, and the antagonist world on the other. Beholding the world today, could anyone maintain that ours is an age of sanity, harmony, virtue, order, and fruitful penitence? No, even if conservatives have held their ground here and there, in general the antagonist world has prevailed.

As I wrote in 1950, in *Queen's Quarterly*, we live in "a world that damns tradition, lauds equality, and welcomes change; a world that has clutched Rousseau, swallowed him down, and demanded prophets yet more radical; a world scarred by industrialism, standardized by the common man, consolidated by government; a world harrowed by war, trembling between the colossi of East and West, and peering over the brink into a gulf of dissolution. . . . The gloomy vaticinations of Burke, which seemed to liberals of Buckle's generation the follies of a deranged old genius, have come to pass: the gods of the copybook headings with fire and slaughter return. Nations dissolving into mere aggregations of individuals; property reapportioned by the political power; great European states ground into powder; tranquil Britain transformed into a socialist commonwealth; the ancient beauty of the Orient ravaged and the empire of India gnawing at her own vitals; the colonial world vomiting out its Europeans, although already metamorphosed by them; the rising on the eastern confines of Europe of a levelling frenzy fierce enough to make Jacobins pale; the passing of riches and might to the Western republic Burke aided—but prosperity acquired in haste and linked with arrogance. Where is the divine guidance Burke discerned in history? Beheld, perhaps, in the punishment of disobedience: 'The Lord made all things for himself—yea, even the wicked for the day of evil.' This horror may have been inevitable; but the last decade of the eighteenth century resounded to Burke's warning, and we still hear its echo, and perhaps can profit. We can salvage: salvaging is a great part of conservatism."

You will perceive that I was not sanguine in 1950. Am I sanguine now? The most that can be said in praise of the conservative cause, some four decades later, is this: the fabric of civilization still hangs together in some quarters of the world. Now and again, over the past two centuries, conservatives have held the line against the forces of the antagonist world; or even have mounted counter-attacks. So I venture to describe for you, very succinctly, ten episodes or actions in which the conservative cause retained or gained some ground.

In the preceding chapter, I endeavored to interest you in ten conservative principles. The number of ten is more difficult to attain when we try to bring to mind ten events associated with conservatives' gains. It would be easy enough to mention elections won, in this country or that, by parties of a conservative inclination; but elections are ephemeral, and the contest between the conservative impulse and the radical impulse is a struggle that transcends little partisan encounters, often no more significant of enduring effect than are baseball or football matches.

So in selecting ten events, I am not discussing primarily the battles of Tweedledum and Tweedledee—of Franklin Roosevelt versus Wendell Willkie, say, or Harold Wilson versus Edward Heath. Instead I am concerned with the conflict between the forces of integration and those of disintegration. By the conservative impulse, I mean the inclination to support a venerable moral order, an established social order, a society of voluntary community, and such healthful institutions as private property and representative government. By the radical impulse, I mean the desire to emancipate all people (whether they like it or not) from moral obligations, to pull down state and church, to bring about an egalitarian collectivism, to discard all the structures of the past. The radical impulse betrays civilization to what Burke called the antagonist world; and into that anti-world most of the peoples of the earth have fallen during the past two centuries.

Here and there, nevertheless, and now and again, the forces of order have withstood successfully, for a time, the forces of disorder—or perhaps have restored order after a time of violence and anarchy. Permit me to suggest, quite arbitrarily, ten such episodes or developments; if you think often better ones, I may readily defer to your judgment. I confine my choices to the two centuries that have elapsed since the American and the French Revolutions, using the term "conservative" in its modern political sense. It would be possible to range through the centuries, picking out in one era or another men or women whom we might label, by analogy, as conservatives; but that exercise might rasp upon liberals' sensibilities. If rarely sanguine, I confess to being sanguinary occasionally. Cicero's order that Catiline's confederates be strangled in the Mamertine prison certainly was a striking event with a conservative purpose, much approved by me; but it was quite unconstitutional; and besides, think of what happened to poor Senator Goldwater when in 1964 he ventured to commend this extremism in the cause of liberty!

Therefore I confine myself to commenting upon events that occurred within the past six or seven generations of mankind, and chiefly within the pale of what we call "Western" civilization. The first of these events came to pass in Philadelphia; and it was a deliberate act of social conservation. I refer to the signing of the Constitution of the United States.

On September 18, 1787, some thirty-nine gentlemen politicians subscribed to the new Constitution, fresh from the pens of Gouverneur Morris and the Committee on Style, there in the Pennsylvania State House, now called Independence Hall. If you contend that the day of the Constitution's ratification, July 2, 1788, is the more significant event, I will not quarrel with you. Yet I prefer the drama of the last day on which the Framers, those most remarkable men, put their quill pens to parchment.

Sir Henry Maine, my favorite historian of the law, wrote a century ago that the Constitution of the United States is the most genuinely conservative document in the history of nations. I will not labor the point. The observance of the Bicentenary of the Constitution of the United States, 1987-1991, should have been a celebration of the triumph of the conservative mind in America, during the closing years of the eighteenth century, over the radical impulse in America. After a dozen years of war and tribulation, some fifty-five gentlemen from twelve states succeeded in contriving, in considerable part by compromise (which conservatives ought never to despise), a framework of government that has survived the gigantic technological, demographic, economic, social, and even moral alterations of the nineteenth and twentieth centuries. Conservatives never built more cleverly than that. Today the United States stands the principal power resisting the triumph of a dreary collectivism throughout the world. Had there come out of the American Revolution what emerged from the French Revolution, all the world today might be one suffocating despotism.

My second event occurs ten years later, in England. Edmund Burke, dying, told his friends to fight on against "the armed doctrine", which today we call ideology, political fanaticism. "Never succumb to the enemy," Burke exhorted them; "it is a struggle for your existence as a nation; and if you must die, die with the sword in your hand; there is a salient, living principle of energy in the public mind of England which only requires proper direction to enable her to withstand this or any other ferocious foe; persevere until this tyranny be past."

That year of 1797 was black for Britain. Yet Burke already had won, although he did not know it. Paine's popular rhetoric did not persuade Englishmen to pull down their inheritance of ordered freedom; while Burke's late writings captured the more lively minds among the rising generation that he had attested at the end of the trial of Warren Hastings. Burke's thought and power of expression it was that brought about a coalition of Whigs and Tories which became the first Conservative party, now the oldest political party in the world. One man's gifts and one man's passion persuaded Britain to fight on, when all allies were lost; and to fight until the strength of the radicals was exhausted.

For a third event with significance for conservatives, I transport you to the House of Representatives, in the little city of Washington, in May, 1824. John Randolph of Roanoke has the floor, speaking with his unsparing mordant wit. He has been fighting internal improvements, intervention in European affairs, and increases in the tariff, that spring; and the South, at least, begins to listen to him earnestly. At this moment Randolph reproaches the enthusiasts for swift progress through public policy. I offer you a brief specimen of his extemporaneous brilliance, unknown in Congress today:

> In all beneficial changes in the natural world, and the sentiment is illustrated by one of the most beautiful effusions of imagination and genius that I ever read—in all those changes, which are the work of an all-wise, all-seeing and superintending providence, as in the insensible gradation by which the infant but expands into manhood, and from manhood to senility; or if you will, to caducity itself, you will find imperceptible changes; you cannot see the object move, but take your eyes from it for a while, and like the index of that clock, you can see that it has moved. The old proverb says, God works good, and always by degrees. The devil, on the other hand, is bent on

mischief, and always in a hurry. He cannot stay, his object is mischief, which can best be effected suddenly, and he must be gone elsewhere.

The causes that Randolph defended all were lost, in his lifetime or little more than three decades later. Yet his words have more meaning to us today, perhaps, than they had for Randolph's contemporaries. As T. S. Eliot puts it, "The communication of the dead is tongued with fire beyond the language of the living."

We turn for our fourth event to New England. Orestes Brownson, an American thinker of most remarkable talents who still is ignored in American universities, but who has fascinated both Mr. Arthur Schlesinger Jr. and myself, in 1840 was the original American Marxist. But by 1848 it was otherwise with him; and only a few months after publication of the *Communist Manifesto*, Brownson refuted Marx in an essay entitled "Socialism and the Church". The understanding of the human condition put forward by Brownson in that essay has confined Marxism in America to dilettantes in universities and a handful of friends of the Soviet Union scattered throughout the land. I give you one passage from "Socialism and the Church":

Veiling itself under Christian forms, attempting to distinguish between Christianity and the Church, claiming for itself the authority and immense popularity of the Gospel, denouncing Christianity in the name of Christianity, discarding the Bible in the name of the Bible, and defying God in the name of God, Socialism conceals from the undiscriminating multitude its true character, and, appealing to our strongest natural inclinations and passions, it asserts itself with terrific power, and rolls on its career of devastation and death with a force that human beings, in themselves, are impotent to resist. Men are assimilated to it by all the power of their own nature, and by all their reverence for religion. Their very faith and charity are perverted, and their noblest sympathies and their sublimest hopes are made subservient to their basest passions and their most grovelling propensities. Here is the secret of the strength of Socialism, and here is the principal source of its danger.

You will recognize in these sentences, written in 1848, the "liberation theology" of our own time. Brownson's writings about the middle of the nineteenth century were events in the sense that they expressed the American revulsion against socialist envy.

For our fifth event, I point to the victory of Benjamin Disraeli over the Liberals in Victorian Britain. "The old Jew gentleman sitting on the top of chaos," as Augustus Hare memorably describes that astute champion of tradition and custom and the chartered rights of Englishmen, of course did not succeed in turning back forever the levelling and disintegrating forces at work in the world; but he did resuscitate an enfeebled resistance to those forces—a resistance that still works within the Tory party. I refer not to the Disraeli of the Reform Bill of 1867, but to the young Disraeli of *Sybil* and the old Disraeli of 1874. Speaking at the Guildhall in that year, he declared that there is more to conservative sentiments than the possession of wealth. "We have been told that a working man cannot be conservative, because he has nothing to conserve—he has neither land nor capital; as if there were not other things in the world as precious as land and capital!" he said then. The working man has liberty, justice, security of person and home, equal administration of the laws, unfettered industry, Disraeli went on. "Surely these are privileges worthy of being preserved! . . . And if that be the case, is it wonderful that the working classes are Conservative?" That argument told in 1874, and it needs to be made again today.

As socialism and nationalism begin to pull the world apart in the last quarter of the nineteenth century and the first quarter of the twentieth, the tide of events runs against the conservative cause. So we must leap down to the struggles of half a century ago, in order to discern conservative resistance to the troops of the antagonist world.

For our sixth event, or rather group of events, then, I look to the defeat or overthrow of communist parties and forces in eastern and central Europe, in the years immediately following the First World War: the rejection of Marxism by the Finns, Poles, Hungarians, Germans, and other nations. The time would come when most of these peoples would be abandoned to Soviet ambition, after all; but for the time being a kind of

frontier was held against Mordor—that is, Moscow. A later sig-
nal event of this sort was the defeat of the Reds in Spain, completed in 1939.

Our seventh event is the defeat of a different ideology: the
Allies' crushing of the Nazis, in 1945; the Western allies, I mean.
It is pleasant to be able to record one major military victory that
helped to sustain order, justice, and freedom. The fortitude of
Britain in general, and of Winston Churchill in particular, made
possible this successful resistance to the enemies of a tolerable
civil social order.

For the eighth event I choose the change of residence of a
man of letters: Aleksandr Solzhenitsyn, exiled from Russia.
Solzhenitsyn's denunciation of the tyranny of ideology did
more to dispel illusions—although not from everybody's
vision—than did any other writing of our time. In 1974
Solzhenitsyn made his way to the West; in 1983, through his
Templeton Address, he expressed with high feeling the essence
of the conservative impulse:

> Our life consists not in the pursuit of material suc-
> cess but in the quest of worthy spiritual growth. Our
> entire earthly existence is but a transition stage in the
> movement toward something higher, and we must
> not stumble or fall, nor must we linger fruitlessly on
> one rung of the ladder . . . The laws of physics and
> physiology will never reveal the indisputable manner
> in which the Creator constantly, day in and day out,
> participates in the life of each of us, unfailingly

granting us the energy of existence; when this as-
sistance leaves us, we die. In the life of our entire
planet, the Divine Spirit moves with no less force:
this we must grasp in our dark and terrible hour.

The ninth event of strong significance for the conserving
of the world of order is the election to the Papacy of the Polish
ecclesiastic now styled John Paul II. A Church swiftly sliding
toward a trivial neoterism, or worse, has been arrested in its
descent; once more the Church begins to speak against the
enemies of order, both order of spirit and social order, and the
heroic character of the Pope, who has known the suffering of
obscure men under grim dominations and powers, gives his
words authority in quarters never Catholic. Rome is the power
that withholds, Cardinal Newman wrote in the middle of the
nineteenth century; and when Rome falls, the Antichrist will
come, in the name of liberation. Two decades ago, that hour
seemed near at hand; but John Paul II, with few to help him,
has faced down the vanguard of the antagonist world.

For our tenth event, I have settled upon the election of
Ronald Reagan to the presidency in 1980. Had a few more
Republicans apprehended the drift of public opinion in the
United States, and understood how the popular rhetoric of Mr.
Reagan spoke to American minds, Mr. Reagan might have been
elected years earlier—even so early as 1964, conceivably—and
much mischief avoided thereby.

Ronald Reagan will be remembered as the President who
restored hope to the American people—even great expectations.

Old sureties that the ritualistic liberal had mocked were unshaken in Ronald Reagan's mind; and President Reagan's reaffirmation of those ancient convictions began to arouse the nation from the discouragement of twenty years or more.

We have yet to elect a Congress of which the majority will be intelligently conservative—much though the times cry out for a genuinely conservative renewal, reaffirmation, and restoration of some measure of order and justice and freedom. Indeed, we have yet to obtain some consensus among people conservatively inclined as to what we mean to conserve.

But we have taken arms against a sea of troubles, friends; and by opposing we may end them. The beginning of the twenty-first century—for a time, it seemed as if humanity would not get so far in time—may mark the beginning of a recovery of right reason and moral imagination. Our Time of Troubles, Arnold Toynbee tells us, commenced with the catastrophic events of the year 1914. Some historians now suggest that our civilization has just begun to recover from the errors and appetites that brought society so close to total surrender to the antagonist world—even our society, so smug about its material acquisitions. If indeed some conservative standards are to be erected soon, there will occur large events worth celebrating; and it is conceivable, that some now living may look back upon the twentieth century as a Bad Old Time when things were in the saddle and rode mankind; a time when nearly all the big events were disastrous. Let us devoutly hope so. We never will succeed in marching to Zion—that gross delusion, indeed, lies behind many of the ruinous events of the past two centuries—but we may aspire to conserve much that deserves saving. Begin to make events, friends, rather than to be overwhelmed by them.

IV

Ten Conservative Books

The political and moral attitude called *conservatism* does not come out of a book; indeed, some of the most conservative folk I have known have been distinctly unbookish. For the sources of a conservative order are not theoretical writings, but rather custom, convention, and continuity. Edmund Burke could imagine nothing more wicked than the heart of an abstract metaphysician in politics—that is, a learned fool or rogue who fancies that he can sweep away the complex institutions of a civilized society, painfully developed over centuries of historical experience, in order to substitute some bookish design of his own for the Terrestrial Paradise. There exists, then, no conservative equivalent of *Das Kapital*; and, God willing, there never will be.

To put this another way, conservatism is not a bundle of theories got up by some closet philosopher. On the contrary, the conservative conviction grows out of experience: the experience of the species, of the nation, of the person. As I pointed out earlier in these discourses, genuine conservatism is the negation of ideology. The informed conservative understands that our twentieth-century social institutions—the common law being a good example of this—have developed slowly by compromise, consensus, and the test of practicality. They did not spring full-grown out of somebody's book; and it is the practical statesman, rather than the visionary recluse, who has maintained a healthy tension between the claims of authority and the claims of freedom; who has shaped a tolerable political constitution.

The Constitution of the United States, two centuries old, is a sufficient example of the origin of conservative institutions in a people's experience, not from abstract treatises. The better-schooled delegates to the Constitutional Convention, among them Hamilton and Madison, would refer now and again to Aristotle or to Montesquieu, by way of reinforcing an argument; yet their own political wisdom, and the Constitution that they framed, were rooted in direct personal experience of the political and social institutions which had developed in the Thirteen Colonies since the middle of the seventeenth century, and in thorough knowledge of the British growth, over seven centuries, of parliamentary government, ordered freedom, and the rule of law. They acknowledged no Omniscient Book as their political oracle; and despite the fancy of various American professors that the Framers were enthusiastic devotees of John Locke, only one speaker at the Convention even mentioned Locke's *Civil Government.*

I have remarked that the conservative mind looks to custom, convention, and continuity for an understanding of the civil social order—not to such artificial constructions as the pretended Social Contract. Let us define our terms, by reference to the larger dictionaries.

Custom is common use or practice, either of an individual or of a community, but especially of the latter; habitual repetition of the same act or procedure; established manner or way. In law, *custom* signifies the settled habitudes of a community, such as are and have been for an indefinite time past generally recognized in it as the standards of what is just and right; ancient and general usage having the force of law.

Convention is the act of coming together; coalition; union. This term also signifies general agreement, tacit understanding, common consent, or the foundation of a custom or an institution. *Convention* implies a customary rule, regulation, or requirement, or such rules collectively, sometimes more or less arbitrarily established, or required by common consent or opinion; a conventionality; a precedent.

Continuity signifies uninterrupted connection of parts in space or time; uninterruptedness; in a culture or a political system, *continuity* implies an unbroken link or series of links joining generation to generation: as the Eastern Orthodox liturgy has it, "ages to ages".

It is possible for books to comment upon custom, convention, and continuity; but not for books to create those social and cultural essences. Society brings forth books; books do not bring forth society. I emphasize this point because we live in an age of ideology, and a good many people—especially professors and graduate students—fall into the curious notion that

all institutions, and all wisdom, somehow are extracted from
certain books. (In religion, this becomes what Coleridge called
bibliolatry.) The Bible is a record of spiritual experiences, not
the *source* of spiritual experiences, really. And from time to
time some student has asked me, after a lecture of mine, "Gee,
Doc, where'd you get all that information? I couldn't find it in
The Book"—that is, the Sacred Textbook, ordinarily a turgid
superficial work written by a mediocre professor whose motive
has been greed. The wisdom of the species is not comprehended
in any seven-foot shelf of books.

So, ladies and gentlemen, if you have been seeking for some
Infallible Manual of Pure Conservatism—why, you have been
wasting your time. Conservatism not being an ideology, it has
no presumptuous crib, the fond creation of some Terrible
Simplifier, to which the ingenuous devotee of political salvation
may repair whenever in doubt. Do not fall into political bibliolatry; in particular, do not regard Kirk's Works as written by
one endowed with the prophetic afflatus.

In those dear dead days almost beyond recall when I used
to keep a bookshop, a small glum man browsed about my tables
and shelves one afternoon, and presently said to me, almost
angrily, "I'm looking for a book that will tell us what to do about
all these modern problems. But it has to be a small book and
there can't be anything about religion in it." Alas, no small book,
or big one either, has been written to tell us honestly and practically what to do about all these modern problems, nor will one
such ever be published, not even by a conservative author. And
if you should be seeking for a sound book of a conservative cast

that has no religion in it—why, you might as well search for the philosopher's stone; or inquire, with Tiberius, what songs the Sirens sang.

Therefore in commending to you, friends, ten important conservative books, I provide you with merely a sampling of the literature of conservatism—not with a corpus of infallible writings on which a zealot might base a conservative Thirty-Nine Articles or a Test Act. Conservative people share a state of mind or a body of sentiments; they do not necessarily all agree on prudential concerns; the variety of conservative approaches to political and moral questions is considerable. I do not argue that these ten books I am about to name are the most important conservative writings: simply that they are intelligently representative of conservative thought. For conservatives do think, even though one conservative scholar, F. J. C. Hearnshaw, remarks that ordinarily it is sufficient for conservatives to sit and think, or perhaps merely to sit. Being no ideologue, the conservative thinker does not fall into the error that the pride and passion and prejudice of mankind may be controlled and directed satisfactory by any set of abstract ideas. To cite the title of a book by my old friend Richard Weaver (who detested that publisher's title to his book), *Ideas Have Consequences*, true; but in politics abstract ideas very often have bad consequences; and the conservative knows that custom, convention, and continuity are forces socially more beneficial than are the fulminations of some gloomy political fanatic. Conservative writing, then, usually is undertaken with some reluctance, and chiefly in reaction against radical or liberal tracts pretending to point out the path to the earthly Zion.

So it was with Burke two centuries ago, and so it is today with Aleksandr Solzhenitsyn.

From my list I have eliminated certain great statesmen, because what they wrote was of little enduring influence, although what they did had large enduring consequences. Also I have left out the great conservative novelists, among them Walter Scott and Benjamin Disraeli and Nathaniel Hawthorne and Robert Louis Stevenson and Rudyard Kipling and Joseph Conrad, because they did not write specifically of conservative political questions, even though their indirect influence upon public opinion may have been vast. In short, I confine myself just now to books directly and unquestionably political in subject and conservative in tone.

In 1955, addressing the London Conservative Union, T. S. Eliot named Bolingbroke, Burke, Coleridge, and Disraeli as the chief conservative men of letters; and of living or recent American writers—quoting from a letter of mine to him—Eliot mentioned Irving Babbitt, Paul Elmer More, Bernard Iddings Bell, and Robert Nisbet. Since Bolingbroke, Coleridge, and Disraeli none of them wrote a one-volume manual of politics that would be readily apprehended by the modern reader, I must pass them by in our discussion. I am going to say something about Burke and Babbitt and Eliot and Nisbet, nevertheless.

Some people may desire to commence their serious study of conservative thought by reading a succinct but sensible manual on the subject. If so, I commend particularly an agreeably slim volume by Robert A. Nisbet, entitled simply

Conservatism: Dream and Reality (University of Minnesota Press), agreeing with everything in it except for Dr. Nisbet's attempt to classify conservatism as an ideology, and his praise of Kirk's Works. Two earlier slim volumes on this subject, both by the same title, *The Case for Conservatism*, were written by Francis Graham Wilson and by Quintin Hogg; Wilson's is back in print. If you desire an anthology of conservative essays, speeches, poems, and tales, *The Portable Conservative Reader*, edited by your servant, is very much in print; if what you seek is an historical analysis of conservative thought, the seventh (and presumably final) edition of your servant's tall book *The Conservative Mind* may occupy your leisure hours for weeks. Now for the ten books to which I particularly direct your attention, as swimming in the main current of conservative thought; I describe them more or less in chronological order.

. . . .

One begins with Burke, for the word "conservative" was not part of the vocabulary of politics until French admirers of that Irish statesman adapted this word to describe the principles of men who would join to the best in the old order of Europe those necessary healthful improvements which would preserve the continuity of civilization. Without Burke's speeches and pamphlets, and especially his eloquent *Reflections on the Revolution in France*, conservatively-inclined people would be intellectually impoverished. As even Harold Laski wrote once, "Burke has endured as the permanent manual without which statesmen are as sailors on an uncharted sea." Foreseeing the revolutions of our time, Burke expounded the principles of social order that conservatives have endeavored ever since to defend.

I have discussed Edmund Burke in several Heritage Lectures. Were it possible, I should like to discuss his contemporary John Adams, in some sense his American counterpart; but much though Adams wrote, no one treatise of his stands out as a seminal work of politics that has greatly influenced men of conservative inclinations. This is a pity, for abundance of wisdom and wit are to be encountered in the ten fat volumes of his writings, edited by his grandson, that were published in 1856; or in the many volumes of the Adams Papers that were published more than a century later. Yet I suppose that very few people have joined me in reading every sentence of Adams that ever was published; so I must pass on for my second conservative book—commending in passing George A. Peek's *The Political Writings of John Adams*, an anthology—to the conservative writer whose influence, at least in America, has been second only to Burke's.

Alexis de Tocqueville's *Democracy in America*, still the best sociological study of our mass-age, was written in dread of the tyranny of the majority and of democratic materialism; the second volume of that great work is strongly influenced by Burke's writings. Tocqueville understood the drift of the American people in the first half of the nineteenth century as did no one else; and the drift still is in the direction he predicted, though we are a century and a half farther down the river.

Incidentally, although Dr. F. A. Hayek abjured the term "conservative" along with the terms "liberal" and "libertarian", nevertheless he acknowledged his discipleship to both Burke and Tocqueville, calling himself an Old Whig, as did Burke; so perhaps he was more of a conservative than he pretended to be.

For our third conservative book, I offer you *The American Democrat*, by James Fenimore Cooper, a contemporary of Tocqueville. Despite the strong surviving popularity of the *Leatherstocking Tales*, even among serious critics of literature, not one-twentieth the number of people have read *The American Democrat* as have read *Democracy in America*; one hopes that the handsome new edition of *The American Democrat* brought out a few years ago by Liberty Fund may find its way into the hands of attentive readers. Its strongest point is Cooper's bold advocacy of the need for honorable leadership in a democratic society.

Chronologically, there now looms up the strong-minded John C. Calhoun; but neither *A Disquisition on Government* nor *A Discourse on the Constitution*, respected though both books are by political scientists, is readily understood by many people nowadays. So for our fourth volume I take from my shelves a book by an ardent Catholic who would be considerably displeased by certain bishops' pastoral letters of recent origin.

I refer to *The American Republic*, published in 1865, by Orestes Brownson, a Catholic Yankee, long-lived and argumentative. One thing on which Mr. Arthur M. Schlesinger, Jr., and I agree is the importance of Brownson. Calhoun and Brownson were the first American public men to use the term *conservative* as a word of praise—so early as the 1840s. Brownson was the first writer to reply, sternly and systematically, to Marx's *Communist Manifesto*. *The American Republic* analyzes this country's unwritten and written constitutions, and describes the American mission of reconciling the claims of authority and of liberty.

Because this book addresses an American audience, I emphasize American books relevant to our national concerns; were I in Britain, I would say more about English and Scottish political writers. In Victorian England the books of James Fitzjames Stephen, W. E. H. Lecky, and Henry Maine were written to withstand the threat of democracy and socialism. As our fifth book, I select Stephen's *Liberty, Equality, Fraternity*—a mordant refutation both of the slogan of the French Revolution and of John Stuart Mill's *On Liberty*. I believe Stephen's powerful assault can be obtained from a reprint house, at a high price.

As the end of the nineteenth century approached, the wittiest and most systematic of English conservative men of letters was W. H. Mallock, the author of more than a score of books, ranging all the way from psychological novels and volumes of travel and memoirs to keen economic analyses. Except for his satirical first book, *The New Republic*, Mallock is read scarcely at all nowadays, and most of his books are unobtainable in the United States except at great research libraries. Yet I strongly urge you to lay your hands, if you can, upon a copy of the sixth conservative book of my choice, Mallock's *Is Life Worth Living?* This polemical work, powerfully written, is a warning against the personal and social ennui that follows upon a general loss of the religious sense: a society bored to death. A new edition of his *Critical Examination of Socialism* has been brought out by Transaction Publishers.

Turn we again to the Americans. During the first three decades of the twentieth century two important critics of literature, Paul Elmer More and Irving Babbitt, were the most intelligent conservatives in this country. It is difficult to choose between More's *Aristocracy and Justice* and Babbitt's *Democracy and Leadership*—the latter available from the Liberty Fund, with an introduction by your servant. But let me recommend, for our present purposes, *Democracy and Leadership* as our seventh book of this confining list. Babbitt courageously endeavored to restore an understanding of the true meaning of *justice,* and to remind his time of the perils of materialistic expansion and centralization, and to defend the ethical purpose of humane letters. Late in 1986, there was published by the National Humanities Institute a new edition of Babbitt's *Literature and the American College*, with a very long introduction by me. Several of Babbitt's and More's books have been reprinted in recent years—a sign of the renewal of conservative thought.

Both before and after the Civil War, half the important conservative books of America have been written in the South. As a noble specimen of the conservative mind of the South, I take for my eighth conservative book *The Attack on Leviathan*, by Donald Davidson, of Tennessee, poet, critic, historian, ballad-collector, champion of the southern inheritance. I happened upon *The Attack on Leviathan* in a college library when

I was a freshman, and it converted me into an adversary of the consolidated mass-state. In *Policy Review's* pages, more than two years ago, I gave some account of how that eloquent book was virtually suppressed by the university press that published it; Davidson, when we met in the 'Fifties, was surprised that I had found a copy anywhere. But the book has been reprinted by another firm, and you ought to seek it out, for it is the most important ignored political work of America in this century. The title of the new edition is *Regionalism and Nationalism in the United States*; it has an introduction by a certain Russell Kirk, and its publisher is Transaction.

Most influential economists have been liberals old style or liberals new style, and sufficiently narrow in their views of human existence. For my ninth conservative work, however, I name *The Social Crisis of Our Time*, by my old friend Wilhelm Roepke, of Germany and Switzerland. This book is an analysis of the menace that Roepke called "the cult of the colossal." Of the many unpleasant consequences of mass society, the worst is proletarianization. We must find our way back to the humane scale, in economics and in politics: "Socialism, collectivism, and their political and cultural appendages are, after all, only the last consequences of our yesterday; they are the last convulsions of the nineteenth century, and only in them do we reach the lowest point of a century-old development along the wrong road; these are the hopeless final stage toward which we drift unless we act. . . ." So Roepke wrote about 1949. Most books of this remarkable social thinker now are quite unavailable in the United States, except for *The Social Crisis of Our Time*.

As my tenth conservative book, I recommend that you read, friends, T. S. Eliot's *Notes towards the Definition of Culture*. President Nixon, in the White House, once asked me what one book he ought to read, the narrow limits of his leisure considered. *Notes towards the Definition of Culture*, I replied; and when he inquired why, I explained that this slim volume touches upon the reasons for the decadence of modern society, the substitution of a bureaucratic specialized elite for a healthy leading class, the relationships that ought to be maintained between men in public station and men of ideas, and what is worth preserving in our culture. More than any other writer of the twentieth century, Eliot stood up for custom, convention, and continuity in society and for the moral order of our common civilization. You should read, too, his other little volume about our civil social order, *The Idea of a Christian Society*. Both volumes remain readily available in bookshops: Eliot's high reputation is difficult to squelch.

There! I have opened the covers of ten books for you—choosing them with some eye to the diversity of the conservative impulse—and have mentioned other good ones. *Reflections on the Revolution in France, Democracy in America, The American Democrat, The American Republic, Liberty, Equality, Fraternity, Is Life Worth Living?, Democracy and Leadership, The Attack on Leviathan, The Social Crisis of Our Time, Notes towards the Definition of Culture*—if you line up those volumes on a shelf and religiously read one chapter in one of them each night, until you have read and digested all ten, you will acquire very considerable political and moral wisdom. Their several authors were an Irish politician, a French traveller and man of law, a novelist in the state of New York, a Catholic journalist, an English judge, an English satirist, a Harvard professor, a Southern poet, a Swiss economist, and an Anglo-American man of letters: not one of them, let it be noted, a professor of political science.

With great ease I could have named for you ten other conservative books, quite as important; some of the alternative ten by the writers I have named today, but others by quite different authors. The literature of conservative opinion, accumulating over two centuries, has grown impressive in its bulk, as in its high quality. The question remains whether one may readily put his hands upon most of it.

You will have observed that I have named not one book, of my ten, by an author still living. That is not for lack of titles from which to choose; rather, I am embarrassed by a wealth of interesting and competent conservative writing today—which is not to suggest that we suffer from a surplus of original genius. Some of the more perceptive conservative minds today are to be encountered in unexpected places: Tage Lindbom, in Sweden, for one, or persecuted Russian writers of the USSR. Among men of high intellectual powers and literary arts still in this land of the living, here in America, are Eliseo Vivas, Andrew Lytle, Cleanth Brooks, and a score more I might name: men of letters of a conservative cast of mind. On the other hand, I note that in the late John East's book about American conservative political thinkers of the past few decades, only one still lives. Eric Voegelin, Willmoore Kendall, Leo Strauss,

Richard Weaver, Frank S. Meyer, Ludwig von Mises—all have departed from this bourne. The last leaf on John East's tree of the Philosophical Founders is yours truly.

. . .

I am reasonably sure that some of you gentle readers must have reflected to yourselves, with respect to the preceding pages, "If so large a body of good or even great books of a conservative character exists, why is it that we infrequently encounter such volumes in bookshops or public libraries? Why were we not introduced to such books in school, college, and university? Why are not books of this sort on the best-seller lists? Why do we read reviews of them—supposing them reviewed at all—only in periodicals of a confessedly conservative persuasion, or in some religious journal, or at most in *The Wall Street Journal*? Why does even *National Review* apparently prefer to review at length books already reviewed by *The New York Review of Books* or *The New York Times*?"

And why, you may have ruminated, are a good many of the old books commended today so long out of print? Why does no publisher make them available, when they are free, most of them, of copyright restraints, and when presumably they would sell as well to the American public as do many serious books of a different school of thought that are readily picked up in bookshops? Why is the publishing of recognizably conservative books, new or old, confined to a few small or smallish publishers, with limited capital and modes of distribution—Regnery

Gateway (having moved its offices to Washington), Sherwood Sugden, Liberty Classics/Liberty Press, occasionally one of the university presses, recently Transaction Books?

Why, because there still prevails a leaden domination over trade-book publishing, and for the most part over scholarly publishing, by yesteryear's climate of ritualistic-liberal opinion. To find a Manhattan publisher for any well-written book that seems to reflect the wisdom of our ancestors is so arduous an undertaking as one of the labors of Hercules—and less attended by success.

This hegemony of an archaic American liberalism, grown perfectly intolerant and flinching at shadows, extends to book-reviewing in the very large majority of both popular and scholarly media of criticism. At the very time when public opinion has shifted massively toward conservative measures and men, the intellectuals of the publishing world have marched off defiantly in an opposite direction. They are very willing, as a breed, to make much money by publishing pornography and reviewing it in a snickering, titillating fashion; but even the prospect of profit will not tempt these lofty-minded editors and reviewers to touch conservative pitch and be defiled.

Of the books I have commended in these pages, the majority still linger in print, but are not readily come by in bookshops or public libraries; while some have been quite unavailable for a long while. Had I named conservative books by authors less famous, I might as well have been writing about the vanished books of Livy's history, for all the chance you might have had of finding a copy to read.

The origins of this anti-conservative mentality among publishers' editors and among reviewers and librarians are worth discussing; for that, however, another essay would be required; and remedies for this discriminatory malady will not soon be found. One palliative might be an injection of capital into publishing firms that know the meaning of custom, convention, and continuity, but apparently (with a few honorable exceptions) the people whom Franklin Roosevelt reproached as Malefactors of Great Wealth think books of small consequence.

At the beginning of this chapter, I remarked that the conservative impulse is not the product of books, but rather of attachment to custom, convention, and continuity. Conservatives are more concerned with real things than with the abstractions of the Academy of Lagado or of Cloud CuckooLand. Nevertheless, fallacious books have had a great deal to do with fetching down the old framework of order in most of the world, during the past two hundred years; and sound books about the human condition and about the civil social order can accomplish much, by rousing a healthy intellectual reaction, to preserve order and justice and freedom.

The number of Americans who read serious books of any sort and form their judgments upon them seems certain to diminish even more rapidly during the remainder of this century than it already has since the Second World War. This diminishing remnant, nevertheless, may amount to that body of unknown persons who, Dicey says, are the real authors of public opinion. The great conservative writers always have addressed a minority of the reading public; but that may be changing, as the reading public is much narrowed and filtered by the gross triumph of videos, cable television, and other dubious entertainments. As Lionel Trilling suggested mournfully in 1950, the literary imagination of the liberals is bankrupt. So it might come to pass, paradoxically enough, that conservative books should command more authority and influence in the twenty-first century than they exercised in the eighteenth century, the nineteenth, or the twentieth.

V

Ten Exemplary Conservatives

I n ways mysterious our political preferences are formed. "When did you decide to become a conservative?" people sometimes inquire of me. But I never did decide: I *found* myself a conservative, once I began to reflect upon such concerns. Others find themselves liberals or radicals, without quite being able to account for that inclination.

Occasionally, nevertheless, we contrive to recall a conversation, a book, a public meeting, a chance encounter, a rebuff, an opportunity, a moment of solitary reflection, or the example of some man or woman, which drew or pushed us in some degree toward a particular view of politics. I think, for example, of a Sunday afternoon in my father's company, resting on a slope high above the village mill-pond, I a little boy. We lay in the shade of great trees; and I recall reflecting on the peace and beauty of the scene, and the great age of the trees—and wishing that everything about us that day might never change. That is the fundamental conservative impulse: the longing for order and permanence, in the person and in the republic.

Or I think of walking with my grandfather, a sagacious and courageous man, along a railway cut through a glacial moraine, we talking of British history—for I had been reading Dickens' *A Child's History of England.* That communion with an old gentleman I admired infinitely, and our reflections that day upon the living past, were among the influences that have prevented me from becoming an evangel of Modernity.

Again, it may be the example of some eminent champion of the permanent things that moves us: some living man, perhaps, or some figure of antique grandeur, dust long ago. His actions shape our beliefs; and we find ourselves applying his convictions and emulating his policies, so far as possible, perhaps in a different age or land.

So I present to you brief sketches of ten people of a conservative cast of mind who did much to form my opinions over the years. I do not suggest that these ten are the grandest figures ever cast in the conservative mold, although the names of two or three of them would appear on almost any informed person's list of great defenders of an old order; I am merely including particular public figures or shapers of ideas who formed *my* conservative mind. Of course I was influenced by a hundred more; but the ones I am about to name worked upon my imagination fairly early—the first eight of them, at least. I refrain here from including any authors whom I discussed much in my earlier disquisition "Ten Conservative Books"—which deletion removes from consideration both Edmund Burke and T. S.

Eliot, the men with whom my book *The Conservative Mind* begins and ends, respectively. Presumably everybody agrees that Burke is the greatest of conservative thinkers; but I omit him here because I have written and said so much about him already, over the past thirty-five years; and about Eliot, too, I have written a big book.

Thus I offer you this day ten exemplary conservatives, with much diversity of talents among them—the most recent among them separated in time by more than two thousand years from the first-born of their number. What they share is an affection for the permanent things, and the courage to affirm that truth was not born yesterday. They are the giants, upon whose shoulders stand such dwarfs as myself. Tall though they loom, I cannot allot many more than three hundred words to any one of them. I hope merely to wake your memories of them, or to induce you to admire them for the first time. Here they are, in diminishing order of antiquity: first, Marcus Tullius Cicero.

In my high-school days, before the ghastly triumph of educational Instrumentalism, a large proportion of the pupils used to study ancient history for a year—and Latin for two years. Thus was I introduced to Cicero, a man of law and philosophy who set his face against a military revolution, and lost, and paid with his head. Conservative was not a term of politics during the first century before Christ, but presumably Cicero would not have objected to being so described, he being something of a philologist: the English word conservative is derived from the Latin conservator, signifying one who preserves from injury, violence, or infraction.

The orations and the life of the defender of the expiring Roman Republic were studied closely in every decent upper school in Britain and America, during the seventeenth and eighteenth centuries and well into the nineteenth. As a high-school senior, I read a novel about Cicero and Caesar, Phyllis Bentley's *Freedom, Farewell*; that led me to Plutarch's life of Cicero, and I recall sitting on my front porch by the railway station, most of one summer, reading Plutarch through, and being moved by Cicero especially.

Cicero died for the old Roman constitution; ever since then, men defending constitutional order have looked to Cicero as their exemplar. As I have said elsewhere, one heroic custom of the early Romans was to "devote" a man to the gods, that through his sacrifice the commonwealth might be forgiven for wrongdoing. To the *mores majorum*, and to the moral law, Cicero gave the last full measure of devotion. At times in his public life, Cicero had been timid or vacillating; yet at the end, the high old Roman virtue was his. That model of virtue endures in the conservative's consciousness. *Roma immortalis* is no vain boast, after all.

Thus my second conservative exemplar is Marcus Aurelius Antoninus, the Stoic emperor. I read him earnestly during my first years as a soldier, I often seated solitary on a sand-dune, the treeless desert stretching far away to grim mountains: appropriately enough, for Marcus Aurelius' book of meditations has been dear to soldiers over the centuries, among them John Smith at Jamestown and Gordon at Khartoum.

About Marcus Aurelius I corresponded with Albert Jay Nock, that strong individualist and essayist, during the last year of Nock's life. "The world has not once looked upon his like," Nock wrote of Marcus, in his essay "The Value of Useless Knowledge", "and his praise is for ever and ever. Yet hardly was the breath out of his body before the rotten social fabric of Rome disintegrated, and the empire crumbled to pieces."

Marcus Aurelius writes of the beauty of a ripe fig, trembling on the verge of deliquescence; I ventured to suggest to Nock that this passage in the Meditations may hint at a certain fascination with decadence; Nock denied it. However that may be, the Emperor acted in a decadent age, corruption all about him, so that, in his phrase, it was necessary for him to "live as upon a mountain", isolated from intimacies. Today's conservatives, too, see about them a bent world.

It was the heroic endeavor of Marcus Aurelius to conserve Romanitas, that grand system of law and order and culture. If he failed—even with his wife, even with his son—still he left an example of integrity that has endured, like his equestrian statue on the Capitoline, down to our time. In Nock's words, "The cancer of organized mendicancy, subvention, bureaucracy and centralization had so far weakened its host that at the death of Marcus Aurelius there was simply not enough producing-power to pay the bills." Eighty years of able Antonine rule "could not prevent the Roman populace from degenerating into the very scum of the earth, worthless, vicious, contemptible, sheer human sculch." We may make comparisons and draw analogies, near the end of the twentieth century. (Nock, by the way, wrote an admirable essay on conservatism, little noticed so far as I know: his model of a conservative is Lucius Cary, Lord Falkland, the mediator between Charles I and the Parliament.)

The lesson I learnt from Marcus Aurelius is the performance of duty. Take this passage from the Meditations—the Emperor being on a hard Danubian campaign when he set down these lines: "In the morning, when thou risest sore against thy will, summon up this thought: 'I am rising to do the work of a man. Why then this peevishness, if the way lies open to perform the tasks which I exist to perform, and for whose sake I was brought into the world? Or am I to say I was created for the purpose of lying in blankets and keeping myself warm?'" With that admonition I steel myself on January mornings at my ancestral village.

Everyone who contends against odds in defense of the permanent things is an heir of Marcus Aurelius.

We leap sixteen centuries to approach my third conservative, Samuel Johnson. That unforgettable moralist and critic sometimes is represented as a blustering bigot; actually the political Johnson was a reasonable, moderate, and generous champion of order, quick to sustain just authority, but suspicious of unchecked power. He was at once the friend and the adversary of Edmund Burke. His note on Whigs and Tories, written in 1781, suggests his reasonableness:

> A wise Tory and a wise Whig, I believe, will agree.
> Their principles are the same, though their modes of
> thinking are different. A high Tory makes government
> unintelligible; it is lost in the clouds. A violent Whig

makes it impracticable; he is for allowing so much liberty to every man, that there is not enough power to
govern any man. The prejudice of the Tory is for establishment; the prejudice of the Whig is for innovation. A Tory does not wish to give more real power to
Government; but that Government should have more
reverence. Then they differ as to the Church. The Tory
is not for giving more legal power to the Clergy, but
wishes they should have a considerable influence,
founded on the opinion of mankind; the Whig is for
limiting and watching them with a narrow jealousy.

At this point it is useful to recall that originally the word
conservative implied a moderate attitude, an endeavor to find
a middle way between extremes. Just that was the mission of
Falkland and, sometimes, of Johnson.

Johnson I read at Behemoth University, called by some
people Michigan State University. (It was a cow college when I
enrolled there.) In morals, the sound sense of Dr. Johnson has
been my mainstay, and *Rasselas* has taught me far more about
human beings and humankind's vanities than has *Candide*.

To Scotland we turn for my fourth conservative, Sir Walter
Scott. Through the Waverley Novels, the Wizard of the North
disseminated Burke's conservative vision to a public that never
would have read political tracts; but Scott's achievement is considerably more than this labor of popularizing political doctrines. For Scott wakes the imagination; he reminds us that we
have ancestors and inherit a moral patrimony; he pictures for

us the virtues of loyalty, fortitude, respect for women, duty toward those who will succeed us in time—and all this without
seeming didactic. As D. C. Somervell puts it, Scott showed, "by
concrete instances, most vividly depicted, the value and interest
of a natural body of traditions."

My mother gave me five of Scott's romances for my eighth
birthday, and I have been reading Scott ever since. Until fairly
recent years, one saw cheap editions of Scott's novels on sale at
British railway kiosks; but modern educational approaches are
effacing that sort of literary taste. I do not mean to desert Sir
Walter: (indeed, I shall re-read *The Antiquary* reasonably soon
at my Michigan fastness.) Popular influence of the novel departed when television was plumped into the living-room of
nearly every household in the western world; I suppose that
relatively few people will read Scott, although books about him
continue to be published; but those who do read him may be
won to his understanding of the great mysterious incorporation
of the human race.

Let us cross the Atlantic now. A Virginian is my fifth exemplary conservative—not George Washington, or George Mason,
or Madison, or Monroe, and certainly not Thomas Jefferson;
but John Randolph of Roanoke, concerning whom I wrote my
first book. Strange to say, Randolph, the enemy of change, was
described at some length in my tenth-grade American history
textbook; I wrote a school paper about him; by 1951, that effort
had grown to a book published by the University of Chicago
Press, *Randolph of Roanoke: a Study in Conservative
Thought*—today published, in a fuller edition, by Liberty Fund.

Randolph's biting wit and extemporaneous eloquence, in the House or the Senate, still ring true against the centralizers, the meddlers in the affairs of distant nations, the demagogues, the men in office who "buy and sell corruption in the gross." Yet it was Randolph's intricate personality and burning emotion, as much as his political perceptions, that drew me to a study of him and of the history of the Southern states. Hugh Blair Grigsby describes Randolph at the Virginia Convention of 1829-30, when Randolph was not far from death's door:

". . . It was easy to tell from the first sentence that fell from his lips when he was in fine tune and temper, and on such occasions the thrilling music of his speech fell upon the ears of that excited assembly like the voice of a bird singing in the pause of the storm. It is difficult to explain the influence which he exerted in that body. He inspired terror to a degree that even at this distance of time seems inexplicable. He was feared alike by East and West, by friend and foe. The arrows from his quiver, if not dipped in poison, were pointed and barbed, rarely missed the mark, and as seldom failed to make a rankling wound. He seemed to paralyze alike the mind and the body of his victim. What made his attack more vexatious, every sarcasm took effect amid the plaudits of his audience." James Madison and James Monroe, near the end of their tether in 1829, listened closely and fearfully to the formidable Randolph, their heads bowed.

It was my study of this master of rhetoric, this hard hater of cant and sham, this American disciple of Burke, that led me deeper into an understanding of Edmund Burke's mind and heart. "Change is not reform!" Randolph cried to the Virginia

Convention; that aphorism I cherish. Would that some chasten-
ing Randolph might stride into today's Senate or House! Henry
Adams, whose ancestors Randolph denounced, called
Randolph of Roanoke "a Saint Michael in politics."

From Southside Virginia we make haste to Salem, in
Massachusetts, to encounter my sixth exemplary conservative,
Nathaniel Hawthorne. My great-aunt Norma thoughtfully gave
me her set of Hawthorne's works when I was about nine years
old, and I have those volumes still, after reading them through
a score of times.

It is significant of the modern temper that for the past three
decades, the typical school anthology of American literature has
found little space for Hawthorne, though a great deal for Walt
Whitman—a disproportion that today, I note, begins to be rem-
edied by some publishers. The anthologists and textbook publishers had sensed the conservatism of Hawthorne, and the flabby
democratism of Whitman is obvious enough. Yet it has been
Hawthorne, not Whitman, who has been taken very seriously at
the higher levels of education and by learned literary critics.

Understanding the reality of sin, Hawthorne was contemptuous of radicals' designs for the perfection of man and society.
It was Hawthorne, you may recall, who said that no man was
ever more justly hanged than was John Brown of Osawatomie.
Hawthorne's *Blithedale Romance* demolishes American utopi-
ans; his short tale "Earth's Holocaust" ridicules the radicals'
fierce endeavor to destroy the civilized past. As did T. S. Eliot,
I take Hawthorne for the most moving and enduring of
American writers.

A fighting, writing President is my seventh exemplary conservative: Theodore Roosevelt. Once upon a time, when my grandfather took his small grandson to the movies, there happened to appear on the screen, briefly, the face of Roosevelt. My grandfather applauded loudly but solitarily, to my embarrassment. Had I then read *Hero Tales from American History*, written by Theodore Roosevelt and Henry Cabot Lodge, I too would have applauded. My grandfather gave me a copy of that book not long later, and I read it most eagerly. How I was stirred, at the age of twelve, by Roosevelt's sketches and vignettes of George Rogers Clark, King's Mountain, the storming of Stony Point, the battle of New Orleans, the death of Stonewall Jackson, the charge at Gettysburg, Farragut at Mobile Bay, the Alamo! When later I came to know Roosevelt's houses at Oyster Bay—where he ran the United States, summers, from a loft-office above a drug store at the principal corners of the village—and in Manhattan, it was as if I were visiting one of my teachers. Much else that Roosevelt wrote has not diminished in vigor. Much that Roosevelt did requires doing all over again.

To apprehend how conservative Roosevelt was, read the venomous chapter about him in that snarling book *The American Political Tradition and the Men Who Made It*, by Richard Hofstadter, a thoroughgoing Marxist if an unconfessed one.

Consider such a passage as this: "The frantic growth and rapid industrial expansion that filled America in his lifetime had heightened social tensions and left a legacy of bewilderment, anger, and fright, which had been suddenly precipitated by the depression of the nineties. His psychological function was to relieve these anxieties with a burst of hectic action and to discharge these fears by scolding authoritatively the demons that aroused them. Hardened and trained by a long fight with his own insecurity, he was the master therapist of the middle classes."

How shocking that a President should be concerned for the middle classes! When Hofstadter sneers with such neurotic malice, one may be quite sure that Theodore Roosevelt was a power for good.

For my eighth conservative, I select that Polish genius who wrote in English, Joseph Conrad. I discovered Conrad early in my high-school years; picked up a second-hand set of his works in Salt Lake City during my years as a sergeant; lost that set in our Great Fire of 1975; and now have replaced most of the burnt volumes. I commend to you especially, with an eye to the literature of politics, his novels *Under Western Eyes*, *The Secret Agent*, and *Nostromo*. Of those, the first shows us Russian revolutionary politics, sad and grisly; the second reveals to us the figure of the Terrorist, yesteryear and today; the third is the most penetrating study ever written of Latin-American politics and character, illustrating Bolivar's mournful observation that whoever tries to establish liberty in Latin America plows the salt sea. Do not neglect Conrad's short stories, notably "The Informer", which I reprint in *The Portable Conservative Reader*.

In Conrad a powerful critical intellect is joined to vast experience of the ways of East and West. The great novelist entertains no illusions about socialism, anarchism, feminism, nihilism, liberalism, or imperialism. Were Conrad, the foe of ideology, writing today—why, he might have difficulty finding a decent publisher, and his novels might be ignored by the mass-media reviewers; but happily for his influence, Conrad's reputation was impregnably established before the present Holy Liberal Inquisition in publishing and reviewing obtained its unsparing hegemony.

Ninth, I call your attention to Richard Weaver, whom I knew well. According to Ambrose of Milan, it has not pleased God that man should be saved through logic. Richard Weaver would have assented to this, knowing as he did the nature of the average sensual man and the limits of pure rationality. Yet with a high logical power, Weaver undertook an intellectual defense of culture and did what he might to rescue order, justice, and freedom from the perverters of language.

Weaver died before his time, in his room—its walls painted black—at a cheap hotel on the South Side of Chicago. He had lived austerely and with dignity, hoping one day to retire to Weaverville, North Carolina, his birthplace. He was a shy little bulldog of a man who detested much in the modern world—with reason. His slim strong book *Ideas Have Consequences*, published in 1948, was the first gun fired by American conservatives in their intellectual rebellion against the ritualistic liberalism that had prevailed since 1933, and which still aspires to dominion over this nation. In 1948 I was a bookseller; and recognizing promptly the virtue of *Ideas Have Consequences*, I organized a display of many copies, sold most of them, and invited Weaver to speak to our George Ade Society in Lansing—perhaps the first time Weaver had been asked to speak, outside the University of Chicago. (Although he was no very effective orator, in one year he was voted the most able instructor in the College of the University of Chicago.)

Among philosophers, Plato was Weaver's mentor; and among statesmen, Lincoln. (Although a declared Southerner, in politics Weaver was a conservative Republican.) Such views did not find him favor in the academy, but he persevered, gaining some ground with his second book *The Ethics of Rhetoric*, and the several volumes of his other essays, published posthumously, have brought a consciousness of enduring truth to many who never saw him or wrote to him. A high consistency and honesty won over, in some degree, even the more hostile of the reviewers of his books.

Some of his closer Chicago friends—their number was not legion—might not see him during the course of an entire year. He never travelled; he endured stoically the ferocious Chicago winters, often wearing two overcoats, one over the other. Once a year he attended a church, and then a high Episcopalian service; the solemnity and mystery of the ritual, strongly though he was attracted by them, overwhelmed his soul: such a feast would last for months. The frugality woven into his character extended even to his very private religion.

No man was less romantic than Richard Weaver—yet none more inveterately attached to forlorn good causes. Vanity he knew not, and he despised the *hubris* of modern times. Although there exist no heirs of his body, the heirs of his mind may be many and stalwart.

Turn we at last to the gentler sex. Once upon a time I wrote a book entitled *The Intelligent Woman's Guide to Conservatism*;

and it would be possible to compile a *Portable Conservative Women's Reader*, for during the past century there have flourished a good many eminent female conservatives.

As my tenth exemplary conservative, then, I designate Freya Stark, the author of several remarkable books of travel in the Levant and Iran. Miss Stark was no politician, but a conservative spirit runs strongly through all her books, particularly her moving volume of essays *Perseus in the Wind* and her important historical study *Rome on the Euphrates*. I began reading the books of Miss Stark (or Mrs. Stewart Perowne, as she became eventually) during my residence in Scotland, and have venerated her ever since. Her brief essay "Choice and Toleration" is included in *The Portable Conservative Reader*.

To apprehend how a civilization undoes itself, one cannot do better than to read attentively her *Rome on the Euphrates*, with its account of the destruction of the western world's middle classes by Roman taxation, centralization, bureaucracy, and foolish war. History does repeat itself, although always with variations. There must be noted one sentence by Freya Stark that every conservative ought to grave upon his lintel—should he possess a house with a lintel—or at least upon his memory: "Tolerance cannot afford to have anything to do with the fallacy that evil may convert itself to good."

. . .

What an *omnium gatherum* of people endowed with a conservative turn of thought and impulse! A Roman orator, a

Roman emperor, a lexicographer, a Scottish romancer, a Virginia politician, a New England "boned pirate", a rough-riding President, a Polish sea-captain-novelist, a recluse at the University of Chicago, a wanderer in antique lands! Yet it was such who formed my own conservative mind; and their very diversity sufficiently demonstrates that conservatism is no ideology, but rather a complex of thought and sentiment, a deep attachment to the permanent things. Incidentally, I have taken the opportunity to pay tribute to some major figures not discussed at any length in my other books, to my shame: President Roosevelt, Dr. Weaver, and Miss Stark.

In the long run, the courses of nations are not determined by the candidates for office or the grandiose administrators whose names bulk large in the daily papers and echo in the television studios; whose names will be quite forgotten, most of them, a decade from now. Napoleon or Pitt, Stalin or Churchill, true, may leave real marks upon the world, for good or ill. Yet it is imagination that governs humankind: so the men and women who alter thought and sentiment are the true movers and shakers of the moral order and the civil social order.

The conservative imagination of the ten people I have presented to you was employed courageously to oppose that disorder which perpetually threatens to reduce the world to chaos. Profiting by their examples, we folk at the end of the twentieth century must rouse ourselves from the apathy of Lotos-land, taking counsel as to how we may defend the permanent things against the wrath of the enemies of order, so fierce and clamorous in our time; or how, at worst, to shore some fragments against our ruin.

VI

The Politics of T. S. Eliot

T urn we now to certain scholars and men of letters—four of them, all men of the twentieth century, all conservative of the permanent things, all of whom I had the honor of calling friend. In reputation the first of these four is T. S. Eliot.

Little more than a century ago, Eliot was born into an intelligently conservative family in St. Louis. His grandfather, a Unitarian minister and a man of mark, founded the Church of the Messiah and Washington University; the Eliots of St. Louis were Republican reformers, active in good causes, pillars of order.

If, visiting St. Louis today, one searches for Eliot's birthplace, one becomes oppressed by a sense of the vanity of human wishes. That Eliot house vanished long ago; the Church of the Messiah, too, was swept away long ago; the whole quarter, once elegant, where the Eliots lived is devastated and depopulated. No memorial to the greatest poet of the twentieth century stands in the city where he was born. Nor in London, except

for the memorial stone in Westminster Abbey, does one encounter any visible trace of Eliot, who never owned a house.
The expectation of change, since Eliot's birth, has been greater
than the expectation of continuity. And the permanent things,
as T. S. Eliot called them—those enduring truths and ways of
life and standards of order—are awash in the flood of sensual
appetite and ideological passion. As Eliot expressed this phenomenon of decadence, referring to standards of education, in
his book *Notes towards the Definition of Culture*, we are "de-
stroying our ancient edifices to make ready the ground upon
which the barbarian nomads of the future will encamp in their
mechanised caravans."

From his youth, Eliot took up the defense of the permanent
things, with some boldness. A great innovator in poetry, he
became a great conservative in morals and politics, so that my
book on conservative thought begins with Burke and ends with
Eliot. At no time in his life was he afflicted by political radicalism. After a decade of residence in London, he announced that
he was a classicist in literature, a royalist in politics, an
anglo-catholic in religion. "I am aware that the second term is
at present without definition," he wrote, "and easily lends itself
to what is almost worse than clap-trap, I mean temperate conservatism. . . ." He would have despised the current American
political label "moderate": the Conservative Party of England
was not nearly conservative enough for T. S. Eliot.

In 1922, poor and overworked in London, he founded a
magazine, *The Criterion*, which endured until January, 1939,
when Europe was about to erupt. The magazine was intended

to work among the educated classes of Europe "an affirmation and development of tradition", as opposed to the dissemination of Marxism and other ideologies among the intelligentsia. Also, though not quite avowedly, the review was meant to work a political resurrection, touching often upon political theory and institutions. Its circulation never exceeded eight hundred copies—George Orwell would have liked to buy it, but lacked the purchase-price—yet it published the writing of men and women of very high talent, and the bound volumes of this periodical remain worth reading earnestly, if need be to the exclusion of any magazine of our own day.

In Eliot's editorial "Commentaries" in that magazine will be found many shrewd or wise observations about politics—short pieces never reprinted. In such observations he impartially scourged the leaders of all political factions in Britain—with the partial exception of Stanley Baldwin, because Baldwin was something of a classical scholar as well as an honest man. Although a high Tory in English political tradition, he never participated in the actions of the Conservative Party—except, late in life, to lecture to the London Conservative Union, in 1955—concerning which memorable lecture, more presently.

Two of Eliot's slim books are concerned in part with political questions: *The Idea of a Christian Society*, published just after the beginning of the Second World War, and *Notes towards the Definition of Culture*, published when socialism had descended upon Britain shortly after that war. Eliot wrote one political or quasi-political poem, *Coriolan*. I have reprinted in

The Portable Conservative Reader his succinct mordant remarks on Marxist critics of literature. Other Eliot observations on politics may be found in certain of his literary essays, notably those on William Bramhall, Charles Whibley, and Machiavelli.

Now this may seem, bibliographically, rather a slight bulk of literary production to justify Eliot's eminence as a leader of conservative opinion. Permit me, then, to explain why Eliot is so much read, and so much respected, by men and women attached to the Permanent Things.

In his lecture on "The Literature of Politics", published in his collection *To Criticize the Critic*, Eliot refers to an essay by your servant, in which I mentioned, as American conservative thinkers, Paul Elmer More, Irving Babbitt, Bernard Iddings Bell, and Robert Nisbet—none of whom had plunged into the hurly-burly of practical politics. Eliot comments upon this separation of serious political writing from political action, "This is not a very healthy state of affairs, unless the views of such writers become more widely diffused and translated, modified, adapted, even adulterated, into action. It seems to me that in a healthy society, there will be a gradation of types between thought and action; at one extreme the detached contemplative, the critical mind which is concerned with the discovery of truth, not with its promulgation and still less with its translation into action, and at the other extreme, the N.C.O. of politics, the man who in spite of relative indifference to general ideas, is equipped with native good sense, right feeling and character, supported by discipline and education. Between these two extremes there is room for several varieties and several kinds of political thinking; but there should be no breach of continuity between them."

A little later in the same lecture, Eliot adds, "To go more directly to the point, a political tradition in which the doctrinaire dominates the man of action, and a tradition in which political philosophy is formulated or re-codified to suit the requirements and justify the conduct of a ruling clique, may be equally disastrous."

Eliot concludes his lecture by remarking that he is not much concerned with those temporary writers of alleged influence, "or with those publicists who have impressed their names upon the public by catching the morning tide, and rowing very fast in the direction in which the current was flowing." Rather, he says, "there should always be a few writers preoccupied in penetrating to the core of the matter, in trying to arrive at the truth and to set it forth, without too much hope, without ambition to alter the immediate course of affairs and without being downcast or defeated when nothing appears to ensue."

Now Eliot was himself one of those few writers, alluded to by him, who have endeavored to get at the political truth, or a more general truth in which political order is involved, and to set it forth: men of talent who labor intellectually in what Eliot called the *pre-political* area. Eliot's moral imagination, his broad learning, and his poetic talents enabled him indeed to penetrate to the core of the matter, when he touched upon the civil social order and that order's relationships to a transcendent order. Conservatively-inclined people on either side of the Atlantic, and farther afield than that, therefore often turn to Eliot's prose, and not infrequently to his verse, for light. In short, Eliot's seminal mind, with its keen perceptions—Eliot's armed vision—opened the way for seekers after intellectual order and moral order and social order to penetrate beyond the cant and slogan of the hour.

For when Eliot in his writings touches upon Hobbes, or Freud, or Marx, or Mannheim, or Shaw, or H. G. Wells, he punctures balloons so deftly as, two centuries earlier, did a very different man of letters, David Hume. Take, for instance, another passage from his lecture on the literature of politics. Eliot remarks that sometimes one is tempted to suspect "that the profounder and *wiser* the man, the less likely is his influence to be discernible." Then he goes on to give a tremendous knock to George Bernard Shaw: "Yet the immediate influence of—shall we say—Mr. Bernard Shaw in the period of his most potent influence, I suppose, at the beginning of this century, must have been more appreciable, and more widely diffused, than that of much finer minds; and one is compelled to admire a man of such verbal agility as not only to conceal from his readers and audiences the shallowness of his own thought, but to persuade them that in admiring his work they were giving evidence of their own intelligence as well. I do not say that Shaw could have succeeded alone, without the more plodding and laborious minds with which he associated himself; but by persuading low-brows that they were high-brows, and that high-brows must be socialists, he contributed greatly to the prestige of socialism. But between the influence of a Bernard Shaw or an H. G. Wells, and the influence of a Coleridge or a Newman, I can conceive no common scale of measurement."

What Eliot gives us is not the posturing glibness of Shaw, but wisdom after the mode of Samuel Taylor Coleridge and John Henry Newman. Incidentally, or accidentally, by showing that a famous innovating poet could reject ideology—socialist, communist, or fascist ideology—Eliot contributed greatly to the prestige of conservatism, in the better sense of that abused word.

Now in remarking that Eliot was pre-political in the sense that he concerned himself principally with ultimate questions, I do not mean that he took little thought for the political exigencies of his era. On the contrary, Eliot was most earnestly, and sorrowfully, concerned with the disasters and the grim prospects of our bent world. His commentaries in *The Criterion* often bore directly on political questions and men of the hour; and indeed a fundamental purpose of his review was to save the world from suicide, through joining together writers and public men of intelligence, in Britain, Europe, and America.

During the years when we met occasionally and exchanged lengthy letters, he was possessed of a good knowledge of practical politics in the United States—he always thinking of himself as an American—as well as a lively familiarity with matters of state in Britain and the Continent. During the 1950s, though alarmed at educational follies in Britain and America, he was not so depressed by public affairs as he had been while editing *The Criterion*, between the World Wars. In December, 1928, the gloomy Eliot had published in his magazine his essay "The Literature of Fascism"—which he rejected, along with the literature of communism. "A new school of political thought is needed," he wrote, "which might learn from political thought abroad, but not from political practice. Both Russian communism and Italian fascism seem to me to have died as political ideas, in becoming political facts." He was no enthusiast for an abstract democracy, an ideology of Democratism; but a healthy democracy, rooted in old institutions, he aspired to restore.

"It is one thing to say," he continued in his article on Fascism, "what is sadly certain, that democratic government has been watered down to almost nothing. . . . But it is another thing to ridicule the *idea* of democracy. . . . A real democracy is always a restricted democracy, and can only flourish with some limitation by hereditary rights and responsibilities. . . . The modern question as popularly put is: 'democracy is dead, what is to replace it?' whereas it should be: 'the frame of democracy has been destroyed; how can we, out of the materials at hand, build a new structure in which democracy can live?'"

Eleven years later, in his little book *The Idea of a Christian Society*, Eliot exhorted liberals and socialists, as war with the Axis powers was imminent, that "The term 'democracy' . . . does not contain enough positive content to stand alone against the forces that you dislike—it can easily be transformed by them. If you will not have God (and He is a jealous God) you should pay your respects to Hitler or Stalin."

For behind the virulent ideologies—substitutes for religion—in the twentieth century, behind the feeble politics of liberalism, behind the ineffectuality of conservatives, Eliot perceived, lay a refusal to admit ethics and theology to political thinking. As he would conclude his lecture on the literature of politics, in 1957: "For the question of questions, which no political philosophy can escape, and by the right answer to which all political thinking must in the end be judged, is simply this: What is Man? what are his limitations? what is his misery and what his greatness? and what, finally, his destiny?"

. . .

I need hardly remark that such principles of politics provoked wrath and ridicule among the intelligentsia of Bloomsbury in Eliot's time—even though Eliot's overwhelming reputation as a poet, and the strength of his personality, somewhat muted outcries against his Toryism. In recent years, many critics have endeavored to ignore Eliot's politics altogether, as irrelevant; while some have reproached him venomously as an enemy of democracy and equality of condition.

It is mildly amusing to find Eliot denounced for his Christian faith and his "feudalist" politics by tenured professors of English, some of them enjoying salaries in excess of one hundred thousand dollars, comforted and cosseted by serried ranks of word-processor operators and go-fers, amply provided with funds for travel and somewhat dubious "research," generously pensioned when they retire from their occasional teaching of a seminar or two—these scholars and gentlemen who preach egalitarian doctrines; these unimaginative pedants who, should a socialist regime ever come to this land, would be mightily reduced in their circumstances and privileges. Eliot was hard pressed for money until late years; and when at length he was awarded the Nobel Prize, the only substantial sum received by him in a lifetime, promptly he was deprived of the lion's share of it by the Inland Revenue.

The Pope of Russell Square, as some called him, from his little office at the firm of Faber and Faber—where I called upon him occasionally, in the 'Fifties—looked down with some contempt upon the crowd of literati of the Left, some of them political simpletons, others unscrupulous opportunists. All that could be said for the London crowd was that they were less silly than the Manhattan crowd of writers or would-be writers; as Eliot put it, "The worst form of expatriation for an American writer is residence in New York City." It is so still.

"It is natural, and not necessarily convincing," he wrote bitingly in 1933, in the pages of *The Criterion*, "to find young intellectuals in New York turning to communism, and turning their communism to literary account. The literary profession is not only, in all countries, overcrowded and underpaid . . . it has much ado to maintain its dignity as a profession at all." Marxism might provide the aspiring writer with both a creed and an assured income. "It is not always easy, of course, in the ebullitions of a new movement, to distinguish the man who has received the living word from the man whose access of energy is the result of being relieved of the necessity of thinking for himself. Men who have stopped thinking make a powerful force. There are obvious inducements, besides that—never wholly absent—of simple conversion, to entice the man of letters into political and social theory which he then employs to revive his sinking fires and rehabilitate his profession."

Eliot lifelong refused to run with these hounds; he subscribed his name to no ideological protests and manifestos; he rejected root and branch British socialism, not to speak of communism, fascism, and naziism; to Ezra Pound's wrath, Eliot was no enthusiast for Social Credit. His rejection of collectivist ideology aside, to what political convictions, realistically speaking, did Eliot adhere? Did his politics consist merely of negations?

Not at all. There are two aspects, or perhaps jurisdictions, of Eliot's practical politics: his British views, and his American views. Permit me first to say something about his American politics, that being the briefer subject.

Eliot wrote to me once that the America for which his family stood had ended with the defeat of John Quincy Adams by Andrew Jackson, in the presidential contest of 1828. (Eliot's distant kinsman Henry Adams made a similar observation.) So one may say that the politics of the Eliot family had been very like the politics of their kinfolk of the Adams family: Federalist so long as a Federalist party cohered, suspicious of levelling democracy, austerely moral, rooted in the culture of New England. These political views and habits were transferred by William Greenleaf Eliot, T. S. Eliot's grandfather, to Missouri. If I may take the liberty of quoting from my own works, a paragraph from my book about Eliot is pertinent here:

"The political exemplar of Eliot's youth had been a gentleman as real to the St. Louis boy as if he still had sat at the head of the dining table on Locust Street: the grandfather he never actually saw, the Reverend William Greenleaf Eliot, 'the nineteenth-century descendant of Chaucer's parson.' That grandfather had been a Christian hero—and a pillar of the visible community, a reforming conservative, as well as a buttress of the community of souls. In St. Louis he had reformed the schools; founded the university, become the apostle of gradual emancipation of the slaves, the champion of national union, the leader in a dozen other turbulent causes of reform—but always in the light of the permanent things. . . . His grandfather's notion of perfectibility, and some other beliefs (among them the grandfather's zeal for prohibiting strong drink), T. S. Eliot would discard; and yet a grandfather like that must weigh more lifelong, for an adherent of Tradition, than all the political metaphysicians in the books."

I having been blessed with a grandfather rather like Eliot's, we got on well when we talked about American politics, Eliot and I. Eliot's profession of royalism, by the way, signified mostly that he supported the English throne, having become a British subject, and that he approved of long-established monarchies elsewhere—such of them as had survived the tooth of time and the frenzy of revolutionaries that had followed hard upon both World Wars. He had not the faintest intention of saddling the United States with a monarch, any more than had his ancestor John Adams (who, nevertheless, had been accused of just such a design): in America, a royal house would have been an unnatural and untenable imposition.

Eliot having written next to nothing about America's practical politics, it is unnecessary here to go farther into his American views, except to remark in passing that he entertained a low opinion of Franklin Roosevelt, and a good opinion of the elder Senator Robert Taft. He sympathized strongly with the group called the Southern Agrarians, and among them was well acquainted with Allen Tate, a frequent contributor to *The Criterion*; he had been influenced by the conservative political convictions of Irving Babbitt (his Harvard mentor) and Paul Elmer More, the chief Humanist critics; he shared their misgivings as to the tendencies of the American democracy, but proposed no alteration of the constitutional framework; so far as he touched upon American remedies, his hope lay in the restoration of learning—a subject he discussed at some length in a series of lectures at the University of Chicago, during 1950. (These "Aims of Education" lectures are included in his collection *To Criticize the Critic*.)

A journal published by the Committee on Social Thought at the University of Chicago, *Measure*, printed Eliot's lectures on education shortly after their delivery. Robert Hutchins, then chancellor of the University of Chicago, published in a following number of *Measure* a rather sharp rejoinder, in which Hutchins said, among other things, that "the only difference between Edmund Burke and T. S. Eliot is that Eliot is a democrat and Burke was not." When next in Chicago, Eliot found himself at a party in his honor, with Robert Hutchins as a guest. Seeking Hutchins out, Eliot inquired of him, in his accustomed very civil manner, "Dr. Hutchins, I am grateful for your trouble in commenting upon my lectures on education; but I am puzzled by your remark about Burke and me. I never have called myself a democrat; and I suppose that Burke, in his age, was more of a democrat than I am in ours. So could you tell me what you meant?"

"But Mr. Hutchins turned his back and walked away. Why did he do that, Dr. Kirk?"

"Because he never had read Burke," I replied. "Hutchins once signed his name to an article attacking Burke that was published in *The Thomist*; but the article was written entirely by someone else; and this is all that Hutchins knows about Burke. You had unveiled his abysmal ignorance of much."

Like many other people in universities, Robert Hutchins was an egalitarian democrat in theory and an exacting autocrat in practice. Eliot had a talent for vexing such people.

. . .

As for English politics, Eliot was a consistent Tory rather than a regular Conservative. (The two partisan labels are not identical: Disraeli thought of changing the party's name back to Tory, after Peel had made it the Conservative party; but Metternich, in exile, dissuaded Disraeli.) Toryism means loyalty to King and Church; the Tories are bound up with the Church of England—and, at least in times past, with the squirearchy, the smaller landed proprietors. So it was with Eliot: he had declared himself a royalist (though, for that matter, nine out of ten English subjects approve of the royal family); he was a most devout communicant of the Church of England, and for some years a churchwarden in London; and he believed that the class of the old county families of England supplied the nation with leaders, in many walks of life, who ought not to be supplanted by an elite, an alleged meritocracy.

Yet the political thinkers and leaders he most admired included the great Whig Edmund Burke—whose name appears
more frequently in Eliot's lectures after, on his decision, Faber
and Faber published my book *The Conservative Mind*. Both in
his early essay on Charles Whibley and his late lecture on the
literature of politics, Eliot comments on four political writers,
masters of literary style, who clearly have influenced his own
views: Bolingbroke, Burke, Coleridge, and Disraeli. (In his essay
on Whibley, he mentions also Lord Halifax.) Eliot's political
thought, in considerable part, is descended from those great
conservatives; it more nearly approximates that of Coleridge,
whom Eliot recognizes as "a man of my own type."

So there is nothing very exotic about Eliot's political principles: they are bound up with English history, the English constitution, and the great divines of the Church of England. Those
very principles dissuaded him from praising the Conservative
party of his day. In June, 1929, when MacDonald and Labour
won the general election, forcing out of office Baldwin's
Conservative government (even though the Conservatives had
obtained a plurality of the popular vote) Eliot found that the
new Lib-Lab cabinet had not one new idea among them. What
might be done, in an hour when fascists and communists were
gaining influence among the intellectuals and among the mass
of voters?

"This is of course a great opportunity—for the Conservative
Party," Eliot wrote in *The Criterion*, "an opportunity which we
are quite sure it will fail to seize. It is the opportunity of thinking in leisure, and of appreciating the efforts of private persons

who have committed some thinking already. The Labour Party is a capitalist party in the sense that it is living on the reputation of thinking done by the Fabians of a generation ago. . . . The Conservative Party has a great opportunity in the fact that within the memory of no living man under sixty, has it acknowledged any contact with intelligence. It has, what no other political party at present enjoys, a complete mental vacuum: a vacancy that might be filled with anything, even with something valuable."

The leaders of the Conservatives were Hollow Men. Eliot feared that the political and social institutions of Britain were giving way; that feeble politicians, belligerent trade unions, a cumbersome bureaucracy, an apathetic public, a Church that no longer held meaning for most English people, an obsession with getting and spending—these phenomena and circumstances were eroding irrevocably the England that Eliot had come to love. For the most part, Eliot's vaticinations would be justified by subsequent events.

In this like Wilhelm Roepke in Switzerland, T. S. set his face against centralized power, whether under "capitalism" or under some socialist regime; he sought to retain a humane society; he knew that no society can long endure—at least no just and free society—without shared religious convictions. The notion that an international "planned economy" and "planned culture" might be contrived was anathema to him. He defended ably, in his last book, a society of classes against a society dominated by elites. There is much more I could say concerning his application of enduring political and social truths to our present discontents and afflictions; but such matters I must leave to your private reading.

Although you may lack time for extensive reading of Eliot's prose, take up at least his *Notes towards the Definition of Culture*, published in 1948—a book I once strongly commended to President Nixon. You will find therein, for one thing, a demolition of Karl Mannheim's proposals for a planned society—indeed, for universal planning. "For one thing to avoid is a *universalized* planning," Eliot writes; "one thing to ascertain is the limits of the plannable."

Probably Eliot would have said, if asked, that the most important passage in this last slim book of his is one concerned with the dependence of our culture, or of any culture, upon religious belief. Here is that passage, in part:

"I do not believe that the culture of Europe could survive the complete disappearance of the Christian Faith. And I am convinced of that, not merely because I am a Christian myself, but as a student of social biology. If Christianity goes, the whole of our culture goes. Then you must start painfully again, and you cannot put on a new culture ready made. You must wait for the grass to grow to feed the sheep to give the wool out of which your new coat will be made. You must pass through many centuries of barbarism. We should not live to see the new culture, nor would our great-great-great grandchildren; and if we did, not one of us would be happy in it."

Since Eliot's death, many unhappy choices have been made in Britain, and the decay that he lamented has continued apace, in several ways—though not in all. The deliberate lowering of intellectual standards in British schools and universities, and formal protestations of disbelief by eminent bishops and archbishops, have been among those dismaying phenomena. Yet it is not possible, Eliot instructs us, to measure the long-run influence of a poet or a philosopher. In the fullness of time, perhaps it will be found that Eliot sowed better than he knew, and that his political and cultural writings will endure along with his great poems, and bear some fruit. We must be very patient, said Eliot, awaiting the dissolution of liberalism and the recovery of tradition.

My friend Eliot did not expect to turn back the clock by any social or literary magic; nor did he fancy that we would be pleased by the result, even were it possible; for we all are creatures of the age into which we have been born. As he expressed this hard truth in "Little Gidding"—

> *We cannot restore old policies*
> *Or follow an antique drum.*

Reading Eliot will not tell us how to balance the federal budget and reduce the national debt—even though the poet of *The Waste Land* was a banker for some years. But his poetry tells us much about the human condition, in its splendor and its misery; and his prose makes us acutely aware of the Permanent Things. I knew Eliot somewhat during his later years, and understand him better now that his ashes lie in the medieval church at East Coker. For, as Eliot wrote in "Little Gidding"—

And what the dead had no speech for, when
living,
They can tell you, being dead: the communication
Of the dead is tongued with fire beyond the language of the living.

VII

Donald Davidson and the South's Conservatism

*L*eviathan is a Hebrew word signifying "that which gathers itself in folds." In the Old Testament, Leviathan is the great sea-beast: "Canst thou draw out leviathan with a hook?" In the seventeenth century, Thomas Hobbes—whom T. S. Eliot calls "that presumptuous little upstart"—made Leviathan the symbol of the state, or rather of mass-society, composed of innumerable little atomic individual human beings.

But here we are concerned with Donald Davidson's Leviathan. In 1938, long before the administration of Lyndon Johnson popularized the slogan "The Great Society", Davidson wrote that his Leviathan is "the idea of the Great Society, organized under a single, complex, but strong and highly centralized national government, motivated ultimately by men's desire for economic welfare of a specific kind rather than their desire for personal liberty." Six decades later, Leviathan looms larger than ever.

The Southern States that once formed the Confederacy have been the most conservative region of America, it is generally agreed. Once upon a time, Richard Weaver told me that Middle Tennessee is the most southern part of the South. There in Middle Tennessee, near the town of Pulaski, in 1893, Donald Davidson was born. Surely Davidson was the most redoubtably conservative of those able American men of letters who have been called the Southern Agrarians. As poet, as critic, as historian, and as political thinker, Davidson was a stalwart defender of America's permanent things during an era of radical change.

Ever since the forming of the Union in 1787, the dominant political tendency in the southern states has been resistance to centralizing power. Far more than any other region, the South has set its face against Leviathan—that is, against the omnipotent swelling nation-state, what Tocqueville called democratic despotism, the political collectivity that reduces men and women to social atoms. Davidson scourged the centralizers—and that at a time when President Franklin Delano Roosevelt was doing much as he liked with the United States of America.

Browsing in 1938 in the library at Michigan State College, an earnest sophomore, I happened upon a new book, published by the University of North Carolina Press, entitled *The Attack on Leviathan*, and subtitled *Regionalism and Nationalism in the United States*. It was written eloquently, and for me it made coherent the misgivings I had felt concerning the political notions popular in the 1930s. The book was so good that I assumed all intelligent Americans, or almost all, were reading it. Actually, as I learned years later, the University of North Carolina Press pulped the book's sheets after only a few hundred copies had been sold: clearly an act of discrimination against conservative views. I had a hand in the reprinting of the book, by another firm, in 1963; and I am happy at having brought out in 1990 a third edition, for Leviathan is as menacing in 1992 as he was in 1938.

Professor Davidson rowed against the tide of opinion among America's intellectuals, in 1938. Centralizing nationalism, he argued, is of necessity tyrannical and enslaving. For a specimen of his method and style, take this passage from his chapter on American literature. He has been criticizing Emerson, and he finds that the opinion-shapers of New York and Boston during the 1930s are Emerson's heirs:

"In our own time, the metropolitan critics are making national prescriptions that are equally partial, though somewhat more confused. In one sentence they assure us that the industrial unification of America is desirable and inevitable; but in the next sentence they declare that the civilization thus produced puts upon us an intolerable spiritual bondage from which the artist cannot escape save through the shibboleths of Marxism and Freudianism. Wearily, they proclaim that America is standardized; but angrily they scorn the rural backwardness of regions that prove to be, after all, less urban than New York. Confidently they announce that America must be industrialized; but they sneer at Mr. Babbitt of the Middle West, the creature of industrialism. They urge the provinces to adopt the intellectual sophistication of the Eastern metropolis; but among themselves they bewail the poverty of the modem temper, which in its sophistication has left them nothing to enjoy."

Now could one write, in this year of 1992, a better description of the mentality of such American intellectuals? One might
substitute, of course, the phrase "the industrial unification of
the world" for that of America; for nowadays the whole of the
world must be subjected to those environmental mischiefs and
social discontents that already have worked immense harm in
the "developed countries".

Davidson was bold enough to defend the agricultural economy against industrial aggrandizement. (Parenthetically it
seems worth remarking that in recent years the dollar volume
of agricultural produce in the industrial state of Michigan has
exceeded the dollar volume of manufactured products.) Bolder
still, he took up the cause of his own region, the South, against
the nationalizers of New York and Washington. He appreciated,
too, other American regions: New England, the Great Plains,
the Lake States, the Pacific coast. But it was the South which
required the service of Davidson's sword of imagination.

"Can principles enunciated as Southern principles, of
whatever cast, get a hearing?" he inquired in *The Attack on
Leviathan*. ". . . It seems to be a rule that the more special the
program and the more remote it is from Southern principles,
the greater the likelihood of its being discussed and promulgated. Southerners who wish to engage in public discussion
in terms that do not happen to be of common report in the
New York newspapers are likely to be met, at the levels where
one would least expect it, with the tactics of distortion, abuse,
polite tut-tutting, angry discrimination and so on down to
the baser devices of journalistic lynching which compose the

modern propagandist's stock in trade. This is an easy and comparatively certain means of discrediting an opponent and of thus denying him a hearing. It is also a fatal means. For if such approaches to public questions are encouraged and condoned, then confusion has done its work well, the days of free and open discussion of ideas are over in the South, only matters of crass expediency can come into the public forum at all, and we face the miserable prospect of becoming the most inert and passive section of the United States, or else of falling into blind and violent divisions whose pent-up forces will hurl us at each other's throats. Then will Jefferson's prophetic vision come true. We shall take to eating one another, as they do in Europe."

Such matters have not much improved since Davidson wrote those sentences, half a century past: the South continues to be treated by Congress as if it were a subject province (in voter-registration especially), and the New York newspapers remain ungenerous.

New York City was to Donald Davidson the abomination of desolation. He and his wife spent their summers at Bread Loaf, in Vermont; and Davidson took extraordinary pains to avoid passing through New York City *en route*. For that matter, he detested sprawling modern cities generally, Nashville included, though he found it necessary to reside most of his life in the neighborhood of Vanderbilt University. To his volume of poems *The Tall Men* (published in 1927) Davidson had a prologue, "The Long Street", the antithesis of the rural Tennessee of yesteryear, that land of heroes. That Long Street—I think of devastated Woodward Avenue, in Detroit—is the symbol of a dehumanized urban industrial culture:

> *The grass cannot remember; trees cannot*
> *Remember what once was here. But even so,*
> *They too are here no longer. Where is the grass?*
> *Only the blind stone roots of the dull street*
> *And the steel thews of houses flourish here*
> *And the baked curve of asphalt, smooth, trodden*
> *Covers dead earth that once was quick with grass,*
> *Snuffing the ground with acrid breath the motors*
> *Fret the long street. Steel answers steel. Dust whirls.*
> *Skulls hurry past with the pale flesh yet clinging.*
> *And a little hair.*

Davidson was a guardian of those permanent things which perish upon the pavements of the Long Street; and an inveterate adversary of the enormous welfare state, which devours the spirit. Those themes run through his verse as through his prose.

Politics, we are told truly, is the art of the possible—and the preoccupation of the quarter-educated. That is, politics ranks low among the works of the mind, if one refers simply to defecated political theory and practice. But Professor Davidson never divorced politics from religion or imaginative literature or tradition. He knew that the greatest works of politics are poetic, from Plato onward. In his later collection of essays entitled *Still Rebels, Still Yankees* (1957) he writes about the dissociation of the poet from society, now "painfully apparent as society has accepted the dominance of science and consequently has become indisposed to accept poetry as truth. . . . In this phase of operations the poet may well become an outright traditionalist in religion, politics, and economics. He examines the defects of modern civilization. He develops a sense of catastrophe. With an insight far more accurate than the forecasts of professional social philosophers, he begins to plot the lines of stress and strain along which disaster will erupt. He predicts the ruin of modern secularized society and makes offers of salvation. These are unheard of or unheeded. Then upon the deaf ears and faceless bodies of modern society he invokes the poet's curse."

Eliot's poetic curse was that famous fatal dismissal, "This is the way the world ends/Not with a bang but a whimper." Davidson, fiercely though he reproached a sensate age, was not quite ready to pronounce a curse upon his time. Tradition still might reassert its old power. Take this passage from his essay "Futurism and Archaism in Toynbee and Hardy" contained in *Still Rebels, Still Yankees*:

> 'You cannot turn the clock back!' is the commonest taunt of our day. It always emerges as the clinching argument that any modernist offers any traditionalist when the question is: 'What shall we do now?' But it is not really an argument. It is a taunt intended to discredit the traditionalist by stigmatizing him a traitor to an idea of progress that is assumed as utterly valid and generally accepted. The aim is, furthermore, to

poison the traditionalist's own mind and disturb his
self-confidence by the insinuation that he is a laggard
in the world's great procession. His faith in an established good is made to seem nostalgic devotion to a
mere phantom of the buried past. His opposition to
the new—no matter how ill-advised, inartistic, destructive, or immoral that new may be—is defined as
a quixotic defiance of the Inevitable. To use a term
invented by Arnold J. Toynbee, he is an Archaist. By
definition, he is therefore doomed.

To abide by Tradition is not to fall into archaism, Davidson
told the rising generation. As for turning back the clock—why,
as Davidson puts it, "Neither can you turn the clock forward,
for Time is beyond human control." When a Futurist uses this
clock metaphor, we perceive "an unconscious revelation of his
weakness. He wishes to imply that his design, and his only, is
perfectly in step with some scientific master clock of cause and
effect that determines the progress of human events. This implication has no basis in reality, since the Futurist actually
means to break off all connection with the historical process of
cause and effect and to substitute for it an imagined, ideal process of quasi-scientific future development which is nothing
more than a sociological version of Darwinism."

Such was the conservative mind of Donald Davidson. If I
have made him seem somewhat abstract—why, that has been my
blunder. He was remarkably versatile: a collector of folk ballads,
a gifted lecturer, a writer of librettos, a historian, even from time

to time active in the troubled politics of Tennessee. He was aware all too well of the huge blunders in public policy during the twentieth century: if one turns to the second volume of his history of the Tennessee River, one finds three chapters accurately exposing the failures of that enormous undertaking, so warmly commended by the liberal press and most Tennessee politicians—yet so founded upon economic and social fallacies.

In person, Davidson was a lean and austere gentleman who smiled rarely; his conversation, nevertheless, was lively, and he was a kindly host. He had been a courageous soldier before I was born, and carried himself like a soldier. To the end he lived with dignity, lamenting the destruction of dignity within universities. Once I walked with him on the campus at Vanderbilt; he told me of how most of the trees there had been felled not long before, to make space for more automobiles. This was bad enough; but to make his indignation perfect, grim rows of parking meters had been installed. A militant survivor from what he called "the old regime", Davidson spoke contemptuously of his university's administrators. Students venerated him. He wrote to me on August 31, 1954: "Living in Nashville and teaching at Vanderbilt University is very hard on a Southern Agrarian, I can assure you. It is, in fact, nothing but warfare, and we can't survive very long without some place to lick our wounds for awhile." (This he wrote from Ripton, Vermont, where he had spent many a summer teaching at the Bread Loaf School.)

Vanderbilt's administration disparaged the Agrarians and, in effect, would not accept Davidson's or Allan Tate's papers as gifts. For that matter, the literate South generally neglected those Agrarians, the most illustrious of southern sons, in their own time. Only when New York paid attention to Tate, Warren, Ransom, Lytle, and others did the South prick up its ears. As that seventeenth-century "Person of No Quality" put it,

> Seven cities now contend for Homer dead,
> Through which the living Homer begged his bread.

I fear I have set down here only a fragmentary summary of Donald Davidson's social thought. But now I pass to some remarks on the Southern Agrarians generally, and to the pressing question of what to do about Leviathan.

. . .

More than sixty years ago, when I was a fourth-grader in the very northern town of Plymouth, Michigan, Twelve Southerners published a book entitled *I'll Take My Stand: The South and the Agrarian Tradition*. That slim volume, a heartfelt defense of the permanent things in the South's culture, has been discussed ever since; a literature of assent or of disapproval has developed about it. Young men and women who come to study with me in my northern fastness discover this literature—even without my having commented on any of it—and read the books, night upon night, even to the witching hour of three.

Christian humanism, stern criticism of the industrial mass society, detestation of communism and other forms of collectivism, attachment to the ways of the Old South in valor and in manners—these were the principles joining the twelve Southern Agrarians who took their stand in Dixieland in 1930. Their twelve essays were approved by T. S. Eliot and some other reflective people at the time the book was published; yet for the most part the Agrarians met with hostility and ridicule. Today their book sometimes meets with understanding, for we are farther down the track to Avernus.

As Louis Rubin says of the Twelve Southerners, *I'll Take My Stand* "is a rebuke to materialism, a corrective to the worship of Progress, and a reaffirmation of man's aesthetic and spiritual needs. And because the South has come so late into the industrial world, it appeals to the hungering memory within the Southerner's mind of the tranquil and leisurely Southern life that existed before the machines and superhighways came. As such the book constitutes both a reminder and a challenge. *What are you losing that you once possessed? Are you sure that you want to discard it entirely?*"

Despite the considerable attention paid nationally to these Agrarian writers, it was not easy for them to find publishers; or, if their writings should be published, to keep them in print. Yet they persisted; and in the long run their high talents as men of letters gave them for some years, about the period of my college days, ascendancy over the realm of letters, even in Manhattan—a mild domination, lingering until recent years, when it was overthrown by the squalid oligarchs of the *New York Review of Books*. (Even here the South has made a successful counterattack, most conspicuously in the homage paid to

Flannery O'Connor and Walker Percy.) As a group, the Agrarians illustrated well the remark made by Lionel Trilling that the twentieth-century writers possessing imagination were not liberals—distinctly not.

The Twelve Southerners, Donald Davidson among them, knew that the South would change. As Stark Young put it in his essay "Not in Memoriam, But in Defense", which concluded their book, "That a change is now in course all over the South is plain; and it is as plain that the South changing must be the South still, remembering that for no thing can there be any completeness that is outside its own nature, and no thing for which there is any advance save in its own kind. If this were not so, all nature by now would have dissolved in chaos and folly, nothing in it . . ."

Yet the South's pace of change has been more rapid, these six decades past, and more overwhelming, than even the gloomiest of the Twelve Southerners expected. Old Nashville, the domicile of the Fugitives and the Agrarians, has been thoroughly demolished and uglified, Strickland's capitol on its hill besieged by the haughty office towers of state and federal bureaucracies, and of teachers' unions. Much else, in Nashville and nearly all the South, has gone by the board—among those losses, the disappearance of Southern architectural styles.

Along with the dwindling of a distinctive Dixie has come relative economic prosperity. It is factory-town prosperity. The rural pattern of existence, which the Agrarians praised, still endures here and there south of Mason's and Dixon's Line, but it has been brutally buffeted during the past sixty years.

Of the Twelve Southerners, only one—Andrew Lytle, novelist and critic—remains here in the land of the living. Modernity has been doing its worst to wipe out Southerners of their sort, in part by sweeping away—in the South and elsewhere—the sort of schooling that men like Davidson and Lytle and Warren profited by. And the welfare state has striven to efface, as impoverished and culturally deprived, the old rural pattern of the South—or, for that matter, of Northern rural counties like that I inhabit—which endured little altered until the building of the "good roads".

Tide what may betide, the Southern Agrarians will loom large in histories of American thought and letters. With liberalism in America now nearly mindless, some of the rising generation in this land are finding in Donald Davidson's prose and verse, and in the writings of other Agrarians, an understanding of personal and social order far removed from desiccated liberal attitudes.

. . .

Six decades after Donald Davidson, Andrew Lytle, Lyle Lanier, Allen Tate, John Crowe Ransom, Frank Owsley, John Gould Fletcher, H. C. Nixon, Robert Penn Warren, John Donald Wade, Henry Blue Kline, and Stark Young took up arms against Leviathan, how goes the fight?

Like the Celts of the Twilight, it seems, the Agrarians have gone forth often to battle, but never to victory. America's farmers now total perhaps five percent of the national population.

The South has been subjugated a second time by the federal government, and endures a second political Reconstruction —although this time the southern economy is far from ruined. Centralization of power in Washington was carried much farther by Lyndon Johnson than ever it had been by Franklin Roosevelt; states still nominally sovereign are reduced to a condition little better than that of provinces. The nationwide television broadcasters are rapidly effacing any remnants of regional cultures. The public educational establishment exhorts its teachers and its charges to sing "The Battle Hymn of the Republic" rather than "Dixie". In many other ways, Leviathan looms far vaster than the monster was in 1930.

And yet the predictions of the Twelve Southerners, like those of Cassandra, are being fulfilled. Our great cities, a hundred Long Streets, are nearly ruined, ravaged by crime, their population corrupted or endangered by deadly narcotics, all community destroyed. Our boasted affluence is given the lie by the swift and sinister growth of a genuine proletariat, voracious and unruly, subsisting at public expense. Our layers of governmental bureaucracy are increasingly inefficient and vexatious. Our legislatures, national and state, seem willing to yield to every demand of a pressure-group, regardless of the true public interest. Our judges, or many of them, have turned demagogues. Our air is polluted badly, our countryside uglified, public taste corrupted. Our children are brought up indulgently on images of terrible violence and gross sexuality. Schooling at every level is reduced to child care, adolescent-sitting, and collegiate mating: humane letters and history are contemned.

While we talk windily still of free enterprise, the industrial and commercial conglomerates move toward oligopoly on a tremendous scale. Religious belief and observance have been first reduced to the ethos of sociability, and then to ignorant discourses on revolution. Leviathan, the monstrous society, has swallowed his myriads.

So I commend the conservatism of the Twelve Southerners. It is not the only mode of conservative thought, but it is an important mode. The authors of *I'll Take My Stand* did not propound a rigorous ideology or display a model of Utopia: their principal purpose it was to open eyes to the illusions of Modernism.

Southern Agrarians proclaimed when I was a child that the southern culture is worth defending; that society is something more than the Gross National Product; that the country lane is healthier than the Long Street; that more wisdom lies in Tradition than in Scientism; that Leviathan is a devourer, not a savior. Study what the Twelve Southerners have written and you may discover that they are no mere Archaists.

"Worn out with abstraction and novelty, plagued with divided counsels, some Americans have said: I will believe the old folks at home, who have kept alive through many treacherous outmodings some good secret of life." So Donald Davidson wrote in his chapter "The Diversity of America". He continued, "Such moderns prefer to grasp the particular. They want something to engage both their reason and their love. They distrust the advice of John Dewey to 'use the foresight of the future to refine and expand present activities.' The future is not yet; it is unknowable, intangible. But the past was, the present is; of that they can be sure. So they attach themselves—or reattach themselves—to a home-section, one of the sections, great or small, defined in the long conquest of our continental area. They seek spiritual and cultural autonomy.... They are learning how to meet the subtlest and most dangerous foe of humanity—the tyranny that wears the mask of humanitarian-ism and benevolence. They are attacking Leviathan."

Amen to that, Donald Davidson, my old friend, now passed into eternity. In these 1990's, half the peoples of the world have risen to strike a blow against Leviathan; so perhaps Davidson's courageous book will be better understood, and by more people, than it was in 1938.

VIII

The Humane Economy of Wilhelm Roepke

P ermit me to offer you some observations concerning Wilhelm Roepke, a principal social thinker of the twentieth century—and, incidentally, the principal architect of Germany's economic recovery at the end of the Second World War. His books are out of print in this country at present, except for *The Social Crisis of Our Time*, of which I brought out a new edition recently. And to my remarks on Professor Roepke I shall add certain related reflections of my own.

Roepke was the confident champion of a humane economy: that is, an economic system suited to human nature and to a humane scale in society, as opposed to systems bent upon mass production regardless of counterproductive personal and social consequences. He was a formidable opponent of socialist and other "command" economies; also a fearless perceptive critic of an unthinking "capitalism". Although German by birth, during the Second World War Roepke settled in Geneva, where he became professor of economics at the Graduate Institute of

International Affairs. There he wrote *Civitas Humana*; *The Social Crisis of Our Time*; *Economics of the Free Society*; *The Solution of the German Problem*; the essays included in the volumes *Against the Tide* and *Welfare, Freedom, and Inflation*. The title of his last book published in America, *A Humane Economy*, was suggested by me.

A gentleman of high courage and a sincere Christian, Roepke set his face against both the Nazis and the Communists. He was intellectually and physically vigorous: an accomplished skier, he always climbed back up the mountainside, rather than riding a chair-lift. Knowing that man is more than producer and consumer, Roepke detested Jeremy Bentham's Utilitarianism, and found that most of his fellow-economists perceived human existence very imperfectly, being blinkered by utilitarian dogmata.

Before turning to Roepke's arguments, I venture to offer some background of his thought, during the disorderly period that followed upon the Second World War, a time during which the idea of grand-scale social planning exercised a malign power. Roepke was the most effective opponent of that *Planwirtschaft*.

That highly speculative division of knowledge which our age calls "economics" took shape in the eighteenth century as an instrument for attaining individual freedom, as well as increased efficiency of production. But many twentieth-century teachers and specialists in economics became converts to a neo-Jacobinism. (Burke defines Jacobinism as "the revolt of the enterprising talents of a nation against its property".) Such doctrines of confidence in the omnicompetence of the state in economic concerns came to predominate in state polytechnic institutes and state universities especially. Quite as eighteenth-century optimism, materialism, and humanitarianism were fitted by Marx into a system which might have surprised a good many of the *philosophes*, so nineteenth-century utilitarian and Manchesterian concepts were the ancestors (perhaps with a bend sinister) of mechanistic social planning. The old Jacobins scarcely realized that their centralizing tendencies were imitative of the policies of the Old Regime; so it is not surprising that recent humanitarian and collectivistic thinkers forget their debt to Jeremy Bentham. Yet the abstractions of Bentham, reducing human beings to social atoms, are the principal source of modern designs for social alteration by fiat.

At the end of the Second World War, centralizers and coercive planners were mightily influential in western Europe and in Britain, and were not missing in the United States. The modern nation-state enjoys effective powers of coercion previously unknown in political structures. But the increase of coercion frustrates the natural course of development; economic theory as a basis for state coercion has repeatedly proved fallible; "planning" destroys the voluntary community and tries to substitute an ineffectual master plan (as, most ruinously, in Iran under the Shah); the goals of state action should be judicial rather than economic; and thus the whole perspective of "social planners" is distorted. In opposition to the dominant school of economic theory just after the Second World War, such economists as Roepke, W. A. Orton, F. A. Hayek, and a handful of others strove to restrain the economic collectivists.

   Although he proved himself very competent to deal with the vast postwar economic difficulties of Germany, a major industrial country, nevertheless Roepke much preferred the social and economic patterns of Switzerland, where he lived from the triumph of Hitler until the end of his life. His model for a humane economy can be perceived by an observant traveller in Switzerland.

· · ·

Professor Roepke seemed to have read everything. He was familiar, for instance, with the social ideas of Calhoun and Fenimore Cooper, concerning which most American professors of economics are densely ignorant. Wilhelm Roepke knew the insights of religion and poetry, the problems of continuity and morality. His book *The Social Crisis of Our Time* is at heart an analysis of the menace that Roepke called "the cult of the colossal". Social equilibrium has been overthrown in our age, Roepke knew. Here are some moving sentences of his concerning that grim subject:

> Men, having to a great extent lost the use of their innate sense of proportion, thus stagger from one extreme to the other, now trying out this, now that, now following this fashionable belief, now that, responding now to this external attraction, now to the

other, but listening least of all to the voice of their own heart. It is particularly characteristic of the general loss of a natural sense of direction—a loss which is jeopardizing the wisdom gained through countless centuries—that the age of immaturity, of restless experiment, of youth, has in our time become the object of the most preposterous overestimation.

Of all our afflictions, Roepke continues, the fruits of moral decay, of consolidation, and of the worship of bigness, the worst is proletarianization. Capitalism may have introduced the modern proletariat, but socialism enlarges that class to include nearly the whole of humanity. Our salvation, Roepke argues, lies in a third choice, something different from either ideological socialism or doctrinaire capitalism.

"Socialism, collectivism, and their political and cultural appenages are, after all, only the last consequence of our yesterday, they are the last convulsions of the nineteenth century and only in them do we reach the lowest point of a century-old development along the wrong road; these are the hopeless final state toward which we drift unless we act," Roepke writes. "The new path is precisely the one that will lead us out of the dilemma of 'capitalism' and collectivism. It consists of the economic humanism of the 'Third Way.'"

That same infatuation with "rationalism" which terribly damages communal existence also produces an unquestioning confidence in the competitive market economy and leads to a heartless individualism which, in Roepke's words, "in the end has proved to be a menace to society and has so discredited a fundamentally sound idea as to further the rise of the far more dangerous collectivism." In such a world, where old landmarks have been swept away, old loyalties ridiculed, and human beings reduced to economic atoms, "men finally grasp at everything that is offered to them, and here they may easily and understandably suffer the same fate as the frogs in the fable who asked for a king and got a crane."

In his chapter "The Splendor and Misery of Capitalism", Roepke examines succinctly the maladies of our present economy and observes that the same economic disharmonies become chronic under socialism. Then he turns to the second part of *The Social Crisis of Our Time*, entitled "Action".

"Socialism—helped by the uprooted proletarian existence of large numbers of the working class and made palatable for them by just as rootless intellectuals, who will have to bear the responsibility for this—is less concerned with the interests of these masses than with the interests of those intellectuals, who may indeed see their desire for an abundant choice of positions of power fulfilled by the socialist state," Roepke instructs us.

Roepke relishes this class of persons as masters of society even less than he does the monopolists and the managers. His object is to restore liberty to men by promoting economic independence. The best type of peasants, artisans, small traders, small and medium-sized businessmen, members of the free professions and trusty officials and servants of the community—these are the objects of his solicitude, for among them traditional human nature still has its healthiest roots, and throughout most of the world they are being ground between "capitalistic" specialization and "socialistic" consolidation. They need not vanish from society, once more they may constitute the masters of society, for Switzerland, in any case, "refutes by its mere existence any cynical doubt regarding the possibility of realizing our program."

Loathing "doctrinaire rationalism", Roepke is careful not to propound an arbitrary scheme of alteration and renovation. Yet his suggestions for deproletarianizing are forthright. Family farms, farmers' cooperatives for marketing, encouragement of artisans and small traders, the technical and administrative possibilities of industrial decentralization, the diminution of the average size of factories, the gradual substitution for the "old-style welfare policy" of an intelligent trend toward self-sufficiency—none of these projects is novel, but they are commended by an economist possessing both grand reputation and sound common sense. To cushion society against the fluctuations of the business cycle, for instance, the better remedy is not increased centralization, a most dubious palliative, but instead the stimulating of men to get a part of their sustenance from outside the immediate realm of financial disturbance. Specialization often works mischief, he says:

"The most extreme examples of this tendency are perhaps some American farmers who had become so specialized and so dependent on their current money incomes that when the crisis came they were as near starvation as the industrial worker. At the other, more fortunate end we see the industrial worker in Switzerland who, if necessary, can find his lunch in the garden, his supper in the lake, and can earn his potato supply in the fall by helping his brother clear his land." Humanizing of economic structure was the kernel of Roepke's proposals. For him, political economy had an ethical foundation.

Roepke was no apologist for an abstraction called "capitalism"—a Marxist term, incidentally, foolishly pinned to themselves by numerous vainglorious champions of economic competition. He knew that the worship of Mammon is damnable.

He spoke always of the human condition, and how we might win our way back to a humane economy. Three decades after Roepke's death, we have lost ground in that endeavor. Washington, London, Tokyo, and Moscow are even more obsessed by the Gross National Product than they were in the 'Fifties, although the paper statistics of the GNP have not produced stability or contentment, and the terrorist walks abroad. There comes to mind the legend inscribed on a chateau's sun-dial, in 1789: "It is later than you think." The nexus of cash payment, never a strong social link, does not suffice to keep down fanatic ideology, nor even to assure prosperity.

. . .

An economy obsessed by an alleged Gross National Product—no matter what is produced, or how—becomes inhumane. A society that thinks only of alleged Efficiency, regardless the consequences to human beings, works its own ruin. Here there comes to my mind a passage from the writings of

W. A. Orton, an American conservative economist, a contemporary of Roepke. In his book *The Economic Role of the State*, Orton ironically describes the cult of Efficiency:

"Let us therefore praise the great god Efficiency," Orton writes. "All he demands is that we make straight his path through the desert and purge the opposition. . . . How much more mastery is evident in the controls of a supersonic plane than in the clumsy splendor of some medieval shrine! How much higher a peak of human achievement! Human? Let us not be too particular about that, for this is where science plays the joker. . . . We arrive at 'justice' without mercy, 'liberation' without liberty, 'victory' without peace, 'efficiency' without effort, 'power' without potency—because the means we collectively employ lie on a plane so different from that of the ends we humanly desire that, the more they succeed, the more they fail. That is the nemesis of all 'great powers' and the end of all who put their trust in them. God knows, this is not a new story."

Detroit, the city I have known best, has worshipped the great god Efficiency. During my own lifetime, Detroit has produced tremendous wealth in goods and services. But the city has been a social failure, and so have most of America's other cities. Once called "the arsenal of democracy", nowadays Detroit, become ruinous and ungovernable, more frequently has been referred to as "the murder capital of America." In Celine's famous novel *Journey to the End of Night*, the journey terminates at Detroit.

In the shocking decay of that great city, one beholds the consequences of an inhumane economy—bent upon maximum productive efficiency, but heedless of personal order and public order. Of course the automobile-manufacturers of Detroit, in the early years of their operation, had no notion of what might be the personal and social effects of their highly successful industrial establishment; nor had anyone else. But they seem still to be ignorant of such unhappy consequences, or else indifferent to the consequences, so long as profits continue to be made. In a later chapter of this book I will take up Detroit again.

My argument is this: unless we begin to think of humanizing our American economy, our cities will continue to disintegrate, and the American people increasingly will grow bored and violent. Some folk in authority are beginning to apprehend that human nature may revolt at having an inhumane scale thrust upon mankind. The failure of high-rise public housing, in city after city, is an illustration of this hard truth. In Newark, New Jersey—a city worse decayed than Detroit, if that be conceivable—the Scudder Homes, a monolith of "housing" thirteen stories high, was demolished by high explosive, life having become intolerable there for the low-income tenants. Town-houses of two or three stories are being built as replacement: a healthy reaction against public housing's anonymous collectivism. New Jersey's manager of the federal Department of Housing and Urban Development, just before the destruction of Scudder Homes, delivered a public address. In his words, "Sophocles said, 'Though a man be wise, it is no shame for him to live and learn.' It is no shame for us to learn from this experience."

Is it so difficult, after all, to convince Americans that simplicity may be preferable to complexity, modest contentment to unrestrained sensation, decent frugality to torpid satiety? If material aggrandizement is the chief object of a people, there remains no moral check upon the means employed to acquire wealth: violence and fraud become common practices. And presently the material production of such a society commences to decline, from causes too obvious for digression here. Our industrial economy, of all economic systems man ever created, is the most delicately dependent upon public energy, private virtue, fertility of imagination. If we continue to fancy that Efficiency and Affluence are the chief aims of human existence, presently we must find ourselves remarkably unprosperous—and wondrously miserable.

Roepke, Orton, Colin Clark, and a few other political economists have been so instructing us for the past half-century. President Bush spoke of bringing about "a kinder, gentler America." That consummation, so much to be desired, requires the humane imagination. And study of the thought of Wilhelm Roepke may nurture that imagination.

IX

Malcolm Muggeridge's Scourging of Liberalism

I n the preceding three chapters, and in this one, I discuss eminent conservative men of letters whom I have known. They have all crossed the bar and put out to sea now. My proclivity for quoting such vanished friends provoked a certain auditor at a large gathering, a few years past, into observing aloud, "Dr. Kirk, you're an anomaly, all of your friends are dead."

Malcolm Muggeridge, the subject of this present chapter, for decades believed himself to be tottering on the brink of eternity, but he survived most of his generation, standing at the height of his fame in his closing years. His many books are so quotable that one is tempted to compose an essay entirely of passages from Muggeridge, unadorned by comments. Restraining myself, nevertheless, I try here to trace the course of Malcolm Muggeridge's abhorrence of the political and moral attitude that is called liberalism.

Muggeridge was the author of the most moving and memorable autobiography of the twentieth century, *Chronicles of Wasted Time*. His memoirs were supposed to run to three volumes, but he did not complete the third, despite friends' expostulations. Yet in 1988 he published a slim volume, written in the third person, entitled *Confessions of a Twentieth-Century Pilgrim*, the concluding portion of which touches upon the religious perceptions of his later years. Young men and women groping for a clue to guide them through the chaos of our age would do well to look into these witty and candid books. Muggeridge was given to quoting this stanza by William Blake:

> *I give you the end of a Golden String,*
> *Only wind it into a ball,*
> *It will lead you in at Heaven's Gate*
> *Built in Jerusalem's Wall.*

At Heaven's Gate Muggeridge has arrived finally, after much stumbling and tribulation and fierce combats with the pen as weapon. Others wandering in a dark wood may profit from both his blunders and his successes.

But it is not Muggeridge the Christian apologist of late years that I mean to eulogize here and now. Rather, I give you Muggeridge the satirist, successor to Aristophanes, Juvenal, Rabelais, and Swift. In an age of general decadence, satire may miss its mark. In the dictionary's definition, satire is "directed to the correction of corruption, abuses, or absurdities in religion, politics, law, society, and letters." Mockingly the satirist contrasts what is with what ought to be, and particularly he contrasts the squalid present with a nobler past.

Yet when standards or norms have been long flouted and almost forgotten, often satire is thrust before blind eyes, or falls upon deaf ears: for not many people remain who recall that once upon time there was talk of virtue. Such is the condition, in large part, of our culture in the latter half of the twentieth century. This considered, Muggeridge's success in waking wits and consciences has been phenomenal. For some fifty-six years, this Muggeridge (to borrow two lines from Ben Jonson) had dared to "strip the ragged follies of the time; Naked, as at their birth." In particular, he had scourged the moral and political folly called liberalism.

A socialist in his upbringing, the young Muggeridge taught for some years in India and Egypt; obtained a post on the staff of the *Manchester Guardian*; and at the age of twenty-nine, accompanied by his wife, Kitty, made his way to Moscow, where he succeeded William Henry Chamberlin as Moscow correspondent of the *Guardian*. The Muggeridges believed earnestly that they were departing from a dying bourgeois culture to participate in a New Civilization, in which the human potential would be fulfilled. They arrived in September, 1932. Within six months, Muggeridge came to know the hideousness of the Communist regime, the Dictatorship of the Proletariat.

"It destroys everything and everyone; is the essence of destruction—in towns, a darkness, a paralysis; in the country, a blight, sterility, shouting monotonously its empty formula—a classless, socialist society—it attacks with methodical barbarity, not only men and classes and institutions, but the soul of a society. It tears a society up by the roots and leaves it dead. 'If we go' Lenin said, 'we shall slam the door on an empty house.'" So Muggeridge wrote in his Moscow diary.

The editor of the *Manchester Guardian* chose not to print much of the truth that Muggeridge sent him from the heart of darkness; in disgust, Muggeridge resigned from that famous newspaper, leaving himself unemployed and in unhappy circumstances. Out of his Russian months came his sardonic novel *Winter in Moscow*, recently republished with an introduction by Mr. Michael Aeschliman.

In that grim and witty book, Muggeridge faithfully describes the cowardice, hypocrisy, and stupidity of the journalists from the West, who rejected or ignored the plain evidences of the Great Famine and the Stalinist terror in the Soviet Union, and praised lavishly the Dictatorship of the Proletariat. England's liberal conscience complacently accepted the horrors of existence in the U.S.S.R., once the Dictatorship was securely established. As Muggeridge writes in *The Green Stick*, the first volume of his autobiography:

> Shaw, the Webbs and the other leading Fabians were . . . strongly opposed to the USSR in its early struggling days; they only began to admire it when it had hardened into an authoritarian terrorist regime. Their admiration turned to besotted adulation when Stalin took on the role, and very much the style, of

the deposed Czar, only more brutally, efficiently and vaingloriously.

Muggeridge's indignation at the folly and the knavery, during his Moscow winter, of both Western visitors to Russia and foreign correspondents posted there, became the recurring theme of his several books and his almost innumerable periodical pieces. Thirty-seven years later, he returned to his commination of the fatuous liberals that he encountered in Moscow.

"In those days, Moscow was the Mecca for every liberal mind, whatever its particular complexion" he would write in 1970. "They flocked there in an unending procession, from the great ones like Shaw and Gide and Barbusse and Julian Huxley and Harold Laski and the Webbs, down to poor little teachers, crazed clergymen and millionaires, and drivelling dons; all utterly convinced that, under the aegis of the great Stalin, a new dawn was breaking in which the human race would at last be united in liberty, equality, and fraternity for evermore. . . . They were prepared to believe anything, however preposterous; to overlook anything, however villainous; to approve anything, however obscurantist and brutally authoritarian, in order to be able to preserve intact the confident expectation that one of the most thoroughgoing, ruthless and bloody tyrannies ever to exist on earth could be relied on to champion human freedom, the brotherhood of man, and all the other good liberal causes to which they had dedicated their lives."

Malcolm and Kitty Muggeridge had arrived in Moscow quite as credulous about the Dictatorship of the Proletariat as were the other visitors whose foolishness he soon would denounce. But they had eyes with which to see; and they departed much wiser and overwhelmed by sadness. They had learned the hard truth about the Communist regime; they had learned the shallowness and falseness of the Western liberal ideology.

So Malcolm Muggeridge rejected liberalism, from 1933 onward. And the liberal establishment rejected him: for after he left the *Guardian* in disgust, he could secure no post with any English paper, being found "too extreme" in his words about the Dictatorship of the Proletariat. An interim appointment in Switzerland with the League of Nations bureaucracy was shameful servitude; the attempt to support his household by occasional free-lance writing soon collapsed. A novel based upon his experiences at the *Manchester Guardian* was suppressed foolishly by its publisher, at the threat of a suit for libel. He came upon an advertisement of an editorial post vacant at an English-language newspaper in India; knowing something of India, he applied, though he had been thinking of suicide. Off he went, perforce, to the *Calcutta Statesman*; but the time would come when he would be the best-known journalist in the world, and the most mordant and dashing adversary of the liberal mentality. His acerbic prose would bring down many an eminent pomposity. One thinks of the lines of John Taylor, the seventeenth-century "Water Poet":

Pens are most dangerous tools, more sharp by odds
Than swords, and cut more keen than whips or
rods.

. . .

This chapter of mine not being a biography of Muggeridge, we turn now to the wit and the invective of his case against liberalism. If one would find a source for his detestation of the liberal mind—aside, that is, from his personal experience of liberalism's impotence in several quarters of the world today—why, that source is the wisdom of Dr. Samuel Johnson, Muggeridge's favorite English writer, so often quoted by him. Johnson died before "liberalism" had become a term of morals and politics; but the self-proclaimed Enlighteners of France, during the age of Johnson, were the intellectual ancestors of our twentieth-century liberals. The commonsensical reasoning of Johnson was Muggeridge's weapon, too; and, later in life, Johnson's reliance upon the authority of Christian teaching. In the eighteenth century, nobody was more "the true-born Englishman" than Samuel Johnson; in the twentieth century, Muggeridge is our best extant example of old English character and the English cast of mind.

What is this liberalism that Muggeridge so valiantly assails? He is not referring to the economic doctrines of Manchester—not primarily, at least. Muggeridge wasn't given to quoting John Henry Newman, but a passage from Newman's *Apologia* may suggest Muggeridge's fundamental objection. Newman remarks that he first heard the word "liberalism" in connection with the opinions of Lord Byron and his admirers. "Afterwards," Newman continues, "liberalism was the badge of a theological school, of a dry and repulsive character, not very dangerous in itself, though dangerous as opening the door to evils which it did not itself either anticipate or comprehend. At present it is nothing else than that deep, plausible skepticism, . . . the development of human reason, as practically exercised by the natural man." Doubt of tradition, authority, things long established; deep corrosive doubt of the long-received belief in a constant human nature; doubt especially of man's power of moral choice, and man's moral responsibility for his actions—these had become the characteristics of liberalism by Muggeridge's day. Their descent from the liberal skeptics of Newman's day, and more remotely from the Enlighteners of Johnson's day, is sufficiently obvious.

Bourgeois society, from which the liberal mentality arose, has been working its own destruction, Muggeridge asserts in *The Green Stick*, far more than any mob of revolutionaries, bourgeois liberals' innovating notions have gnawed at the footings of personal and social order. Two bourgeoisie—"a typical Viennese general practitioner, and a British Museum Reading Room *enragé*—Freud and Marx—. . . undermined the whole basis of Western European civilization as no avowedly insurrectionary movement ever has or could," Muggeridge writes, "by promoting the notion of determinism, in the one case in morals, in the other in history, thereby relieving individual men and women of all responsibility for their personal and collective behaviour."

Muggeridge's most burning piece of invective against twentieth-century liberalism, "The Great Liberal Death Wish", was first published in 1970, and is reprinted in my anthology *The Portable Conservative Reader*. He commences his slashing essay with a reference to his Moscow experiences in 1932-33, and then proceeds to trace the misfortunes brought on by liberalism—which, he was to declare later, will bring to pass the disintegration of Christendom.

The fundamental error of liberalism is its false gospel of automatic and ineluctable progress, Muggeridge reasons. This fallacy grew out of infatuation with Darwin's theory of natural selection. He despises the evangels of Scientism: ". . . a Herbert Spencer, or a poor, squeaky H. G. Wells, ardent evolutionist and disciple of Huxley, with his vision of an earthly paradise achieved through science and technology; those twin monsters which have laid waste a whole world, polluting its seas and rivers and lakes with poisons, infecting its very earth and all its creatures, reaching into Man's mind and inner consciousness to control and condition him, at the same time entrusting to irresponsible, irresolute human hands the instruments of universal destruction. . . .

"The enthronement of the gospel of progress necessarily required the final discrediting of the gospel of Christ, and the destruction of the whole edifice of ethics, law, culture, human relationships and human behaviour constructed upon it. Our civilization, after all, began with Christian revelation, not the theory of evolution, and, we may be sure, will perish with it, too—if it has not already."

With T. S. Eliot and Donald Davidson, whose work I discussed in a preceding chapter of this book, Malcolm Muggeridge tells us that as Christian belief is rejected, so modern civilization stumbles down to dusty death. So thought the novelist Robert Graves; so the historian Eric Voegelin; so the sociologist Pitirim Sorokin. Culture arises from the cult; when the cult dissolves, so in time does the culture. Thus Muggeridge's declaration that the destruction of religious belief causes the collapse of modern society is not peculiar to him; but he expresses this shattering judgment with high sardonic power. Take this passage from "The Great Liberal Death Wish":

"It is, indeed, among Christians themselves that the final decisive assault on Christianity has been mounted; led by the Protestant churches, but with Roman Catholics eagerly, if belatedly, joining in the fray. All they had to show was that when Jesus said that His kingdom was not of this world, He meant that it was. Then, moving on from there, to stand the other basic Christian propositions similarly on their heads. As, that to be carnally minded is life; that it is essential to lay up treasure on earth in the shape of a constantly expanding Gross National Product; that the flesh lusts with the spirit and the spirit with the flesh, so that we can do whatever we have a mind to; that he that loveth his life in this world shall keep it unto life eternal. And so on. One recalls a like adjustment of the rules in Orwell's Animal Farm. A whole series of new interpretative 'translations' of the Bible have appeared supporting the new view, and in case there should be any anxiety about the reception of these adjustments in Heaven, God, we are told on the best theological authority, has died."

Christian faith arose upon belief in Christ's promise of the resurrection of the flesh and the life everlasting. What liberalism seeks is not the life eternal, but the oblivion of death: the liberals' doctrinaire advocacy of contraception and abortion is evidence of their overpowering death-wish. Copulation without population is their obsession.

"If sex provides the mysticism of the great liberal death wish," in Muggeridge's words, "it needs, as well, its own special mumbo-jumbo and brainwashing device; a moral equivalent of conversion, whereby the old Adam of ignorance and superstition and the blind acceptance of tradition is put aside, and the new liberal man is born—enlightened, erudite, cultivated. This is readily to hand in education in all its many branches and affiliations. To the liberal mind, education provides the universal panacea. Whatever the problem, education will solve it. Law and order breaking down?—then yet more statistics chasing yet more education; venereal disease spreading, to the point that girls often are found to be infected?—then, for heaven's sake, more sex education, with tiny tots lisping out what happens to mummy's vagina when daddy erects, as once they did the Catechism; drug addiction going up by leaps and bounds, especially in the homes where television is looked at . . .—surely it's obvious that what the kids need is extra classes under trained psychiatrists to instruct them in the why and the wherefore of narcotics."

Muggeridge touches in this article, and elsewhere, upon the liberals' perverse attachment to whatever political causes are hostile to things established in our civilization; why any friends to British or American interests are denounced by the liberals as reactionaries. One instance—"Why, in a world full of oppressive regimes and terrorist practices, in England the venom and fury of the liberal mind should pick on the white South Africans with particular spleen when their oligarchic rule only differs from that of a dozen others—Tito's, Franco's, Ulbricht's, Castro's, etc.—in that they happen to be anxious to be on good terms with the English."

The liberal mentality seems bent upon annihilation of the convictions and circumstances that have made possible a liberal democratic society. Everywhere today's liberals demand more freedom. But freedom from what? Why, freedom from that order, public and personal, which has nurtured justice and true liberty. The typical latter-day liberal is not aware that his proposals and his actions are life-denying; nay, he fancies that they are life-enhancing; nevertheless, he is driven by his unrecognized death-wish. Down with civilization, that we may be liberated from all restraints! Indulge me in two more quotations, from the concluding pages of Muggeridge's burning essay.

"I see the great liberal death wish driving through the years ahead in triple harness with the gospel of progress and the pursuit of happiness," Muggeridge cries prophetically. "These our three Horsemen of the Apocalypse—progress, happiness, death. Under their auspices, the quest for total affluence leads to total deprivation; for total peace, to total war; for total education, to total illiteracy; for total sex, to total sterility; for total freedom, to total servitude. Seeking only agreement based on a majority, we find a consensus based oñ a consensocracy, or oligarchy of the liberal mind. . . ."

Malcolm Muggeridge abandons all hope for this temporal world of ours, this society in love with death, willing its own dissolution. I have quoted many times the final paragraph of his overwhelming jeremiad:

> As the astronauts soar into the vast eternities of space, on earth the garbage piles higher; as the groves of academe extend their domain, their alumni's arms reach lower; as the phallic cult spreads, so does impotence. In great wealth, great poverty; in health, sickness; in numbers, deception. Gorging, left hungry; sedated, left restless; telling all, hiding all; in flesh united, forever separate. So we press on through the valley of abundance that leads to the wasteland of satiety, passing through the gardens of fantasy; seeking happiness ever more ardently, and finding despair ever more surely.

. . .

A decade ago, Malcolm and Kitty Muggeridge visited us at Mecosta for three days. We ought to have read aloud Whittier's *Snowbound*, for a great blizzard descended upon us all. The occasion was one of the seminars sponsored by the

Intercollegiate Studies Institute, which are held from time to time at our house of Piety Hill. "Pilgrims in the Dark Wood of Our Time" was the general title I had given to the seminar; possibly that put into Mr. Muggeridge's mind the title of his most recent book, *Confessions of a Twentieth-Century Pilgrim.* On a Saturday afternoon, my wife and I took the Muggeridges walking in a dark wood of spruces and pines planted by me thirty years before, on my ancestral acres. We have a photograph of the four of us cheerful in a snowy grove, Malcolm wearing a black fur cap, Kitty with a scarf wound over her face, Annette laughing in green cap and muffler, I bareheaded and burly. This perhaps was, and is, one of those moments when, as T. S. Eliot puts it, time and the timeless intersect: the four of us may experience through eternity that wintry stroll.

In his lectures to our ISI seminar, Mr. Muggeridge was so despairing of our bent twentieth-century culture that the undergraduates in our audience took me for a carefree optimist, by contrast. Corrupted by our intellectual delusions, Muggeridge told our seminar; intoxicated by our affluence; betrayed by our own gadgets—why, modernity is not long for this world, and good riddance!

The triumph of television seals our doom, he declared: mass inanity and the manipulation of public opinion, the overwhelming of decent taste, the undoing of books and schooling—these are the gifts of the boob-tube. It is not possible to un-invent television.

Now it was by his regular and unforgettable appearances on television for the British Broadcasting Company that

Malcolm Muggeridge had grown famous and prosperous, in the 'Sixties: his craggy face with its deep-set eyes, his urbanity of manner, his sharpness of wit, had won him an immense audience of viewers. The man who speaks from the television screen to gullible millions possesses power: but Malcolm Muggeridge rejected such power.

As Ian Hunter writes in his able biography of Muggeridge, he "has always been fascinated and repelled by the spectacle of power and those who wield it. . . . Power is to the collectivity, he believes, what lust is to the individual—'an expense of spirit in a waste of shame' in Shakespeare's elegant phrase. Through the practice of half a century of journalism, and particularly since the advent of television, he has been brought in contact with prime ministers, potentates, and despots, people who have achieved power over their fellowmen by acclamation, birth, persuasion, the ballot box, or the barrel of a gun. Its effect on almost all of them, he has observed, is to corrupt—not in the more obvious sense in which Lord Acton spoke of power corrupting, but in subtler, more insidious ways; principally, by diverting their attention from what is enduring, true, and worthwhile to what is evanescent, circumstantial, and tawdry. 'Here am I, Captain of a Legion of Rome' runs an inscription Muggeridge is fond of quoting, 'who served in the Libyan desert and learns and ponders this truth—there are in life but two things, love and power, and no man can have both.'

"His view has partly been shaped by his own experiences . . . of ballot boxes and interminable parliamentary debates in Paris and London and Washington, which finish up in societies so aimless and enfeebled that they are unable to resist either external aggressors or internal terrorists, yielding simultaneously to barbarians from without and within, and in their last legislative gasp striving to extinguish individual freedom through the closed shop and individual life through legalized abortion."

Choose love, not power, Muggeridge tells us. He does not show our society any way of escape from Avernus; but he does exhort us, as souls, to seek our salvation with diligence.

It is a sign of Malcolm Muggeridge's genuineness that children take to him. Our second daughter, Cecilia, ten years old when the Muggeridges made their way to our abode in the Michigan backwoods, sat in the front row during Mr. Muggeridge's lectures, quietly observant. Later we asked her, "Cecilia, did you understand what Mr. Muggeridge was saying?" She replied demurely, "Not everything, but more than I expected." She has been wise ever since.

We lodged Malcolm and Kitty in our own large bedchamber, which has a fireplace; for English people—and no couple were more English than the Muggeridges—are very fond indeed of open fires. Now at that time our youngest daughter, Andrea, aged three years, was in the habit, about the witching hour, of creeping into our room from her own, and snuggling herself between her parents. Our house, by the way, is notoriously haunted.

Forgetful that her parents had resigned their room to the English guests, tiny Andrea . . . but here I turn to a report from Kitty Muggeridge.

"We had a visitor in our room last night," Mrs. Muggeridge told us, "a small figure in white. It came silently, and crawled into bed between us."

"It looked at Malcolm, and next at me. Then, after an interval, it said, 'I'd better be going now,' and departed."

"How long did it stay?" we asked Mrs. Muggeridge.

"Long enough so as not to give offense by leaving," she told us.

As a pilgrim for eight decades in this dark wood of our time, Malcolm Muggeridge had beheld the destruction of much and the ugly alteration of more. Yet, like Democritus, he was always laughing. "All that I can claim to have learnt from the years I have spent in this world is that the only happiness is love," he writes in the first chapter of *The Green Stick*, "and that the world itself only becomes the dear and habitable dwelling place it is when we who inhabit it know we are migrants, due when the time comes to fly away to other more commodious skies."

So, sincerely, wrote the most convincing satirist of our age. At whatever risk, ever since 1932 Malcolm Muggeridge had uttered the truth. One of his harder truths is that liberalism now has become rotten to the core. Somewhere Muggeridge remarks that people learn not from exhortation, but from experience. Before this century is out, doubtless the surviving votaries of liberalism will be taught some more disagreeable lessons.

X

Popular Conservatism

I s the American conservative movement, which began to take form forty years ago, now enervated and disheartened, plodding down the track to Avernus?

Nay, not so. The political and social attitudes that are called conservative have been deeply rooted in the United States; and nowadays the leaders of both great political parties—dull dogs though those leaders may be—have grown aware of the practical advantage of bearing the label "conservative". The amusing post-convention attempt made by the Democrats in 1988 to represent Governor Dukakis as a prudent and frugal New England conservative of the approved pattern, and Senator Bentsen as the Old Gentleman with the Black Stock, is sufficient illustration of the realism that has descended even upon elements of the Democratic party; while that party's 1988 platform, accepted by delegates best classified as ritualistically liberal, was an attempt to assure the voting public that Democrats, too, are attached to the Permanent Things. Far from entering now an era of political innovation, we Americans may look upon the spectacle of two parties professedly conservative. It does not necessarily follow that either party must be *intelligently* conservative: my present point is merely that our principal public men today have come to recognize the great strength of what I call Popular Conservatism.

When I say "popular conservatism", I do not mean "populist conservatism". A Populist, whose basic conviction is that the cure for democracy is more democracy, conserves nothing—even though he may wish to do so. Populism, in effect, is what Walter Bagehot called "the ignorant democratic conservatism of the masses". It is the tendency later called Populism that Tocqueville dreaded when he wrote that the triumph of democracy might lead to the stagnation of the society of the future, all change being resisted by the conservatism of mediocrity and complacency. Populism declares, in the mordant sentence of Mark Twain, "One man is as good as another, or maybe a little better." In American politics, the populist attitude is typified by the following true anecdote of the presidential election of 1960.

To a friend of mine, an employer, came one of his employees at the end of October, to discuss the presidential candidates. He told my friend that he—let us call him Smithson—never had voted before, but had determined to vote on November 7, 1960. For which candidate he should vote, he could not make up his mind. The dialogue went much as follows:

> Smithson: "Gee, boss, I don't know nothin' about them two guys Nixon and Kennedy, except what I see on TV. What'll I do?"

Employer: "Jack Smithson, the thing for you to do is not to vote; stay home."

Smithson: "Oh, I got a right to vote; I'm gonna vote, all right."

Employer: "You lost that right when you stopped paying attention to politics; or maybe you never started paying any attention, Jack."

Smithson: "Don't give me that: I gotta right to vote. Why, if it wasn't for voters like me, them smart guys would be runnin' everything in Washington."

Populism is a revolt against the Smart Guys. I am very ready to confess that the present Smart Guys, as represented by the dominant mentality of the Academy and of what the Bergers call the Knowledge Class today, are insufficiently endowed with right reason and moral imagination. But it would not be an improvement to supplant them by persons of thoroughgoing ignorance and incompetence.

No, there prevails in America a conservative understanding of a popular character that is not Populism. It runs through both great political parties, though whether it is sufficiently expressed by either party's measures varies with times and circumstances. To put the matter very succinctly, the large majority of Americans prefer the devil they know to the devil they don't know: that is the essence of conservatism. "What is conservatism?" Abraham Lincoln inquired in an election address. "Is it not preference for the old and tried over the new and untried?" He so affirmed, declaring himself conservative.

Neoterists, preferring the new and untried to the old and tried, do not make much headway in America's practical politics—not if the general public comes to understand what the neoterists are about.

Over the past several decades, opinion polls have revealed that the word "conservative", as a term of politics, is distinctly preferred by the American public over the terms "liberal" and "radical". Most Americans do not think that society is perfectible—so far as they can be said to think at all about such matters—and are not disposed to march to Zion at the heels of some political enthusiast. The ideologue they reject with commendable decisiveness: that is what happened to Jesse Jackson at Atlanta and elsewhere. So far as any political theory influences popular opinion in these United States, it is political empiricism: the test of the nation's political experience. The Constitution of the United States is revered, even if, given a knowledge-test about the Constitution, most voters might score poorly.

Of course few American citizens think of themselves as empiricists, or subscribe consciously to any other mode of philosophy. They are governed, rather, by their acceptance of institutions and traditions. Once, in my presence, the late Eric Voegelin was asked by a professor, "Dr. Voegelin, don't your students at Louisiana State find your doctrines strange?"

"Not at all," Voegelin replied, urbanely. "They never have heard of any other doctrines."

So it is with the great American public: they never have heard of a doctrinal alternative to the assumptions and institutions upon which the American Republic is founded. They know the words "Marxism" and "Communism", true—but as devil-terms merely, anathema among labor-union members especially. Whatever their discontents of the hour, the large majority of Americans—nay, a vast majority—are basically conservative in that they do not dream of undoing America's social order or America's established political structures.

Do not think I claim overmuch. Readers may be inclined to inquire at this point, "If Americans are so conservative, why is it that the present Congress repeatedly has enacted measures advocated by rather extreme liberal lobbyists and publicists?"

There exist two reasons for this paradox of a conservative electorate and a liberal Congress; either of these reasons would be worth extended discussion. Here I can touch upon them only very briefly.

The first reason is that the United States today does *not* suffer from what Tocqueville dreaded, "the tyranny of the majority"; rather, America labors under the tyranny of minorities—but minorities aggressive, intolerant, well financed, and cleverly directed. I mean the feminist minority, the black-militant minority, the welfare-rights minority, the pistol-packing minority, the industrial-merger minority, the blight-South-Africa minority, the Zionist minority, the homosexual minority, the animal-rights minority. Coherent and vindictive, such groups claim to have power to make and unmake members of Congress—who often are timid, if blustering, creatures. Thus the conservative impulses and prejudices of the general American public frequently are ignored by the majority in the Congress and in the state legislatures, not to mention the Executive Force.

The second reason is that most Americans, though conservative enough in their general views, are unable to distinguish between conservative and liberal or radical candidates, very commonly—especially when all candidates claim to be more or less conservative. Nor is this the worst of it: for most American citizens do not perceive the character or probable consequences of new legislation, until well after such measures have been enacted and have begun to have unpleasant results. (Repeal, I scarcely need add, is very difficult: the various lobbies that secured enactment in the first place are zealous to impede reaction.) The public is left complaining of some new meddling by the bureaucracy or of some new exaction by the Internal Revenue Service; but what's done is done, and can't be undone, it appears—or can't be undone, short of some immense wave of public protest. Conservatives are not given to intimidation by street demonstration and police-bashing.

So I repeat that the overwhelming majority of Americans are conservative enough in their political inclinations, if often frustrated in the actual policies carried on by public authorities. Can I be more specific about these conservative attitudes or prejudices that are so prevalent in this American Republic? I offer you the following several assumptions or inclinations that are general among American conservatives.

First, they take a religious view of the human condition; they believe in a moral order of more than human contrivance; and they grow alarmed at increasing secularization of American society, both through the agency of the state and commercialized sensationalism.

Second, they resent increasing concentration of power in the agencies of government and in the economy.

Third, they retain confidence in the Constitution of the United States and in America's prescriptive political institutions and principles.

Fourth, they set their faces against communism and all other ideologies.

Fifth, they believe in protections for private property, a competitive economy, and diversity of economic rewards.

Sixth, they emphasize private rights, voluntary community, and personal opportunity.

And one might name other major assumptions of American conservatives; but time runs on, runs on. Let me repeat here that relatively few conservatively-inclined citizens, if required to make a formal statement of their political convictions, could give us such a summary as I have just now presented: Americans are not given to abstract doctrine and theoretic dogma in politics. Nevertheless, one may subscribe implicitly to a sort of creed without being able to repeat it from memory.

Ordinarily conservatives in this country have much to say about felt grievances, but relatively little to say about political first principles. They are dismayed at the decay of our great cities, angered by public policies that have injured public instruction, deeply resentful of inflation of the dollar, uneasy at new taxes, alarmed by the decay of private and public morality, opposed to abortion-on-demand, suspicious of central direction. On specific issues of this sort, they may be roused to political action, or at least to vote; but sustained resistance to the great grim tendencies of our age often is quite another matter. Such is our present popular conservatism—less vociferous during the 'Eighties than earlier, because a popular conservative public man was lodged in the White House from 1981 to 1989.

For Ronald Reagan, Mr. President of these United States, was regarded as the apotheosis of America's popular conservatism. Had the Republicans nominated him for the presidency in 1968, say, the recent history of this country might have been very different. I am not saying that Reagan was successful in everything he had undertaken; he found himself baffled in much; but in difficulty he was sustained by the conservative understanding that politics is the art of the possible.

I was invited to meet with President Reagan in the Oval Office a day or two after his return from Moscow—which was no retreat. He stood there erect and smiling, ruddy of face, ineffably cheerful, American confidence incarnate, eager to take the campaign trail in advocacy of Mr. George Bush's candidacy. As the photographer clicked pictures of us, Mr. Reagan told me jokes; all of his jests seem original with him; anyway, I never heard them before. I offer you one specimen—a fabrication of his, I hasten to remark.

He and Gorbachev had been riding together in a Soviet limousine, Mr. Reagan told me, through the Russian countryside. Gorbachev had with him in the car a KGB agent, and Reagan a Secret Service man. They were passing a tall cataract; Gorbachev ordered their driver to stop.

"Jump down that waterfall!" Gorbachev com-
manded the Secret Service man—who declined to
do so.

"Why do you disobey my order?" the master of
all the Russias demanded.

"Because, sir, I have a wife and three children,"
the Secret Service man declared.

Gorbachev turned to the KGB agent: "Jump down
that waterfall!" The agent obeyed.

Horrified, the Secret Service man scrambled down
to the foot of the waterfall, where he found the KGB
man, battered and bruised, but wringing out his clothes.
"Why did you obey him?" the American gasped.

"Because I have a wife and three children."

The President, actor that he was, thus succeeded in at once
entertaining me and assuring me that he was no naive enthusiast for Glasnost. Later, responding in a holograph note to my
letter informing him of the death of our old friend Lawrence
Beilenson, he remarked that he had read Colonel Beilenson's
wise book *The Treaty Trap*. He ought not to be underestimated
as a statesman: he understood the grisly power against which
American policy contends.

As everyone well knows, Mr. Reagan was the catalyst that
brought together the disparate elements of American conservatism in 1980, giving them control of the Executive Force. We
may not look upon his like again. For we may elect presidents
with fuller knowledge of the federal government, or presidents

with a better command of foreign affairs, or presidents abler in finance—but we are unlikely to find, ever again, a president who so perfectly represents America's popular conservatism.

Ronald Reagan really was the Western hero of romance, the conservative's exemplar in public life: audacious, dauntless, cheerful, honest—and skilled at shooting from the hip. William Butler Yeats tells us that everyone ought to make a mask for himself, and wear it, and become what the mask represents. Decades ago, Ronald Reagan put on the mask of the Western hero, in Hollywood, and truly lived the part, and became the Western hero. He proved that when, shot and trampled upon outside a Washington hotel, he joked irrepressibly with his wife and with the doctors who worked nip and tuck to save his life. So it is that no matter what blunders President Reagan may have made in office, he became the most popular public man in half a century and more.

And in the eyes of the typical American conservative, Mr. Reagan's occasional failures were eclipsed by his large accomplishments during eight years in office. His administration achieved virtually full employment, greatly reduced inflation of the dollar, lowered interest rates drastically, reduced income taxes for many and temporarily swept away inheritance taxes by the federal government, restrained the bureaucracy somewhat, and opened the way for reforms of public instruction. In foreign policy, Mr. Reagan's Lebanese and Iranian blunders had been counterbalanced by his dramatic successes in Grenada and Libya. If some conservative journalists reproach his administration for not having undone liberalism root and

branch—why, the typical American voter sensibly never expected Ronald Reagan to work miracles: politics is the art of
the possible, and from the first Reagan did not command a
majority in either house of Congress.

If, then, I am asked to declare what the typical American
conservative believes in—why, he believes in Ronald Reagan
and Mr. Reagan's general principles and prejudices. Mr. Reagan
did not create the American conservative character, of course;
but he embodies it.

Yet, charismatic personalities aside, can I offer an image of
the sort of people who subscribe to this popular American conservatism, and did so before Mr. Reagan took to practical politics, and still continue to do so now that Mr. Reagan has returned to his little ranch-house there in oldfangled California,
in the unspoilt country behind Santa Barbara? Why, yes.

The person attached to America's popular conservatism is
a person who reads *The Reader's Digest*. He is practical, not very
imaginative, patriotic, satisfied for the most part with American
society, traditional in his morals, defensive of his family and
his property, hopeful, ready for technological and material improvements but suspicious of political tinkering. His name is
legion, and so is hers. Like conservatives in other lands, he and
she are the salt of the earth.

His opinions on current affairs coincide with, and in part
are formed by, *The Reader's Digest*, more widely circulated than
all the other conservative magazines combined. In the *Digest*,
it is not editorializing, but the general content and tone of the
many articles, that tend to shape opinion. When I was a boy,

before *The Reader's Digest* sprang into existence, a principal conservative influence among periodicals was *The Saturday Evening Post*, with an admirable editorial page; but that influential weekly was broken by Demon TV, which took away many former readers and, worse still, the bulk of the popular magazines' advertising revenue. Of the weekly and monthly popular periodicals of the 1930s and 1940s, only the *Digest* still is a power in the land.

Of course I do not mean that the *Digest* alone shapes the mind of the representative American conservative. The most widely-circulated newspaper in America (counting its several regional editions) is the *Wall Street Journal*, with the best editorial page in the land, read faithfully by what we may call the upper strata of the conservative public. Of serious fortnightlies, monthlies, and quarterlies of a conservative tendency, none has a mass circulation: the biggest is *National Review*, with some 170,000 copies per issue, read by perhaps a quarter of a million people—that is, one tenth of one per cent of the American population. (It is considerable consolation that the liberal and radical periodicals of opinion are no more widely circulated than are the conservative ones.) My immediate point is that popular conservatism has a *Reader's Digest* mentality, rather than a *National Review* mentality.

As for television, of course conservatives are influenced by the boob-tube as are Americans of other persuasions. But the conservative tends to be less credulous when he views TV news and the like: he may be fairly well aware of how the war in Indo-China, for instance, was reported. He may even have grasped the hard truth that seeing ought not to lead infallibly to believing—at any rate, not seeing through somebody else's distant TV camera.

Our hypothetical representative conservative, popular variety, then, is a person of fairly modest means who reads his monthly *Digest*, probably takes a grain of salt when he reads his local daily paper or watches television, aspires to send his offspring to college, owns a decent house or apartment, works industriously, does some thinking about society's ills and prospects, and perhaps takes arms occasionally against the sea of troubles that begins to flood the corner where he is. He is resolved to resist alien designs and Marxist influences, but he has no really passionate interest in foreign affairs. Neither is he a zealot for an abstraction (and a Marxist abstraction, at that) called "democratic capitalism"; he is willing to let the rest of the world mind its own business, if the rest of the world will refrain from troubling him. He distinctly is not a rich man bent upon enlarging corporate mergers; indeed, he tends to resent the consolidation of banks, airlines, and Lord knows what else—having found that he was better served when more competition existed. He abhors the politics of race and of gender; he votes for conservative candidates when he can contrive to identify them, but he cannot be described as a political "activist". He goes to church, or least encourages his children to attend. He would like to have a short way with drug-pushers and muggers. For him, "liberal" is a nasty label; and even the Democratic National Convention took note of that distaste, in 1988.

Some Democratic candidates for high office seem to think that most Americans reel on the brink of destitution, and calculate their speeches accordingly; they obtain about five per cent of the votes in primary or election, much to their chagrin. Some Republican candidates for high office apparently take it that most Americans live by large capital gains, and wish public policies shaped accordingly; such Republicans, too, win about five per cent of the votes. For ninety per cent of the American electorate is neither really rich nor really poor, or in any event does not think of itself as rich or poor; and that ninety per cent of the population is concerned primarily for order and security, rather than infatuated with the dreams of avarice, or moved by the vice of envy. So conservatives, already a majority in American's sentiments, have the prospect of becoming a huge permanent majority.

Popular conservatism has become something more than the inclination or the mood of the 'Eighties. Notwithstanding the political cyclical theories of Mr. Arthur M. Schlesinger, Jr., the Age of Roosevelt is not going to come round a second time; as Heraclitus instructs us, we never step in the same river twice.

Conservatism is not going to become unpopular in America; so the question before us is not whether it will be supplanted by a new liberalism, but rather if a high degree of intelligence and imagination may be infused, these next few years, into the popular conservative yearning. Some of us, having labored in that vineyard for four decades, pray that the harvest may be sweeter than the grapes of wrath.

XI

A Dispassionate Assessment of Libertarians

The term *libertarianism* is distasteful to people who think seriously about politics. Both Dr. F. A. Hayek and your servant have gone out of their way, from time to time, to declare that they refuse to be tagged with this label. Anyone much influenced by the thought of Edmund Burke and of Alexis de Tocqueville—as were both Professor Hayek and this commentator—sets his face against ideology; and libertarianism is a simplistic ideology, relished by one variety of the folk whom Burckhardt called "the terrible simplifiers".

Nevertheless, I have something to say, just now, favorable to today's libertarians in the United States; later I shall dwell upon their vices. With your indulgence, I will make three points about persons calling themselves libertarians that may warm the cockles of their rebellious hearts.

First, a number of the men and women who accept the label "libertarian" are not actually ideological libertarians at all, but simply conservatives under another name. These are people who perceive in the growth of the monolithic state, especially during the past half-century, a grim menace to ordered liberty; and of course they are quite right. They wish to emphasize their attachment to personal and civic freedom by employing this twentieth-century word derived from *liberty*. With them I have little quarrel—except that by so denominating themselves, they seem to countenance a crowd of political fantastics who "license they mean, when they cry liberty."

For if a man believes in an enduring moral order, the Constitution of the United States, established American ways of life, and a free economy—why, actually he is a conservative, even if he labors under an imperfect understanding of the general terms of politics. Such Americans are to the conservative movement in the United States much as the Liberal Unionists have been to the Conservative Party in Britain—that is, close practical allies, almost indistinguishable nowadays. Libertarians of this description usually are intellectual descendants of the old "classical liberals"; they make common cause with regular conservatives against the menace of democratic despotism and economic collectivism.

Second, the libertarians generally—both the folk of whom I have just approved, and also the ideological libertarians—try to exert some check upon vainglorious foreign policy. They do not believe that the United States should station garrisons throughout the world; no more do I; in some respects, the more moderate among them have the understanding of foreign policy that the elder Robert Taft represented. Others among them, however, seem to labor under the illusion that communist ideology can be dissipated by trade agreements—a notion really fatuous. I lack time to labor this point here; I shall take it up again in my following chapter about the Neo-Conservatives, who in foreign policy tend toward an opposite extreme. Let it suffice for the present for me to declare that so far as the libertarians set their faces against a policy of American domination worldwide—why, I am with them. I part with them when they forget that the American government nowadays, in Burke's phrase of two centuries ago, is "combating an armed doctrine", not merely a national adversary.

Third, most of the libertarians believe in the humane scale; they vehemently oppose what Wilhelm Roepke called "the cult of the colossal". They take up the cause of the self-reliant individual, the voluntary association, the just rewards of personal achievement. They know the perils of political centralization. In an age when many folk are ready—nay, eager—to exchange their independence for "entitlements", the libertarians exhort us to stand manfully on our own feet.

In short, the libertarians' propaganda, which abounds, does touch upon real social afflictions of our time, particularly upon repression of vigorous and aspiring natures by centralized political structures and by the enforcement of egalitarian doctrines. With reason, many people in many lands, near the end of the twentieth century, are discontented with the human condition; the more able among the discontented look about for some seemingly logical alternative to present dominations and powers; and some of those discontented—the sort of people who went out to David in the Cave of Adullam—discover libertarian dogmata and become enthusiasts, at least temporarily, for the ideology called libertarianism.

I say *temporarily*: for an initial fondness for libertarian slogans frequently has led young men and women to the conservative camp. Not a few of the people who have studied closely with me or who have become my assistants had been attracted, a few years earlier, to the arguments of Ayn Rand or of Murray Rothbard. But as they read more widely, they had become conscious of the inadequacies and extravagances of the various libertarian factions; as they had begun to pay serious attention to our present political difficulties, they had seen how impractical are the libertarian proposals. Thus they had found their way to conservative realism, which proclaims that politics is the art of the possible. Therefore it may be said of libertarianism, in friendly fashion, that often it has been a recruiting-office for young conservatives, even though the libertarians have had not the least intention of shoring up belief in custom, convention, and the politics of prescription.

There! I have endeavored to give the libertarians their due. Now let me turn to their failings, which are many and grave.

For the ideological libertarians are not conservatives in any true meaning of that term of politics; nor do the more candid libertarians desire to be called conservatives. On the contrary, they are radical doctrinaires, contemptuous of our inheritance from our ancestors. They rejoice in the radicalism of Tom Paine; they even applaud those seventeenth-century radicals the Levellers and the Diggers, who would have pulled down all land-boundaries, and have pulled down, too, the whole framework of church and state. The libertarian groups differ on some points among themselves, and exhibit varying degrees of fervor. But one may say of them in general that they are "philosophical" anarchists in bourgeois dress. Of society's old institutions, they would retain only private property. They seek an abstract Liberty that never has existed in any civilization—nor, for that matter, among any barbarous people, nor any savage. They would sweep away political government; in this, they subscribe to Marx's notion of the withering away of the state.

One trouble with this primitive understanding of freedom is that it could not possibly work in twentieth-century America. The American Republic, and the American industrial and commercial system, require the highest degree of cooperation that any civilization ever has known. We prosper because most of the time we work together—and are restrained from our appetites and passions, to some extent, by laws enforced by the state. We need to limit the state's powers, of course, and our national Constitution does that—if not perfectly, at least more effectively than does any other national constitution.

The Constitution of the United States distinctly is not an exercise in libertarianism. It was drawn up by an aristocratic body of men who sought "a more perfect union". The delegates to the Constitutional Convention had a wholesome dread of the libertarians of 1786-87, as represented by the rebels who followed Daniel Shays in Massachusetts. What the Constitution established was a higher degree of order and prosperity, not an anarchists' paradise. So it is somewhat amusing to find some old gentlemen and old ladies who contribute heavily to the funds of the libertarian organizations in the mistaken belief that thus they are helping to restore the virtuous freedom of the early Republic. American industry and commerce on a large scale could not survive for a single year, without the protections extended by government at its several levels.

"To begin with unlimited freedom," Dostoevsky wrote, "is to end with unlimited despotism." The worst enemies of enduring freedom for all may be certain folk who demand incessantly more liberty for themselves. This is true of a country's economy, as of other matters. America's economic success is based upon an old foundation of moral habits, social customs and convictions, much historical experience, and commonsensical political understanding. Our structure of free enterprise owes much to the conservative understanding of property and production expounded by Alexander Hamilton—the adversary of the libertarians of his day. But our structure of free enterprise owes nothing at all to the destructive concept of liberty that devastated Europe during the era of the French Revolution—that is, to the ruinous impossible freedom preached by Jean Jacques Rousseau. Our twentieth-century libertarians are disciples of Rousseau's notion of human nature and Rousseau's political doctrines.

Have I sufficiently distinguished between libertarians and conservatives? Here I have been trying to draw a line of demarcation, not to refute libertarian arguments; I shall turn to the latter task very soon.

. . .

Before I essay that task, however, let me illustrate my discourse by a parable.

The typical libertine of 1992 delights in eccentricity—in private life as in politics. His is the sort of freedom, or license, that brings on social collapse. Libertarianism and libertinism are near allied. As that staunch Victorian conservative James Fitzjames Stephen instructs us, "Eccentricity is far more often a mark of weakness than a mark of strength." G. K. Chesterton remarks that true genius is not eccentric, but centric.

With respect to libertarian eccentricity, their dream of an absolute private freedom is one of those visions which issue from between the gates of ivory; and the disorder that they would thrust upon society already is displayed in the moral disorder of their private affairs. Some keen readers will recall the article on libertarianism in *National Review*, a few years ago, by that mordant psychologist and sociologist Dr. Ernest van den Haag, who remarked that an unusually high proportion of professed libertarians are homosexuals. In politics as in private life, they demand what nature cannot afford.

The enemy to all custom and convention ends in the outer darkness, where there is wailing and gnashing of teeth. The final emancipation from religion, the state, moral and positive law, and social responsibilities is total annihilation: the freedom of deadly destruction. When obsession with an abstract Liberty has overcome personal and public order—why, then, in Eliot's lines, we are

> ... *whirled*
> *Beyond the circuit of the shuddering Bear*
> *In fractured atoms.*

Just that is the theme of my parable—or rather, of Chesterton's parable, for I offer you now a hasty synopsis of G. K. Chesterton's story "The Yellow Bird"—which too few people have read, though it was published in 1929. Chesterton knew that we must accept the universe that was created for us.

In Chesterton's tale, there comes to a venerable English country house a guest, Professor Ivanhov, a Russian scholar who has published a much-praised book, *The Psychology of Liberty*. He is a zealot for emancipating, expanding, the elimination of all limits—in short, a thoroughgoing libertarian.

Ivanhov, under the shelter of an old English roof and enjoying not merely all English liberties but also the privileges of a guest, proceeds to put into practice his libertarian doctrines. He commences his operations by liberating the yellow bird, a canary, from its cage; once out the window, the canary is harassed by the wild birds of the woods. The next day Ivanhov proceeds to liberate his host's goldfish by smashing their bowl. On the third day, resolved not to endure imprisonment in the arching "round prison" of the sky that shuts in the great globe itself, Ivanhov ends by blowing up the beautiful old house to which he had been welcomed—thus annihilating his residence and himself.

"What is liberty?" inquires a spectator of these libertarian events—Gabriel Gale, Chesterton's mouthpiece. "First and foremost, surely, it is the power of a thing to be itself. In some ways the yellow bird was free in the cage. It was free to be alone. It was free to sing. In the forest its feathers would be torn to pieces and its voice choked for ever. Then I began to think that being oneself, which is liberty, is itself limitation. We are limited by our brains and bodies; and if we break out, we cease to be ourselves, and, perhaps, to be anything."

The Russian psychologist could not abide the necessary conditions of human existence; he must eliminate all limits; he could not endure the "round prison" of the overarching sky. But his alternative was annihilation for himself and his lodging; and he embraced that alternative. He ceased to be anything but fractured atoms. That is the ultimate freedom of the devoted libertarian. If, *per impossible*, our American society should accept the leadership of libertarian ideologues—why, this Republic might end in fractured atoms.

Notwithstanding, there is something to be said for the disintegrated Professor Ivanhov—relatively speaking. With reference to some remarks of mine in a public lecture at Washington, there wrote to me Mr. Marion Montgomery, the Georgia critic and novelist: "The libertarians give me the willies. I prefer the Russian anarchists, who at least have a deeply disturbed moral sensibility (that Dostoevsky makes good use of), to the libertarian anarchists. There is a decadent fervor amongst some of the latter which makes them an unwelcome cross for conservatism to bear."

Just so. The representative libertarian of this decade is humorless, intolerant, self-righteous, badly schooled, and dull. At least the old-fangled Russian anarchist was bold, lively, and knew which sex he belonged to.

It is not well-intentioned elderly gentlemen who call themselves libertarians that I reproach here; not, as I mentioned earlier, those persons who, through misapprehension, lend their names and open their checking accounts to "libertarian" publications and causes and extravagances. Rather, I am exposing the pretensions of the narrow doctrinaires or strutting libertines who have imprisoned themselves within a "libertarian" ideology as confining and as unreal as Marxism—if less persuasive than that fell delusion.

Why are these doctrinaire libertarians, with a few exceptions, such peculiar people—the sort who give healthy folk like Marion Montgomery the willies? Why do genuine conservatives feel an aversion to close association with them? Why is an alliance between conservatives and libertarians inconceivable, except for very temporary purposes? Why, indeed, would any such articles of confederation undo whatever gains conservatives have made in recent years?

I give you a blunt answer to those questions. The libertarians are rejected because they are metaphysically mad. Lunacy repels, and political lunacy especially. I do not mean that they are dangerous: nay, they are repellent merely. They do not endanger our country and our civilization, because they are few, and seem likely to become fewer. (Here I refer, of course, to our home-grown American libertarians, and not to those political sects, among them the Red Brigades of Italy, that have carried libertarian notions to bolder lengths.) There exists no peril that American public policies will be affected in any substantial degree by libertarian arguments; or that a candidate of the tiny

Libertarian Party ever will be elected to any public office of significance: the good old causes of Bimetallism, Single Tax, or Prohibition enjoy a more hopeful prospect of success in the closing years of this century than do the programs of Libertarianism. But one does not choose as a partner even a harmless political lunatic.

What do I mean when I say that today's American libertarians are metaphysically mad, and so repellent? Why, the dogmata of libertarianism have been refuted so often, both dialectically and by the hard knocks of experience, that it would be dull work to rehearse here the whole tale of folly. I offer you merely a few of the more conspicuous insufficiencies of libertarianism as a credible moral and political mode of belief. Such differences from the conservatives' understanding of the human condition make inconceivable any coalition of conservatives and libertarians.

. . .

First, the great line of division in modern politics, as Eric Voegelin reminds us, is not between totalitarians on the one hand and liberals (or libertarians) on the other: instead, it lies between all those who believe in a transcendent moral order, on the one side, and on the other side all those who mistake our ephemeral existence as individuals for the be-all and end-all. In this discrimination between the sheep and the goats, the libertarians must be classified with the goats—that is, as utilitarians admitting no transcendent sanctions for conduct.

In effect, they are converts to Marx's dialectical materialism; so conservatives draw back from them on the first principle of all.

Second, in any tolerable society, order is the first need. Liberty and justice may be established only after order is reasonably secure. But the libertarians give primacy to an abstract Liberty. Conservatives, knowing that "liberty inheres in some sensible object", are aware that freedom may be found only within the framework of a social order, such as the Constitutional order of these United States. In exalting an absolute and indefinable "liberty" at the expense of order, the libertarians imperil the very freedom that they praise.

Third, conservatives disagree with libertarians on the question of what holds civil society together. The libertarians contend—so far as they endure any binding at all—that the nexus of society is self-interest, closely joined to cash payment. But the conservatives declare that society is a community of souls, joining the dead, the living, and those yet unborn; and that it coheres through what Aristotle called friendship and Christians call love of neighbor.

Fourth, libertarians (like anarchists and Marxists) generally believe that human nature is good and beneficent, though damaged by certain social institutions. Conservatives, to the contrary, hold that "in Adam's fall we sinned all": human nature, though compounded of both good and evil, cannot be perfected. Thus the perfection of society is impossible, all human beings being imperfect—and among their vices being violence, fraud, and the thirst for power. The libertarian pursues his illusory way toward a Utopia of individualism—which, the conservative knows, is the path to Avernus.

Fifth, the libertarian asserts that the state is the great oppressor. But the conservative finds that the state is natural and necessary for the fulfillment of human nature and the growth of civilization; it cannot be abolished unless humanity is abolished; it is ordained for our very existence. In Burke's phrases, "He who gave us our nature to be perfected by our virtue, willed also the necessary means of its perfection—He willed therefore the state—He willed its connection with the source and original archetype of all perfection." Without the state, man's condition is poor, nasty, brutish, and short—as Augustine argued, many centuries before Hobbes. The libertarians confound the *state* with *government*; in truth, government is the temporary instrument of the state. But government—as Burke continued—"is a contrivance of human wisdom to provide for human *wants*." Among the more important of these wants is "a sufficient restraint upon their passions. Society requires not only that the passions of individuals should be subjected, but that even in the mass and body, as well as in the individual, the inclinations of men should frequently be thwarted, their will controlled, and their passions brought into subjection. This can be done only *by a power out of themselves*; and not, in the exercise of its function, subject to that will and to those passions which it is its office to bridle and subdue." In short, a primary function of government is restraint; and that is anathema to libertarians, although an article of faith to conservatives.

Sixth, the libertarian fancies that this world is a stage for the ego, with its appetites and self-assertive passions. But the conservative finds himself in a realm of mystery and wonder, where duty, discipline, and sacrifice are required—and where the reward is that love which passeth all understanding. The conservative regards the libertarian as impious, in the sense of the old Roman *pietas*: that is, the libertarian does not respect ancient beliefs and customs, or the natural world, or love of country.

The cosmos of the libertarian is an arid loveless realm, a "round prison". "I am, and none else beside me," says the libertarian. But the conservative replies in the sentence of Marcus Aurelius: "We are made for cooperation, like the hands, like the feet."

These are profound differences; and there exist others. Yet even if conservative and libertarian affirm nothing in common, may they not agree upon a negative? May they not take common ground against totalist ideology and the omnipotent state? The primary function of government, conservatives say, is to keep the peace: by repelling foreign enemies, by administering justice domestically.

When government undertakes objectives far beyond these ends, often government falls into difficulty, not being contrived for the management of the whole of life. Thus far, indeed, conservatives and libertarians hold something in common. But the libertarians, rashly hurrying to the opposite extreme from the welfare state, would deprive government of effective power to conduct the common defense, to restrain the unjust and the passionate, or indeed to carry on a variety of undertakings clearly important to the general welfare. With these failings of the libertarians plain to behold, conservatives are mindful of Edmund Burke's admonition concerning radical reformers: "Men of intemperate mind never can be free. Their passions forge their fetters."

Thus in the nature of things, conservatives and libertarians can conclude no friendly pact. Adversity sometimes makes strange bedfellows, but the present successes of conservatives disincline them to lie down, lamblike, with the libertarian lions.

• • •

By this time, possibly I have made it sufficiently clear that I am no libertarian. I venture to suggest that libertarianism, properly understood, is as alien to real American conservatives as is communism. The typical conservative in this country believes that there exists an enduring moral order. He knows that order and justice and freedom are the products of a long and often painful social experience, and that they must be protected from abstract radical assaults. He defends custom, habit, tested institutions that have functioned well. He says that the great virtue in politics is prudence: judging any public measure by its long-run consequences. He is attached to a society of diversity and opportunity, and he is suspicious of any ideology that would rule us by a single abstract principle, whether that principle is "equality" or "liberty" or "social justice" or "national greatness". He recognizes that human nature and society cannot be perfected: politics remains the art of the possible. He adheres to private property and free economic enterprise; he is aware that decent government, repressing violence and fraud, is necessary for the survival of a healthy economy.

What the doctrinaire libertarians offer us is an ideology of universal selfishness—at a time when the country needs more than ever before men and women who stand ready to subordinate their private interests, if need be, to the defense of the Permanent Things. We flawed human creatures are sufficiently selfish already, without being exhorted to pursue selfishness on principle.

XII

The Neoconservatives: An Endangered Species

The author of these pages recklessly confesses to being one of the few survivors of the original intrepid band of Neoconservatives. Very early in the nineteen-fifties, some of us who declared our belief in the Permanent Things were so denominated by our adversaries; but we did not clasp the epithet to our bosoms as a badge of honor—unlike the people who, a quarter of a century later, pleaded guilty as charged, and gloried in their shame.

To put the matter another way, the terms "New Conservative" and "Neo-Conservative" began to appear in certain journals nearly forty years ago. They were applied to such writers as Robert Nisbet, Peter Viereck, Daniel Boorstin, Clinton Rossiter, and your servant. When commentators and critics of that remote epoch entertained sentiments kindly in some degree toward such literate obscurants, they used the term "New Conservative"— implying that misguided though such relatively youthful reactionaries might be, still they probably meant well, and occasionally displayed glimmerings of sense; nay, more, that now and again such New Conservatives even made suggestions worth discussing, though perhaps *per accidens*.

Such were the opinions of our friendlier critics. But journalists and professors who thought less well of us pinned upon us the dread label "Neo-Conservatives", knowing us for symptoms of the recrudescence of a loathsome plague called reaction, enemies of all progress, oppressors of the poor, either tools of the bloated capitalist or else toadies of feudal barons, simpletons enamored of the superstitions of the childhood of the race. The worst fears of these evangels of secular progress came to be realized; they were true prophets. For indeed revived conservative doctrines were disseminated throughout the land by our malicious typewriters, and the American people were arrested in their march toward an earthly Zion.

Yet we scribbling conservatives at the beginning of the 'Fifties, or at least most of us, did not eagerly accept the appellation "New Conservative", nor yet that of "Neo-Conservative". Some of us merely styled ourselves conservatives, being well aware that conservatism is nothing new; others of our kidney preferred to bear no dog-tag.

Presently it came to pass, during the reign of King Lyndon the Dealer, that the media of opinion began to recognize the existence of a loose league of other persons whom we may call the New Neoconservatives, so to speak. This fresh horde of dissenters from Holy Liberalism were men and women of Manhattan, for the most part, and of Jewish stock chiefly—although they recruited some Protestant and Catholic auxiliaries. At one time or another, nearly all of them had professed to be radicals or ritualistic liberals—that a long time ago, in the case of their leaders. These are the Neoconservatives so much praised or drubbed nowadays. Mr. Irving Kristol and his associates accepted without much protest the "Neoconservative" tag pinned to them by their adversaries— much as Whigs and Tories, during the seventeenth century, had come to wear as badges of honor the derisive epithets thrust upon them by enemies.

Although I paid no very close attention to the emerging of these late recruits to the conservative moment, I did welcome their appearance, perceiving that not a few among them were people of talent and energy, active in serious journalism and in certain universities, and giving promise of the rise of conservative or quasi-conservative opinions among the Jewish intelligentsia of New York in particular—a class previously given over to radicalism or a disintegrated liberalism. Perhaps I expected too much of these Manhattan allies.

When the late Michael Harrington smote them hip and thigh, I was not taken aback: such an assault was to be expected from a syndicalist. When Mr. Peter Steinfels, editor of *Commonweal* then, poured the vials of his scorn upon their devoted heads in a book entitled *The Neoconservatives*, I was puzzled that Mr. Joseph Sobran, in the pages of *National Review*, found some substance in Steinfels' acerbic criticisms; I encouraged Dr. Frank Annunziata to write for my quarterly *University Bookman* a defense of these Neoconservatives against Steinfels.

Although one may trace the beginnings of Neoconservatism of the Manhattan sort back to the year 1965, the ladies and gentlemen of that political sect did not loom large for me until the early years of the Reagan administration. I was mildly startled when, in 1980, Mr. George Gilder, addressing the Heritage Foundation, declared emphatically that he was no Neoconservative. (He found them insufficiently capitalistic, and morally inferior to Mrs. Phyllis Schlafly.) In short, I was prejudiced in favor of these Prodigal Sons, come home to a conservative patrimony, who have been denominated the Neoconservatives. How earnestly they founded magazine upon magazine! How skillfully they insinuated themselves into the councils of the Nixon and Reagan administrations! How very audaciously some of them, a decade ago, proclaimed their ability to alter the whole tone of the *New York Times*! (That was a consummation devoutly to be wished, but it turned out to be a mere delusory hope of the Neoconservatives; the *Times* remains unregenerate.) Yet their *hubris* in that instance notwithstanding, the Neoconservatives certainly displayed enterprising talents in their early years.

For some persons who are called, or who call themselves, Neoconservatives, my approbation is undiminished. Who would not welcome to an alliance so ardent a polemicist as Michael Novak, such prudent sociologists as the Doctors Berger, such redoubtable educators as Diane Ravitch, such sound scholars as Nathan Glazer? Often such opponents of nihilism and fanatic ideology contend in the Academy against bitter enemies who outnumber the Neoconservative professors many times over. Let us sustain them!

Yet in general the Neoconservative group have not made many friends nor influenced many people, despite talents for self-publicizing. As Mr. Ben Hart, tongue somewhat in cheek, observed to me about the Neoconservatives while we were arranging a lecture, "There are only about three of them." They have no true political constituency, not even in Manhattan—or perhaps especially not in Manhattan. They have shown no great literary skill: I fear that few books by Neoconservatives will still be read in the year 2000. Neoconservatives have tended regrettably to become a little sect, distrusted and reproached by many leaders of what we may call mainline conservatives, who now and again declare that most of the Neoconservatives are seeking place and preferment chiefly.

I offer you two specimens of the rejections of the Neoconservatives that I encounter nowadays in many quarters. My first extract is from a letter recently received from a highly distinguished historian. "I have burned my bridges with most (not all) of the Konservatives, and especially with the neo-conservatives, who are selfish and uninstructed radicals and progressives, wishing to pour cement all over the country and make the world safe for democracy, well beyond the dreams of Wilson," he writes to me. "A feeling for the land, for its conservation, and for the strong modesty of a traditional patriotism (as distinct from nationalism) none of them has."

My second instance of the spreading distaste for Neoconservatives comes from a well-known literary scholar. "It is significant that when the Neo-Cons wish to damn any conservative who has appealed for a grant to a conservative foundation, they tell the officers of the foundation that the conservative is a fascist," he states. "I believe that the chief enemy of American conservatism has not been the Marxists, nor even the socialist liberals in the Democratic Party, but the Neo-Conservatives, who have sabotaged the movement from within and exploited it for their own selfish purposes."

What is a Neoconservative, really? Is he, as Harrington and Steinfels saw him, a liberal who has turned his coat opportunistically? Is he primarily a seeker after power and the main chance? Or is he a man who has new ideas about the defense of the Permanent Things? For my part, I have wished that certain so-called Neoconservatives whose views and lives I approve, like certain Libertarians for whom I retain a fellow-feeling, would content themselves, as do I, with the simple old badge Conservative.

Be that as it may, I predict that within a very few years we will hear little more of the Neoconservatives. Some will have fallen away, and others will have been merged in the main current of America's conservative movement, and yet others' pert loquacity will have been silenced by the tomb. After all, the leading Neoconservatives are not new people; they have become old people already, as have I myself. We have it on the considerable authority of Mr. Irving Kristol, as cited by Mr. Michael Novak, that—campfollowers excluded—in number the Neoconservatives are but sixty.

During 1988, there was published in *Commentary* a charmingly naive essay by Dan Himmelfarb, in which it was argued that the children and grandchildren of extant Neoconservatives would come to form a Sacred Band, calling themselves Neoconservatives life-long, and destined to rule the American roost. This dream ignores the fact that things initially new do not long remain new; everything changes, yesteryear's novelty ceasing to charm.

Self-proclaimed political elites do not long endure in this democratic republic; but the Neoconservatives prefer to ignore Experience—a hard master, Experience, Benjamin Franklin says. Those who ignore history are condemned to repeat it, as Santayana reminds us. Deficient in historical understanding as in familiarity with humane letters, most of the Neoconservatives lack those long views and that apprehension of the human condition which form a footing for successful statecraft. Often clever, these Neoconservatives; seldom wise.

. . .

Having dreed the weird of that faction called the Neoconservatives, I proceed to praise them. For despite the seeming harshness of the judgments I uttered a few paragraphs ago, I have many sympathies with these Neoconservatives, and admiration for some of them. Permit me, then, to touch upon their achievements.

First, in a time when riotous students and urban mobs did much as they pleased; in an era when the Academy and the learned societies were dominated by radical doctrinaires; when the blunders domestic and foreign of the Johnson administration enfeebled the nation—why, at that juncture the Neoconservatives came forward, proclaiming that politics is the art of the possible; and did their best in the cause of sound sense. They drubbed liberals' sentimentalism and scorned radical fanaticism. In that hour they maintained stoutly the rule of law and the politics of prudence.

Second, we are in debt to the Neoconservatives for their founding of several intelligent serious journals—somewhat narrow in their scope and in their readership and in their circle of contributors, perhaps, but containing valuable articles on public policy, education, and other major issues of the day. These publications have helped to demonstrate that, after all, conservatives are not so stupid as John Stuart Mill fancied them to be.

Third, in the realm of domestic politics as least, the Neoconservatives began discussion of practical alternatives to mere social drifting; they, or some of them, knowing that the national clock could not be turned back to the year 1928, endeavored to frame public policies which would meet realistically the necessities of the concluding three decades of the twentieth century.

Fourth, in foreign policy the Neoconservatives opposed manfully—or, in the case of Ambassador Kirkpatrick, womanfully—the designs and menaces of the Soviet Union. They have been aware that America was not merely opposing a national rival, but (graver peril) combatting an armed doctrine—as Burke said of British resistance to the Jacobins two centuries ago. Sometimes, true, they have been rash in their schemes of action, pursuing a fanciful democratic globalism rather than the true national interest of the United States; on such occasions I have tended to side with those moderate Libertarians who set their faces against foreign entanglements.

And not seldom it has seemed as if some eminent Neoconservatives mistook Tel Aviv for the capital of the United States. Yet by and large, I think, they have helped to redeem America's foreign policy from the confusion into which it fell during and after the wars in southeastern Asia. In this they have redressed the balance in the conduct of foreign affairs. In a little while, nevertheless, I shall set down some misgivings about possible long-run consequences of their understanding of America's international undertakings.

. . .

Earlier I remarked that the Neoconservatives are often clever, but seldom wise. Eliot's lines from *The Rock* may be applied to them:

> *Where is the wisdom we have lost in knowledge?*
> *Where is the knowledge we have lost in information?*

In their publications, the Neoconservatives thrust upon us a great deal of useful information, and obviously are possessed of considerable knowledge of the world about us. But in the understanding of the human condition and in the apprehension of the accumulated wisdom of our civilization, they are painfully deficient.

An instance of this lack of wisdom is the Neoconservatives' infatuation with ideology. On the platform of the Heritage

Foundation, a few years past, Mr. Irving Kristol and I exchanged views on the subject of "ideology"; we differed forcibly. He and various of his colleagues wish to persuade us to adopt an ideology of our own to set against Marxist and other totalist ideologies. Ideology, I venture to remind you, is political fanaticism: at best, it is the substitution of political slogans for real political thought. Ideology animates, in George Orwell's phrase, "the streamlined men who think in slogans and talk in bullets."

In my first chapter I warned conservatives against the curse of ideological infatuation; so I do not propose here to digress at any length on that grim subject. I refer you, rather, to the recently-published collection of Dr. Gerhart Niemeyer's essays, entitled *Aftersight and Foresight*. In his essay "Ideas Have Also Roots", Professor Niemeyer reproves Mr. Kristol for his unfortunate advocacy of a "Republican ideology", and goes on to describe the unhappy infiltration of ideological illusions into American politics.

"Ideology is not confined to communists and fascists," Dr. Niemeyer writes. "We, too, have our share of it, and it shows in our policies. All modern ideologies have the same irrational root: the permeation of politics with millenarian ideas of pseudo-religious character. The result is a dreamworld. Woodrow Wilson dreamed both of 'a world safe for democracy', and of 'enduring peace', a 'world safe from war'. More recently, our national leaders have talked about 'creating' a new society, a 'Great Society', and to that end making 'war against poverty', 'war against hunger', 'creating new men', 'making the world new as at the beginning', building 'a city shining on a hill'. All these presume that man could create himself, implying that he is not a creature, dependent on God, but the master of his own soul and destiny. Civilizational activities are given the character of salvation and thus stamped with a label of sacredness."

A very recent example of this puerile infatuation of the Neoconservatives with "a new ideology" or "an American ideology" is a very lengthy, highly pretentious article by Mr. Michael Novak in the fall, 1988, number of that now altered periodical *This World*. Entrenching himself behind a formidable array of footnotes, but ignoring scholarly studies of ideology, Mr. Novak advocates ideology as "an indispensable but secondary guide to social action." Unlike many Neoconservatives, Mr. Novak does pay some respects to religion in this essay—conveniently ignoring the unpleasant fact that all ideologies are anti-religions, or inverted religions. But the reader may suspect, unjustly, that Mr. Novak's sentiments are much like those of the late Robert S. Kerr, long senator from Oklahoma, who was given to intoning from time to time, "God always has His arm around my shoulder." In his role of Humpty Dumpty, Novak presumes to redefine this word ideology: he instructs us that "Ideology is a guiding vision of future social action." Words mean, of course, whatever Humpty Dumpty and Michael Novak wish them to mean.

In the light of this definition, one heartily endorses the off-hand remark of President George Bush that he does not relish "this vision thing". Visionary politics, as Dr. Niemeyer emphasizes in the paragraph I quoted earlier, do not open our way to an Earthly Paradise.

What is this ideology that Kristol and Novak would have us embrace? Why, the ideology of a term Mr. Novak has popularized, "Democratic Capitalism."

By vigorous advocacy of Democratic Capitalism, by doctrinaire attachment to that ideology, Mr. Novak is saying in effect, Marxism will be undone and the American people will be given a vision of social perfection. What a feeble reed to put into one's hand!

Not caring to break a butterfly on the wheel, I offer you merely a very succinct refutation of the strange notion that the ideology called Democratic Capitalism can set our collective American steps aright. First of all, the phrase is a contradiction in terms; for capitalism is not democratic, nor should it be, nor can it be. The test of the market is not a matter of counting noses and soliciting votes; and the mark of capitalism is not the fallacy that "one man is as good as another, or maybe a little better," but large decisions by shrewd entrepreneurs and managers. Nor is there any egalitarianism in the distribution of the rewards of a market economy.

Second, "Capitalism" is a word popularized by Karl Marx; it implies that the selfish accumulation and enjoyment of capital is the sole purpose of our present society, soon to be overthrown by the proletariat. "Capitalism" is represented as a complete system, moral, intellectual, political, and economic: an ideology has been devised by the greedy capitalists to serve as a false front for this enslaving of the workers of the world. Such is the Marxist argument; and Novak appears to be fulfilling Marx's prophecies by cobbling up just such an ideology.

Now in truth our society is not a "capitalist system" at all, but a complex cultural and social arrangement that comprehends religion, morals, prescriptive political institutions, literary culture, a competitive economy, private property, and much more besides. It is not a system designed to secure and advance the interests of great possessors of capital goods unjustly acquired. Do Neoconservatives, in the role of Burckhardt's "terrible simplifiers", think they will gain the affections of the peoples of the world by actually declaring Americans (and their allies) to be the very capitalist exploiters the Marxists have been denouncing all these years? By promulgating an ideological manifesto that offers nothing better than a utopia of "democratic" creature-comforts?

As for the "democratic" aspect of this Neoconservative ideology, "the Constitution of the United States is not for export," as Dr. Daniel Boorstin puts it. To expect that all the world should, and must, adopt the peculiar political institutions of the United States—which often do not work very well even at home—is to indulge the most unrealistic of visions; yet just that seems to be the hope and expectation of many Neoconservatives. (Mr. Kristol does not go so far.) Such naive doctrine led us into the wars in Indo-China—the notion that we could establish or prop up in Viet Nam a "democracy" that never had existed anywhere in southeastern Asia. Such foreign policies are such stuff as dreams are made of; yet they lead to the heaps of corpses of men who died in vain. We need to ask ourselves whether the Neoconservative architects of international policy are very different from the foreign-policy advisors who surrounded Lyndon Johnson.

Let me make myself a little clearer in this matter by repeating here what I wrote five years ago in my review of Dr. Jeane Kirkpatrick's two volumes of speeches and papers. Mrs. Kirkpatrick declares that the United States should pursue a foreign policy of advancing "human rights", rather than one of the national interest; and she tells us, in effect, that only democratic governments are legitimate governments. That is the Neoconservatives' ideological dogma.

Yet Ambassador Kirkpatrick remarks that we ought not to reject the alliance of autocratic or authoritarian states (as distinguished from totalist regimes) which share with America the will to resist communism. So ought she not to base her argument for "legitimacy" upon the existence of "constitutional government" or "constitutional order, justice, and freedom", or "representative government", or simply "tolerable government", rather than insisting upon an abstract "democracy"?

For the word "democracy" has come to resemble an old hat which everybody wears and nobody respects. As she observes herself, some of the most oppressive regimes in our world pretend to be democracies. And have not democracies often been unholy alliances between a successful demagogue and a greedy mob?

Is the government of Saudi Arabia—distinctly not democratic—less legitimate than the government of the typical Marxist "people's republic"? Is the government of Israel, a garrison state, illegitimate because it excludes from full civic participation one-fifth of its population, on ethnic and religious grounds—scarcely a democratic principle of just government?

Most of the world never was satisfactorily democratic in the past, is distinctly undemocratic today, and has no prospect of decent democracy in the future. Were the United States to insist upon the attainment of democracy (plus capitalism) by every nation-state with which it has satisfactory relations, before long our principal trading-partner might be Switzerland. The United States cannot be forever unsettling the governments of client states, or small countries, or of allies, on the ground that they are not sufficiently democratic in obedience to the doctrines of Rousseau, or that they "discriminate" against somebody or other, or that they prefer traditional economies to a full-blown abstract capitalism. One thinks of the aphorism of the late Madame Nu: "If you have the United States for a friend, you don't need any enemies." Successful foreign policy, like political success generally, is produced through the art of the possible—not through ideological rigidity. It will not do for the Department of State to repeat, like an incantation, "Democracy good, all other government bad."

In short, I am saying that a quasi-religion of Democratic Capitalism cannot do duty for imagination and right reason and prescriptive wisdom, in domestic politics or in foreign relations. An ideology of Democratic Capitalism might be less malign than an ideology of Communism or National Socialism or Syndicalism or Anarchism, but it would not be much more intelligent or humane.

. . .

You will have gathered that I am disappointed, generally speaking, with the Neoconservative faction. I had hope that they might bring lively imagination into the conservative camp; instead, they have urged conservatives to engage in ideological sloganizing, the death of political imagination.

I had expected the Neoconservatives to address themselves to the great social difficulties of America today, especially to the swelling growth of a dismal urban proletariat, and the decay of the moral order. Instead, with some exceptions, their concern has been mainly with the gross national product and with "global wealth". They offer few alternatives to the alleged benefits of the Welfare State, shrugging their shoulders; and the creed of most of them is no better than a latter-day Utilitarianism.

I had thought that the Neoconservatives might become the champions of diversity in the world; instead, they aspire to bring about a world of uniformity and dull standardization, Americanized, industrialized, democratized, logicalized, boring. They are cultural and economic imperialists, many of them.

I had conjectured that the Neoconservatives might be so many new brooms sweeping clean: that they would set new standards of political rectitude, and leaven healthily the lump of the stolid conservative interest. Instead, they have behaved as if they were the cadre of political machines of a type all too frequently encountered in American political history—eager for place and preferment and power, skillful at intrigue, ready to exclude from office any persons who might not be counted upon as faithful to the Neoconservative ideology. Often, backstairs, they have seemed more eager to frustrate their allies than to confute those presumptive adversaries the liberals and radicals. The strategy of Volpone or of Sir Giles Overreach, nevertheless, may prove vain in the long run; and so it is coming to pass nowadays with the Neoconservatives.

Do I then write "Ichabod!" upon the lot of them? Nay, not so. Among them, as I mentioned earlier, are men and women who have risen superior to the foibles and fallacies that have marred the Neoconservative clique generally; and it would be a great pity for the American nation to lose the talents of such people. And whatever blunders the Neoconservatives have made from time to time, all the same they have stirred up some intellectual activity among conservatives generally, no easy thing to do.

In the *Wall Street Journal*, on August 22, 1988, Mr. Irving Kristol expressed his concern as to whether Mr. George Bush has the motivation to learn anything, and disparaged "managerial skills" in government. He urged the appointment to cabinet posts of "superior academics"—presumably of the Kristol kidney. "For the real political talents," Mr. Kristol wrote in a revealing passage, "are quick-wittedness, articulateness, a clear sense of one's ideological agenda and the devious routes necessary for its enactment." Machiavelli!

Such have been the talents of the Neoconservatives in Washington during the past eight years—clever creatures, committed to an ideology, and devious in attaining their objects. The seven cardinal virtues go unmentioned. (The virtue of prudence, according to both Plato and Burke, is the virtue most needed in the statesman.) Where is the wisdom we have lost in knowledge, Neoconservatives? Where is the knowledge we have lost in information?

Mr. Bush, not grown up in the backbiting ideological jungle of New York City, seems unlikely to accept Mr. Kristol's councils. For George Bush is no ideologue and no intellectual, praise be: rather, he is, as Kristol writes, "a fine gentleman of good breeding, a true patriot, an experienced, reliable and trustworthy public servant." Later in the same article, incidentally, Mr. Kristol makes it clear enough that he is no respecter of fine gentlemen: he commends Mrs. Thatcher for having in her cabinet "none of the traditional aristocratic coloration", and rejoices that the present Conservative majority in the House of Commons has fewer members "who have gone to Eton or Harrow, Oxford or Cambridge".

It is a reasonable presumption that Mr. Kristol and certain of his colleagues would prefer to install in the White House some person who might be astutely manipulated by Neoconservative ideologues. Mr. Bush has far too much practical experience of federal office to be so managed by the "first-class academic brain trust" that Mr. Kristol desires to establish in the White House. "In politics, the professor always plays the comic role," Nietzsche wrote. So it is coming to pass with the Neoconservatives, of whose "guiding vision" the Bush people are skeptical.

Do I think, what with my mordant comments in this portion of my book concerning conservative factions, that after four decades of striving the conservative impulse withers in the sere and yellow leaf, ready for a bonfire on All Hallows' Eve? Not at all.

Already, despite the complexion of the majority in the Congress, the conservatives are dominant in public policy. No longer does one hear talk of the promise of Neoliberalism.

It is to be hoped that the conservative movement of the 'Nineties will resemble Cicero's Optimates—"the party of all good men." Some of us, once upon a time, had fixed lifelong in our brains, through the standard exercises in typewriting manuals, Cicero's exhortation: "Now is the time for all good men to come to the aid of their party." Even publicans, sinners, and Neoconservatives may do battle for the Permanent Things.

XIII

The Cultural Conservatives

In practical politics, what we call the conservative movement in America, I repeat, is a coalition of several interests and bodies of opinion. It is only in their opposition to Leviathan that the several factions join forces. Among these factions, it seems to me, the most imaginative is the body of persons called "cultural conservatives" or "traditionalists".

The term *cultural conservative* is at least four decades old. From time to time it has been applied to me, though I never have so denominated myself. What has been meant by this term? Why, presumably those who employ it have regarded a "cultural conservative" as a person who endeavors to preserve the customs, the institutions, the learning, the mores of a society, as distinguished from men and women whose immediate interest is in practical political activity of a conservative cast. The implication of some writers who draw this line of demarcation seems to be that nasty though conservative politicians are, possibly some feeble defense may be made for the good, if foolish, intentions of mere cultural conservatives.

In truth, the advocates of cultural conservatism recognize that although in our Father's house are many mansions, they are not all on the same floor. The culture which these Cultural Conservatives hope to conserve is a complex of elements that make possible the functioning of our present society; and that have given us a civilization which in some respects is the most successful ever to arise. This existing culture is rooted in earlier Hebraic, classical, and Christian cultures. For the most part, it came across the Atlantic from Europe. Commonly we call it "Western" culture—although that term is rather an awkward one. (Is Jerusalem "west"? West of what? We used to say that Jerusalem lies in the Levant—that is, the East.)

Still more specifically, friends to cultural conservatism, as it is expressed in today's controversies, aspire to preserve and renew the permanent things in the American social order: the American mores praised by Alexis de Tocqueville, the framework of laws, the private rights, the hearty old customs, the patterns of family affection, the diffusion of private property, the protections against arbitrary power, the vigor of local community, the confidence that life is worth living. They believe that there exists a moral order to which humankind should conform. They do not believe that life is mostly an exercise in getting and spending. Nor do they think that culture was born yesterday.

In 1987 there was founded in the city of Washington an Institute for Cultural Conservatism. The Institute's task is

Herculean: the reinvigoration of American culture in the sense that a nation's culture is the complex of convictions, folkways, habits, arts, crafts, economic methods, laws, morals, political structures, and all the ways of living in community that have developed over the centuries. The Institute's framers have declared, with some courage, "The politics that carry us into the twenty-first century will be based not on economics, but on culture."

This attachment to folkways, traditions, and well-rooted beliefs and institutions may be regarded as a kind of sociological understanding of culture—although not the sociology of the positivists. It is concerned, that is, with a general and popular culture: a culture in which the mass of Americans participate, whether or not they are quite conscious of being in this sense "cultured" or "acculturated". Marxist doctrinaires might attach to this pervasive American culture the label "bourgeois". The tag is not quite accurate or adequate; for that word, of nineteenth-century European usage, implies a certain social pattern that scarcely exists today and never did prevail in the United States, with the possible exception of yesteryear's Boston, Philadelphia, or Charleston. However that may be, bourgeois culture has had many merits; and if Marxists wish to call the popular culture of the United States "bourgeois", there is little point in denying that soft impeachment. To put the matter another way, cultural conservatives endeavor to uphold the better features of American civilization, of the life we know and live—recognizing, true, that not everything in today's culture deserves praise, and that prudent, gradual change may be the best means for preserving the permanent things.

Yet intelligent cultural conservatives make themselves defenders of something more than the common culture which the American population has inherited. For they try to uphold, as well, that understanding of culture which champions the cultivation of mind and conscience; what is often called "high culture". If we may call the popular culture democratic, let us call this higher culture aristocratic: both aspects of culture are necessary to an enduring civilization. It is not a question of conflict between "democratic" and "aristocratic" modes of culture: as T. S. Eliot wrote, in the healthy culture of a people, the differing levels of culture flourish in symbiosis.

The culture, the civilization, that the Cultural Conservatives hope to reinvigorate is, in large part, the American manifestation of what is called Christian civilization, that great culture originated in a little cult of Galileans two thousand years ago. It is indebted for much to the earlier Hebraic and classical cultures, but in its works, moral and material, it has become the most resplendent of all civilizations, ever since culture began. Nowadays that latter-day Christian culture begins to seem decadent; some people say that already we live in a post-Christian era. The Cultural Conservatives labor to arrest the decay, or even to renew what has faded. They appeal "to all fair and open-minded people, including those who decline to affirm a religious belief personally," welcoming allies. Their principles, however, are founded upon the Christian understanding of the human condition; and what they are determined to conserve is not nineteenth-century Utilitarianism, nor the twentieth-century ideology of Democratism, but

Christian civilization as it has been realized in American beliefs, customs, habits, and institutions.

. . .

Our inherited culture is involved in grim difficulties. I suppose that most educated people nowadays will assent to that statement. Four decades ago, not long after the Second World War, I often encountered people who waxed indignant at my venturing to suggest the possibility of cultural decadence among us. It is otherwise now.

Sometimes, true, I come upon men and women well satisfied with our world, and with their diversions—rather nasty diversions, not infrequently—therein. Yet these are not what I call tranquil people; instead they bring to mind a couplet by Adam Mickiewicz:

> *Your soul deserves the place to which it came,*
> *If having entered Hell, you feel no flame.*

Some years ago I was seated in the parlor of an ancient house in the close of York Minster. My host, Canon Basil Smith, the Minster's Treasurer then, a man of learning and of practical faith, said to me that we linger at the end of an era: soon the culture we have known will be swept into the dustbin of history. About us, as we talked in that medieval mansion, loomed Canon Smith's tall bookcases lined with handsome volumes; flames flared up from his coal fire. Was all this venerable setting of culture, and much more besides, to vanish away as if the Evil Spirit had grasped it in his talons? Basil Smith is buried now, and so is much of the society that humorous, high-minded cleric of the North Country ornamented and tried to redeem. As we sat beside his fireplace, I thought him too gloomy then; but already much that he predicted has come to pass.

On the occasion of my final visit to him, indeed, there occurred a small but significant incident nearly related to my dread that our culture rustles in the sere and yellow leaf. The bells of York Minster had pealed over the city for centuries, every Sunday morning. But in the year of my visit, the proprietor of Young's Hotel, across a medieval street from the Minster, had complained that the tolling disturbed the slumbers of his guests who had been at their potations the preceding night. With a meekness of a sort not enjoined by Jesus of Nazareth, the archbishop and chapter—Canon Smith dissenting, I doubt not—had agreed not to ring those confounded bells early on the Sabbath. The decaying "sensual culture" (as Pitirim Sorokin would call it) had triumphed over a remnant of an enfeebled "idealistic culture". With increasing speed, this process continues in Britain, America, and other lands. The dismissal of the sacred: that rejection lies at the heart of our cultural tribulations. But I run on too fast. If we are to arrest the decay of our culture, first we must diagnose the malady called *decadence*.

In the ten-volume *Century Dictionary*, published at the beginning of this century, we encounter this succinct definition of the word decadence: "A falling off or away; the act or process of galling into an inferior condition or state; the process or state of decay, deterioration." The term "The Decadence", in historiography, specifically refers to the closing centuries of the Roman empire. Is twentieth-century civilization suffering from ills very like those of fifth-century Roman civilization? But, postponing an answer to that inquiry, let us pursue our business of definition.

A lively, if dismaying, book on the subject of decadence is C. E. M. Joad's *Decadence: a Philosophical Inquiry* (1948). Professor Joad wrote that a society or an individual that has become decadent has "dropped the object"; or, in terms less abstract, in a decadent state people have lost any aim, end, or object in life; to decadent folk, life has no significance except as mere process or experience; they live as dogs do, from day to day. The essence of the decadent understanding of the human condition, in Joad's phrases, may be found "in the view that experience is valuable or is at least to be valued for its own sake, irrespective of the quality or kind of the experience, and in the appropriate beliefs about life, morals, art and society which entail and are entailed by this view, together with the scales of values and modes of taste associated with these beliefs."

Joad sets down certain characteristics of a decadent society: luxury; skepticism; weariness; superstition; preoccupation with the self and its experiences; a society "promoted by and promoting the subjectivist analysis of moral, aesthetic, metaphysical and theological judgments." Anyone who does not recognize the acuteness of Joad's analysis here—why, he must lead a life singularly sequestered.

The mordant wit of C. Northcote Parkinson, in *The Law of Longer Life* (1978), is directed toward the history of social decadence. Parkinson distinguishes six stages, historically regarded, through which civilizations pass on their way to dissolution. Here are those stages, very briefly put:

First, political over-centralization, as in Babylon, Persepolis, Rome, Peking, Delhi, Paris, and London.

Second, inordinate growth in taxation, which becomes "the means of government interference in commercial, industrial, and social life. . . . Taxation, taken to the limit and beyond, has always been a sign of decadence and a prelude to disaster."

Third, "the growth of a top-heavy system of administration." A great characterless political machine develops. "Those who are theoretically men of power have surprisingly little real authority, being caught up in a machine which moves slowly in some unintended direction."

Fourth, "promotion of the wrong people." In the labyrinth of political bureaucracy, "To have original ideas would be a bar to success. This situation is probably inevitable and eternal but the same tendency, in a decadent society, rubs off on other people. . . . The whole society, as well as the whole organization, becomes lethargic and cumbersome, routine-ridden and tame."

Fifth, "the urge to overspend." After years and decades of excessive public expenditure, "Lacking the courage to reduce its expenditure, lacking the means of improving the revenue (the taxes having hit the ceiling), the government incurs a vast debt and loads it on to the shoulders of some future generation."

Sixth, "liberal opinion"—that is, a feeble sentimentality which weakens the minds and the wills of a great part of a nation's population. "What concerns our argument is not that the world's do-gooders are mistaken but that their attitude is decadent. They are moved by sentiment rather than by reason and that is itself a symptom of decay. Still more to the point, their interest is solely in the present and for them, too, the future is merely the end."

Hard truths! Both writers, I believe, are painfully correct. And yet neither, it seems to me—at least in the preceding passages—has touched directly on the principal cause of the ruinous decay of great cultures. The recent writer who describes that principal cause most movingly is Aleksandr Solzhenitsyn, in his address on receiving the Templeton Prize, in 1983. I give you this one passage:

"Over half a century ago while I was still a child," Solzhenitsyn said, "I recall hearing a number of older people offer the following explanation for the great disasters that had befallen Russia: 'Men have forgotten God; that's why all this has happened.'"

For culture comes from the cult. For the past three centuries, the cult of our civilization—that is, the Christian religion—has been declining in power. The principal reason for this decay has been the growth of the anti-cult of scientism, which is by no means the same thing as natural science. John Locke's religious rationalism has trickled down, among great many of the educated or half-educated of our own time, to perfect indifference or positive hostility toward a transcendent religion. And so the culture itself, the core of which was faith, begins to fall to pieces.

A cult is a joining together for worship—that is, the attempt of people to commune with a transcendent power. It is from association in the cult, the body of worshippers, that human community grows. This basic truth has been expounded in recent decades by such eminent historians as Christopher Dawson, Eric Voegelin, and Arnold Toynbee.

Once people are joined in the cult, cooperation for many other things becomes possible. Systematic agriculture, armed defense, irrigation, architecture, the visual arts, music, the more intricate crafts, economic production and distribution, courts and government—all these features of a culture arise gradually from the cult, the religious tie. And especially a web of morals, rules for human conduct, is the product of religious beliefs.

Out of little knots of worshippers, in Egypt, the Fertile Crescent, India, or China, there grew up simple cultures, for those joined by faith can dwell together in relative peace. Presently such simple cultures may develop into complex cultures, and those intricate cultures into great civilizations. American culture of our era is rooted, strange although the fact may seem to many, in tiny gatherings of worshippers in Palestine, Greece, and Italy, thousands of years ago. The enormous material achievements of our civilization have resulted, if remotely, from the spiritual insights of prophets, and sages.

This historical truth came home to me, decades ago, when I was strolling through the Chicago Institute of Art. I came upon a half-darkened corridor in which, on either side, was displayed an exhibition of miniature models of medieval buildings, composing a town. And at the far end of the exhibit, in a case dominating the display, was the model of a Gothic cathedral. The placard below that building read much as follows: "This exhibition fitly culminates in the great church, the center of all human activity, the mother of architecture and the other arts, the core and source of civilization." At that time I was a fairly thoroughgoing secularist, never having been baptized, let alone being a communicant of any church The legend beneath the miniature cathedral, nevertheless, struck me with some force: first, because it was posted in a building maintained by public funds (what of the first clause of the First Amendment?); second, because what the legend said was historically true, although never put to me so visually before. Civilization, the civilization we have known, is the child of the church's culture.

How is it that we human beings, in our savage state two-legged wolves, subject only to our ravening egos, moved by lust, avarice, envy, and other deadly sins—how is it that we are able to dwell in a civil social order, most of us abstaining from violence and fraud? Because we have acquired moral habits. But what authority lies behind the habits, giving them sanction? Without religious convictions, we would be so many Cains, every man's hand against every other man's, and society could not cohere. Out of the cult comes moral order, without which even the simplest culture could not flower.

But suppose that with the elapse of centuries, faith diminishes and the cult withers. What then of a civilization that has been rooted in the cult? What occurs when the only remaining ardent adherents to the cult are literalists who mistake tradition's symbols of transcendence for mere chronicles of miraculous or inexplicable events? G. K. Chesterton instructs us that all life being an allegory, we can understand it only in parable. But what if the teachings of mechanists and materialists have so perverted the popular imagination that allegory and parable no longer are apprehended?

∎ ∎ ∎

So it has come to pass, in the closing years of the twentieth century. With the weakening of the moral order, "Things fall apart . . . mere anarchy is loosed upon the world." The Hellenic and the Roman cultures went down to dusty death after this fashion. And since the seventeenth century, Christian doctrine has been losing its hold upon the mind and the heart of the peoples of what is now called the West and once was called Christendom. From time to time, some reinvigoration of Christian belief has occurred, in forms so widely varying as Wesleyan enthusiasm at the end of the eighteenth century and the influence of Chateaubriand's book *The Genius of Christianity* early in the nineteenth century; but in general rationalism, skepticism, and the indulgence of will and appetite have tended to win the field.

Many books have been published on this large subject of the decline of the influence of religious convictions, I cannot well enter upon details here. For the moment, I state merely that my own study of such concerns has led me to conclude that a culture, a civilization, cannot long survive the extinction of belief in a transcendent order that brought the culture into being. For an understanding of the character and importance of religion unlike the "fundamentalism" often assailed in liberal papers and by persons like Mr. Norman Lear, I refer you to such twentieth-century scholars as Mircea Eliade, Rudolf Otto, Jaroslav Pelikan, and Christopher Dawson.

How are we to account for the widespread decay of religious impulse and religious conviction? (Here I remark that the survival of churches as humanitarian or political organizations does not signify that religious faith has survived.) It seems clear enough that the main cause of the loss of the idea of the holy is the attitude called "scientism"—that is, the popular notion that revelations of natural science, over the past two centuries and longer, somehow have demonstrated the obsolence of the church's claims; have informed us how men and women are naked apes merely; have pointed out that the ends of existence are production and consumption merely, that happiness is the gratification of sensual impulses; that notions of the resurrection of the flesh and the life everlasting are superstitions of the childhood of the race. Upon these scientistic assumptions, elevated to an ideology by John Dewey and his colleagues, public schooling is conducted nowadays, implicitly or explicitly.

This view of the human condition has been called *reductionism*; it reduces human beings almost to mindlessness; it denies the existence of the soul. This attitude, called by Christopher Dawson "secular humanism", is scientistic but not scientific: for it is a far cry from the understanding of matter and energy that one finds in the addresses, during recent years, of Nobel prize-winners in physics, say.

As Arthur Koestler remarks in his little book *The Roots of Coincidence*, yesteryear's scientific doctrines of materialism and mechanism ought to be buried with a requiem of electronic music. Once more, in biology as in physics, the scientific disciplines enter upon the realm of mystery.

Yet the great public always suffers from the affliction called cultural lag. If most people continue to fancy that the vulgarized scientific theory of a century ago is the verdict of all scientists today, will not the religious understanding of life continue to wither, and civilization continue to crumble?

Perhaps; and yet, scientists being to the modern populace what priests were to the medieval populace, scientific techniques and speculations might themselves undo the reductionist notion of the human condition, and restore general awareness of the transcendent. The Christian doctrine of the resurrection of the flesh and the life everlasting, for instance, was inexplicable in terms of natural science when Saint Paul enunciated it; and to nineteenth-century men of science it was a teaching plainly incredible. Yet we now know that the nineteenth-century understanding of matter—including the human body—was mistaken. Twentieth-century physicists instruct us that you and I are composed of negative and positive particles of electricity, as is all other matter; that, in short, we are energy, rather than solid substance; and that energy may neither be added to nor destroyed—merely transmuted. What once has been assembled, and then dispersed, may be assembled once more. Conceivably these bones may rise again.

It is my argument that the elaborate culture we have known stands in grave peril; that our civilization may expire of lethargy, or be destroyed by violence, or perish from a combination of both evils. Cultural conservatives, believing that life remains worth living, begin to address themselves urgently to means by which a restoration of our inherited culture may be achieved. They, far more than the other factions sometimes called conservative, require the moral imagination. The restoration of learning, humane and scientific; the reform of many public policies; the brightening of the corners where we loiter—such approaches are open to those among the rising generation who look for a purpose in life.

Such a restoration, painstaking labor of reason and imagination, cannot be accomplished by the ideologue, the violent revolutionary. Conceivably the politics of this country, after the end of this century, may be much more concerned with the reinvigoration of culture than with the economic issues that have dominated elections, most of the time, for the past seven decades. And whether or not modern people are given a Sign from on high, those men and women who are urgently concerned for the moral order, and for the survival of a high culture, need to repair to culture's source—the religious perception of what we are or ought to be, here below.

Toward a Prudent Foreign Policy

M odern civilization's Time of Troubles, we are told by
Arnold Toynbee, commenced in 1914. Four years
later, the worst blow to the received political and
social order was struck by the triumph of the Bolsheviki in
Russia. But in the year of our Lord one thousand nine hundred
ninety-two, it begins to appear that once more it may become
possible to speak with some confidence of the Permanent
Things. Old concepts of order, justice, and freedom may prevail, after all. God willing, much that is worth keeping may be
conserved, here near the end of the twentieth century. It is one
of the marks of human decency, Eliseo Vivas instructs us, to be
ashamed of having been born into the twentieth century.
Perhaps we may atone for the century's sins by overthrowing,
at the end of the century, the fourth Horseman of the
Apocalypse, Revolution.

Already America's conservatives have won a grand victory,
after seven decades of struggle. From President Wilson's

dispatch of troops to the Russian arctic to President Reagan's expedition to Moscow for conferring with Gorbachev, the American Republic wrestled with the Russian bear; and the Western concept of ordered freedom contended against the ideology of Marxism. Alexis de Tocqueville foresaw that tremendous contest, which now has been decided in favor of the United States of America and in favor of the politics of prudence and prescription.

The final encounter was won by an elderly and eminent conservative, Mr. Ronald Reagan. When he took the presidential oath of office, Mr. Reagan was thoroughly unacquainted with foreign affairs. And yet, with the exception of his failure in Lebanon, President Reagan was wondrously successful in foreign policy. He restored the vigor of the American economy, so that the oligarchs in the Kremlin perceived the Soviet Union's weakness in the face of American productivity. He commenced work upon the Strategic Defense Initiative, and the masters of the Soviet empire, even the imperialists of the Red Army, knew to their sorrow that they could not find the resources to match that shield against nuclear rockets. He sent a rocket into the very parlor, literally, of the malign dictator of Libya; and the masters of the Soviet system opened their eyes wide at his audacity. The Communists of Russia and the Communists of Cuba seized upon the island of Grenada, to make another base of it; but President Reagan promptly dispatched a military force to Grenada, shot some of the Russians and the Cubans in the course of the operation, and shipped back to Moscow and to Havana, as released prisoners, the rest of their men. This action told the rulers of the Evil Empire that Mr. Reagan, given to calling bluffs, did not fear those ten-feet-tall Russians. Besides, already the Soviet Union sporadically depended, for very sustenance, upon shipments of American wheat. It was borne in upon Gorbachev and his colleagues that they must rethink, retrench, and resign numerous ambitions, lest they perish: for the old actor from the Californian ranch, quick on the draw in his films, had outgunned them.

In general, prospects abroad for American conservatives are more cheerful than they seemed in the heyday of Chairman Johnson, say; and in particular, bright in eastern Europe just now. Permit me, then, to sum up America's gains in international affairs; and next to utter, Cassandra in trousers though you may think me, certain vaticinations of a cautionary character.

．．．

First, my friends, you and I are in at the death of the Marxist ideology. Because any ideology—that is, a theory of fanatic politics promising the terrestrial paradise—is illusory, eventually the consequences of the ideology are perceived by most people to be ruinous; and then, God willing, a healthy reaction occurs. That has happened, after seven decades, in Russia; it is happening today in China; it has been occurring in the African, Asiatic, and Latin-American states that succumbed to Communist ideologues during the past forty years. In Europe, only Serbia endures Communist masters still. And that country has been cast out of the United Nations.

The practical consequences of Marxist doctrine are so thoroughly exposed that before long Marxism will find defenders only in the American academy. Marxism pretended to be a moral system as well as an economic and political panacea. Now some first principles of morals, at least, and some workable assumptions about politics and economics, any people must have. What beliefs will fill the vacuum left by the evaporation of Marxist dogmata?

Conceivably some alternative ideology might take hold upon the minds and emotions of peoples who recently have freed themselves from Marxism—some other dogmatic and treacherous system that immanentizes the symbols of transcendence. Yet what such an ideology might amount to, no man can say; perhaps it would be an abstract and aggressive nationalism. Or some naive Americans speak windily of an "ideology of democracy"—but about democratism I will have something to say presently.

The better hope is that there may succeed to Marx's dialectical materialism, in Russia, eastern Europe, and much of Africa, a renewed Christian belief, already resurgent in Poland, Rumania, Lithuania, Hungary, Slovenia, and elsewhere. Persecution stimulates, rather than stifles, a people's religious faith—provided that the state's persecution is not perfectly effectual, as it was not in the Roman empire, and has not been even in the Soviet Union or its satrapies. The long history of the Jews attests this truth. And when the survival of a nation is bound up with the survival of a church, as in Poland and Ireland, religion becomes stronger than ever ideology might be.

No religious creed supplies satisfactorily a plan of politics and economics: the purpose of religious faith is the ordering of the soul, not the ordering of the state. But religious dogmata do offer answers to ultimate questions; while ideology cannot convincingly answer such questions.

Now, Communist illusions having been repudiated, in much of the world men and women may turn again to what Marx had called, falsely, "the opiate of the people": to the religious understanding that, among other hard truths, teaches why man and society are not perfectible, here below.

It is even conceivable that the resurgent Christian belief of eastern Europe may be communicated to a fair number of people in these United States, where increasingly both Protestant and Catholic churches have suffered from the inroads of ideology or of secular humanism. However that may be, Marxist ideologues can take some small comfort from the knowledge that their ideology will not be altogether effaced from this earth. For as John Lukacs remarks, "There will always be Communists—in New York."

In foreign policy, no longer will our Department of State be contending with the fanatic irrationalism of ideology, in Europe, Asia, or Africa—or, at any rate, not by the beginning of the twenty-first century, I believe. Great states and small are beginning to settle for politics as the art of the possible. Marx's insistence on the inevitability of Communism's triumph has been refuted totally—and almost overnight.

Forty years ago, Whittaker Chambers gloomily believed that in choosing the American cause of order, justice, and freedom, he was joining the losing side. It is said that Henry Kissinger, at the height of his influence in Washington, privately believed that his diplomatic endeavors were only postponing the eventual triumph of Communism and the Soviet Union. How very different is our present prospect! One thinks of Edmund Burke's rejection of historical determinism, at the end of his days, in his first *Letter on a Regicide Peace*. Providence, or mere individual strong wills, or chance, Burke says, abruptly may alter the whole apparent direction of a nation. "I doubt whether the history of mankind is yet complete enough, if ever it can be so, to furnish grounds for a sure theory on the internal causes which necessarily affect the fortune of a State," as Burke puts it. It is possible, he mentions, that great and sudden changes in the affairs of nations may be the consequence of "the occasional interposition and the irresistible hand of the Great Disposer." One may speculate on whether, during the past three years, the Great Disposer's instrument may have been the Great Communicator, Mr. Reagan.

Be that as it may, the power of Marxist ideology, menacing even the United States for the past century and a half, appears to be broken. And the power of the Soviet empire, too, has been broken into pieces. The question even arises of whether Moscow will retain effective control of any territories beyond Great Russia. Civil war may consume the energies of what, for some seventy years, was the Soviet Union. No longer can the Russian system compete in armaments with the United States; that competition, which sorely tried the finances of the United States, worked the ruin of that enormous domination which extended from the Baltic to the Pacific.

Thus it has come to pass that the United States faces no rival power worthy of the name. China is sunk in poverty and hopelessly misgoverned; the British and French empires gave up the ghost four decades ago; Japan is strong economically, but not big enough to contest the mastery of the world; even a reunited Germany, chastened by the misfortunes of a half century ago, will not aspire to exercise a hegemony over Europe, let alone to box seriously with the United States. Henry Luce and Richard Nixon used to say that the twentieth century must be the "American Century"; but that aspiration may be fulfilled, instead, in the twenty-first century.

Aye, nowadays America alone is a great power in the world, with resources—both military and financial—sufficient, in most respects, unaided to secure her national interest against all comers. But this vast questions looms up: how should the United States employ the powers of its ascendancy? Are we Americans fulfilling a manifest destiny, the mission of recasting every nation and every culture in the American image?

. . .

Recently various American voices have proclaimed enthusiastically that soon all the world, or nearly all of it, will embrace a New World Order, presumably what is called "democratic capitalism". It is the assumption of these enthusiasts that the political structure and the economic patterns of the United States will be emulated in every continent, forevermore.

This attitude brings to mind a character in the best of American novels, George Santayana's *The Last Puritan*. That character is Cyrus P. Whittle, a Yankee schoolmaster, very like the type of academic that dominates American universities at the present hour. Whittle teaches "American history and literature in a high quivering voice, . . . as if he were driving a long hard nail into the coffin of some detested fallacy. . . . His joy, as far as he dared, was to vilify all distinguished men. Franklin had written indecent verses; Washington—who had enormous hands and feet—had married Dame Martha for her money; Emerson served up Goethe's philosophy in ice-water. Not that Mr. Cyrus P. Whittle was without enthusiasm and a secret religious zeal. Not only was America the biggest thing on earth, but it soon was going to wipe out everything else; and in the delirious dazzling joy of that consummation, he forgot to ask what would happen afterwards."

Just so: what sort of world would this projected universal Americanization produce? Ever since the Second World War, American publicists have been describing the Earthly Paradise to be created by the establishing of "democratic capitalism" in every land—even though the phrase "democratic capitalism" is of recent origin, a bit of neoconservative cant. For instance, in 1951 there was published in the British periodical *The Twentieth Century* an article entitled "The New American Revolution". Its author was a David C. Williams, director of research for the Political Action Committee of the AFL-CIO.

His sentences are interestingly similar to certain outpourings of the new Endowment for Democracy and other organs of "global democracy".

"This twentieth century manifestation of the American Revolution has been aptly called 'the revolution of rising expectations,'" Williams wrote. "Americans insist that it would be under way even if there were no such thing as Communism in the world. . . . The agents of this new revolution are the numerous officials, business men, technicians, and trade unionists whom the American Government is sending abroad. . . . American business men have the task of convincing their European counterparts that it pays to modernize, and to produce for the masses rather than the classes. They can assure their European friends that it is possible for them to achieve as a group the position of highest prestige in their communities, displacing landowners, civil servants, and officers of the armed forces from their traditional places of honor."

Thus American energy is to become a revolutionary influence rather than a conservative, deliberately appealing to cupidity, class envy, and the itch for change: so Williams argued. In Asia, he continued, we Americans will help to "break down the traditional bonds of caste and family which prevail" and "drive the handicraft producers to the wall." Will there be anguished protests? So much the worse for reactionaries. We will condescend to educate them out of their prejudices:

"The new American revolution is not to everyone's taste," Williams declared unflinching. "Those whose traditional positions of prestige will be overturned of course abhor it. But perhaps the greatest spiritual distress is felt by European and Asian intellectuals. To them, the American way of life appears crass and vulgar. Many American intellectuals would agree with them. But they would also warn them that the logic of mass production and mass markets cannot be resisted. The 'happiness' which the average man wants, and will get, is not yet that of the esthete. The Communists of Eastern Europe showed a sound instinct of self-preservation when they banned American jazz as a corrupting influence. Cheap music, cheap comic books, Coca-Cola, and cars are what the people want—understandably, because they have had no opportunity to learn to want, or to obtain, anything better. Culture can no longer be preserved by being made the monopoly of the favored few. The much harder task lies ahead of educating the masses to want better and more satisfying things than they do now."

So America's contribution to the universal "democratic capitalism" of the future (David C. Williams' premises granted) will be just this: cheapness, the cheapest music and the cheapest comic-books and the cheapest morality that can be provided. This indeed would be the revolution of revolutions, the Gehenna of universal monotony and mediocrity. This is Cyrus P. Whittle, telling himself that not only is America the biggest thing on earth, but America soon is going to wipe out everything else; and in the dazzling delirious joy of that consummation, forgetting to ask what will happen afterward.

This advocacy of an American-directed culture of materialism is not confined to publicists for the great labor unions. A few years after Williams wrote, I found myself at a large

assembly in the city of Washington, a speaker sandwiched between Vice-President Nixon and the gentleman then president
of the Chamber of Commerce of the United States. This latter
speaker read aloud an address written for him by a Grub Street
hack of the libertarian persuasion, in which he declared that
America, happily, was a revolutionary power, not at all conservative; and that it would be American policy, world-wide, to
efface archaic cultures and sell to such backward peoples no
end of American goods and services; also to bestow upon such
peoples democratic ways of politics, whether or not the recipients might welcome American-style democracy.

Here I interject a general proposition of mine bearing some
relation to American foreign policy. It seems to be a law governing all life, from the unicellular inanimate forms to the
highest human cultures, that every living organism of every
genus and species endeavors, above all else, to preserve its
identity. Whatever lives tries to make itself the center of the
universe; it resists with the whole of its power the endeavors
of competing forms of life to assimilate it to their substance
and mode. Every living thing, as part of a species, prefers even
death as an individual, to extinction as a distinct species. So if
the lowliest alga struggles fatally against a threat to its peculiar
identity, we ought not to be surprised that men and nations resist
desperately—perhaps unreasoningly—any attempt to assimilate
their character to some other body social. This resistance is the
first law of their being, extending below the level of consciousness. There is one sure way to make a deadly enemy, and that is
to propose to anybody, "Submit yourself to me, and I will

improve your condition by relieving you from the burden of your own identity and by reconstituting your substance in my image."

Just that, in effect, was what the Russian Communists said, at the end of the Second World War, to the unfortunate inhabitants of the Baltic states. And today we behold the successful reaction of those peoples. Can we suppose that forced-draft Americanization, in the name of the abstraction "democratic capitalism", would be much more cordially received throughout the world than forced-draft Russianization in the name of "proletarian dictatorship"?

Let me call to the attention of the zealots for global democracy—that is, of course, American-directed democracy— certain ruinous results which have occurred, and are occurring today, when in the name of "democracy" or of "democratic capitalism" the government of these United States has intervened to thrust some approved pattern of democratic institutions upon some nation-state whose political culture is far removed from the politics of North America. I will not go so far as to describe Lyndon Johnson's endeavor to bomb the Vietnamese of the North into being good democrats; this zealous attempt was unsuccessful. Rather, in that land let me remind you of how President Diem was found insufficiently democratic by President John F. Kennedy and Ambassador Henry Cabot Lodge; how, therefore, Kennedy and Lodge, at the urging of the "Gung-Ho boys" in the Department of State, connived with certain ruthlessly ambitious military men in South Vietnam to overthrow, and promptly murder, President Diem, the only leader who might have held back the

Communists of the North. The consequence? Why, nowadays the South of Vietnam, like the North, is a grinding and impoverished "people's democracy", Marxist style. What a triumph of the democratic dogma!

Or consider what is happening in the Republic of South Africa today, the politics of that land having been found insufficiently democratic by the present Congress of the United States, the wise and temperate statesmen of the United Nations General Assembly, and other deliberative bodies in various quarters of the world. Because Jeremy Bentham's and Earl Warren's doctrine of "one man, one vote" has not been applied to the Bantu peoples of South Africa—whose political tradition is thoroughly undemocratic, consisting rather of the rule of hereditary chiefs who succeed through the matrilineal principle of descent—severe economic penalties are imposed upon the only political order in Africa which adheres to parliamentary government and the prescriptive rule of modern law.

It has been the deliberate policy of certain political interests in the United States to bring down that constitutional government by any possible means, regardless of consequences. "Let justice be done, though the heavens fall!" Already the heavens are falling in Natal, where different Bantu peoples and factions struggle fiercely one against another. Will such "liberation" be carried so far as it was in the Congo, now Zaire, where today the brutal despot Mobutu rules absolutely, supported by Washington and the bankers of New York? What a charming democratic prospect for South Africa! But there being lands beyond Stirling and men beyond Forth, the government of

South Africa may find economic salvation, at least, through new trade-treaties with the states of eastern Europe. The new governments of Hungary, Czechoslovakia, Poland, and other countries are not under the illusion that proletarian dictatorship, or its African equivalent, is an expression of true democracy.

In short, I venture to suggest that it would be highly imprudent for the government of the United States to set about undermining regimes that do not seem perfectly democratic to the editors of *The Progressive*—whether that undermining be worked through the suasion and the money of the Endowment for Democracy, or through the CIA and the military operations of this land of liberty. There has come into my hands a recent document of the Department of the Army and the Department of the Air Force, entitled "Military Operations in Low Intensity Conflict". Even the modified version of this report which I have obtained discusses such measures as equalizing of incomes in "host nations" or "Third World countries" as a means of aiding insurgency or counter-insurgency; and touches upon political and economic measures which American forces intervening in such lands might implement. I suspect that behind these military designs lies an impulse to "democratize" oldfangled orders in the Third World, by force if need be. This is the ideology of democratism, advocated—for instance—by the International Security Council, an unofficial group made up principally of veteran Cold Warriors. Brief sentences must suffice here to suggest the rather belligerent notions of this Council: "An artificial ideal of noninvolvement should not be the benchmark against which the profile of an American policy is judged. This is particularly applicable to a policy that directly promotes the values and practices of democracy." So write the publicists of this International Security Council.

What complacent asininity! A politicized American army, operating abroad, would be no more popular, soon, than the Red Army has been. An imposed or induced abstract democracy, thrust upon peoples unprepared for it, would produce at first anarchy, and then—as in nearly all of "emergent" Africa, over the past four decades—rule by force and a master. About 1956, Chester Bowles, previously head of the Office of Price Administration, was writing and lecturing about how gratifyingly democratic lands like Angola and Mozambique would become, under American tutelage, once the colonial oppressor was forced out. Yet ever since Portuguese administration ended, Angola and Mozambique have been tormented by civil war; certainly Archbishop Tutu, of South Africa, is aware that African states nowadays are far worse off, in terms of liberty and order, than they were when governed by European administrators. For what Tocqueville called "the tyranny of the majority" we see all about us.

If by the word "democratic" is meant the complex of republican political institutions that has grown up in the United States, over more than two centuries—why, the new paper constitutions now being discussed in eastern Europe cannot magically reproduce American history. If by "capitalism" is meant the massive and centralized corporate structures of North America—why, massive and centralized state capitalism is precisely what the self-liberated peoples of eastern Europe are endeavoring to escape. The differing nations of our time must find their own several ways to order and justice and freedom. We Americans were not appointed their keepers.

I have been suggesting—not to blind eyes, I trust—that a soundly conservative foreign policy, in the age which is dawning, should be neither "interventionist" nor "isolationist": it should be prudent. Its object should not be to secure the triumph everywhere of America's name and manners, under the slogan of "democratic capitalism", but instead the preservation of the true national interest, and acceptance of the diversity of economic and political institutions throughout the world. Soviet hegemony ought not to be succeeded by American hegemony. Our prospects in the world of the twenty-first century are bright—supposing we Americans do not swagger about the globe, proclaiming our omniscience and our omnipotence.

Why engage in wars halfway around the world, at incalculable expense in men and money? As Burke, two centuries gone, said of the Pitt government's strategy against revolutionary France (with respect to the Netherlands), "A war for the Scheldt? A war for a chamberpot!" And later, "The blood of man should be said but to redeem the blood of man. The rest is vanity: the rest is crime."

A war for Kuwait? A war for an oil-can! The rest is vanity; the rest is crime.

A Republican administration in Washington contrived American entry into the Spanish-American War. Since then, until 1991, it was Democratic governments of the United States that propelled the United States to war, if sometimes through the back door: the First World War, the Second World War, the Korean War, the Indo-Chinese wars. But an unimaginative, "democratic capitalist" Republican regime, early in 1991, committed the United States, very possibly, to a new imperialism.

For Mr. Bush's "New World Order" may make the United States detested—beginning with the Arab peoples—more than even the Soviet empire was. Mr. Bush's people hinted at their intention of stationing an American military "presence" permanently on the Persian Gulf, to insure the steady flow of petroleum to the consumers of the United States. Increasingly, the states of Europe and the Levant may suspect that in rejecting Russian domination, they exchanged King Log for King Stork.

President Bush's assembling of half a million men in the deserts of Arabia, and then bullying and enticing Congress into authorizing him to make war, sufficiently suggests that conservative views are not identical with the measures of the Republican party. We learn from the saturation-bombing in Iraq that genuine conservatives—as distinguished from arrogant nationalists—have a hard row to hoe when they endeavor to teach the American democracy prudence in foreign relations; and that the exercise of foreign politics, as of domestic politics, is the art of the possible.

XV

The Behemoth State: Centralization

Presumably most of my readers are aware that the word "federal" does not mean "central". But the Congress of the United States, in recent decades, and frequently the Executive Force, too, have been behaving as if unable to discern any distinction between the two terms. That way lies the collapse of the Constitution.

A simple instance of this occurred on Capitol Hill during the Hundredth Congress. We now have a new statute that prohibits servants of the federal government—and they are legion—from lodging in hotels (lodging at public expense, anyway) that do not have sprinklers in the ceilings of bedchambers. A few exemptions are granted, chiefly to hotels that stand less than four stories high. The act's premise is that by excluding non-complying hotels from federal patronage, virtually all innkeepers will find it necessary to install sprinklers (cost about $1,500 per room). The justification for this thoughtful legislation is that over the past six years, more than four hundred persons have died in hotel fires in the United States. (Even I can master short division: this statistic, in effect, tells us that the hotel-fire death rate, per annum, per state, has been 1.34 persons. I do not have to hand statistics as to age and gender; at any rate, about one and one-third people, averaging the country over, have died in the average state in the average year, 1983-1989. It is well, of course, to save lives; but a great many more lives might be saved by prohibiting the sale of skis through act of Congress, or by a federal statute requiring all holders of real property to sprinkle salt on their sidewalks, whether part of the public way or private, after every snowfall.)

My present point, however, is not the prudence or the expense of the act now on the statute books, but rather the political consequences of decreeing that the federal government shall prescribe and regulate all sorts of concerns previously left to the police powers of the several states and local agencies of government, or left to the sensible management of individuals, households, and firms. The Sprinkler Act is a sufficient instance of the continuing conversion of this country from a federal union for specified purposes to a centralized plebiscitary democracy, in which little discretion of choice is left to states and local communities, let alone private citizens.

Behold Behemoth! While Americans are congratulating themselves and Europeans upon the collapse of socialist states beyond the demolished Iron Curtain, there continues to expand here in North America the empire of what Alexis de Tocqueville called "democratic despotism". This is a grim tendency toward total centralization of which conservatives have long complained, in somewhat vague terms, but to which they have offered, so far, little effective resistance. Permit me to quote to you a very percipient passage in Tocqueville's *Democracy in America*:

> I think, then, that the species of oppression by which democratic nations are menaced is unlike anything that ever before existed in the world; our contemporaries will find no prototype of it in their memories. I seek in vain for an expression that will accurately convey the whole of the idea I have formed of it; the old words *despotism* and *tyranny* are inappropriate; the thing itself is new, and since I cannot name, I must attempt to define it.
>
> I seek to trace the novel features under which despotism may appear in the world. The first thing that strikes the observation is an innumerable multitude of men, all equal and all alike incessantly endeavoring to procure the petty and paltry pleasures with which they glut their lives. Each of them, living apart, is as a stranger to the fate of all the rest; his children and his private friends constitute to him the whole of mankind. As for the rest of his fellow citizens, he is close to them, but he does not see them; he touches them, but he does not feel them; he exists only in himself and for himself alone; and if his kindred still remain to him, he may be said at any rate to have lost his country.
>
> Above this race of men stands an immense and tutelary power, which takes upon itself alone to

secure their gratification and to watch over their fate. That power is absolute, minute, regular, provident, and mild. It would be like the authority of a parent if, like that authority, its object was to prepare men for manhood; but it seeks, on the contrary, to keep them in perpetual childhood; it is well content that the people should rejoice, provided that they think of nothing but rejoicing. For their happiness such a government willingly labors, but it chooses to be the sole agent and only arbiter of their necessities, facilitates their pleasures, manages their principal concerns, directs their industry, regulates the descent of property, and subdivides their inheritances; what remains, but to spare them all the care of thinking and all the trouble of living?

Thus it every day renders the exercise of the free agency of man less useful and less frequent; it circumscribes the will within a narrower range and gradually robs a man of all the uses of himself. The principle of equality has prepared men for these things; it has predisposed them to endure them and often to look on them as benefits.

Tocqueville has in mind here, obviously, a central government the intentions of which are beneficent. But suppose that some intentions are not beneficent? Or that legislation might be intended to harass or to punish a class, a faction, or some minority? Where, under centralized government, would the dissidents hide? At the moment, however, let us confine our-selves to acts and decisions of centralized power which, on their face, seem intended—if perhaps in error—to confer benefits upon the public. Many such examples might be cited; I confine myself to two, both of which occurred during the presidential administration of Lyndon Johnson.

The first of these had to do with governmental inspection of meat. Some inspectors from the federal Department of Agriculture happened to visit Arizona, and there came into conflict with Arizona's state meat-inspectors. The two sets of officials parted in wrath, the gentlemen from Washington men-acing the Arizonans that they would be taught their place. Back in the seats of the mighty, these bureaucrats sent word to their departmental superiors, and thence to the President of the United States, that ill-inspected and potentially poisonous meat was being approved for public sale by Arizona's negligent meat-inspectors. On learning this dread secret, President Johnson saw opportunity for making the American nation aware of his solicitude for their well-being: the Great White Father revealed the iniquities of Arizona to a frightened people, crying out emphatically, "Get rid of rotten meat! Get rid of rot-ten meat!"

A complaisant Congress very, very promptly passed a new act regarding the inspection of all meat, much extending the jurisdiction and the activities of that branch of the Department of Agriculture, and subjecting all state meat-inspecting bureaus to federal jurisdiction. How thoughtful for the welfare of the American people, from sea to shining sea!

But others, not federal employees, looked into this affair, and the *Wall Street Journal* published in some detail an account of what had occurred. It was discovered, tardily, that in truth standards of meat-inspection had been high, not low; that in fact Arizona did not approve rotten meat of any sort; and that all this fuss had arisen out of minor disputations between federal and state officials. This revelation embarrassed and angered President Johnson, who had assumed that the Washington inspectors were honest and not spiteful; but he could scarcely go back on television, this time to cry, "Bring back rotten meat! Bring back rotten meat!" Nor did the Congress trouble itself to repeal the statute, so recently enacted, that made state meat-inspection standards wholly subordinate to federal regulations. Since then, federal courts have ruled that if a state has higher standards than the federal ones, nevertheless the state must admit within its jurisdiction meats that meet merely the lower federal standard. A mad world, my masters!

Indulge me, ladies and gentlemen, in one more instance of this arrogating of power over not merely over state jurisdictions, but over the American bedroom—nay, the very bed and bedding. A federal agency abruptly ruled that all new mattresses manufactured must be of the inner-spring type—whether or not customers should prefer a plain cotton mattress or at any rate separate springs and mattress. This ukase, promptly enforced, put out of business many small makers of mattresses; it profited, however, big standard manufacturers who charged high prices; it appeared that lobbyists for the big mattress-making corporations had been at work efficiently in

Washington. As for the American citizen who might prefer a simpler mattress and a cheaper, or for a person like your servant this writer, who possesses several ancestral antique beds that no inner-spring mattress will fit—why, says Uncle Sam to such reactionaries, "Be comfortable, damn you, and expect to pay for it!"

I have not been able to ascertain under what fantastic interpretation of existing statutes the federal agency in question was able to prescribe the sort of mattress Americans must sleep upon. How could this possibly lie within the prescriptive jurisdiction of the general government—or, for that matter, within the police powers of the several states? Yet done the thing was. A related arbitrary regulation employed the pretext of securing the health of children—though of course that protection, too, ordinarily has been exercised by state and local authorities, or by voluntary organizations.

This latter instance of federal *pleonexia* had to do with articles of nightware meant for use by children. From on high in Washington it was decreed that all pyjamas, nightgowns, and the like must be manufactured of fire-retardant fabrics, if children were to wear them and shops were so to display them. This measure was supposed to prevent infants from being burned alive in bed; much mention was made of the number of persons annually slain or scarred as a result of smoking in bed, though I, at least, had been unaware that small children were given to smoking in bed. Enforced for a time, this paternal legislation caused severe loss to makers and retailers of standard children's nightware who had large stocks on hand; also it conferred large commercial advantages upon those progressive manufacturers who already, doubtless through foresight and humane concern, were producing large quantities of fire-retardant nightware for little tots.

But alas and lackaday! Scientific studies, within a few months, coincidentally revealed that fire-retardant nightware indubitably has caused skin cancer, respiratory troubles, and other physical afflictions. The federal regulations in question were quietly rescinded, I believe; and I fancy that it is now permitted for us to clothe our infants with mere unadulterated cotton or wool.

I have chosen these relatively harmless and mildly amusing instances of the excessive zeal of the Washington bureaucracy to centralize practically everything, ladies and gentlemen, lest I be taken for a dreadful scare-monger. Now and again some well-intentioned elderly lady assures me, benignly, "Uncle Sam knows what's best for us." I decidedly am not of that opinion. Thorough political and economic centralization works ills much graver than the quality of meats, the distribution of bedsprings, and the fabrics of nighties. For my part, I am of the opinion that Tocqueville, rather than Uncle Sam, knows what's best for us. Let me add that both John Adams, Federalist, and Thomas Jefferson, Democratic Republican, would have been astounded and indignant at the degree of centralization already well established among us, two centuries after the Constitution of the United States had commenced to function. I fancy that neither one would have insisted upon a sprinkler being installed in his bed-chamber, at the expense of a perversion of the Constitution.

The pretexts for giving a veneer of seeming constitutionality to the concentration of power at Washington have been various. Our recent act to install sprinklers in hotel bedrooms is one of the less extravagant apologies—that is, it amounts merely to a refusal to pay the bills of federal employees who lodge at inns that have no sprinklers in bedrooms. (Of course every hotel in this country must be thoroughly inspected to ascertain the number of sprinklers.) Another and somewhat more severe form of compulsion is the refusal to pay any monies from the federal treasury to non-complying persons and institutions, as in the case of colleges and universities coerced into Affirmative Action programs and the like. Yet another method in the withdrawal of tax exemptions from institutions otherwise entitled to such exemption, as in the case of Bob Jones University. The most common method employed to induce states and cities, and various voluntary associations, to submit to federal regulation is the matching grant-in-aid, often on a very large scale. And in a number of instances the Congress and the Executive Branch have not troubled themselves to look for excuses in the Constitution: they simply have pushed through a piece of legislation, of national scope, without bothering to inquire whether by any stretch of the imagination such an act could be regarded as authorized by some provision of the Constitution.

In consequence of all this, the federal character of the United States, this country's chief contribution to the art of governance, has been fading to a shadow of a shade. And where Congress hesitated, the Supreme Court rushed in to nationalize the whole political structure. More mischief of this sort was accomplished during the reign of King Lyndon than during any other period of American history—considerably more, incidentally, than was accomplished during the reign of King Franklin—but in general the leaders of either major political party have made no strong effort to resist consolidation of power; and, after all, it has come about by degrees, not as a result of any announced design. No doubt a well-publicized plan for systematic centralization would have been hotly rejected by the American electorate; and among those opponents of deliberate centralization would have been a good many liberals.

A decay of historical consciousness among Americans has had its part in reducing resistance to the concentration of decision-making powers in the general government. Here I offer you two paragraphs written by C. Northcote Parkinson, the deviser of Parkinson's Law. Professor Parkinson declares that political centralization is the initial cause of a nation's decadence.

"The first stage on the downward path is one of over-centralization," Parkinson wrote in 1978. "Everything is done to eliminate or neutralise all but the main and central seat of administration. The lesser centres of power are either provincial governments or organizations which can be classified as religious, financial, military, or economic: an arch-bishopric, a national bank, a military command or a major industrial or trading group. The attempt to centralize all power in the one capital city and, indeed, in its administrative quarter, means the assimilation of all possible rival institutions from monasteries to television stations, from harbour authorities to charitable foundations. All these can be eliminated in the name of democracy or efficiency, and the result is the creation of the one government machine into which all problems are fed and from which all wisdom is to emerge. All that is initially lost is the likelihood of the government's having to listen to informed criticism from outside its inner circle of officials. Thereafter the problems centre upon the growing size and complexity of the central administration. As the civil servants multiply there is an ever-increasing distance between the citizen and the nameless people who will ultimately decide upon his application, protest, or appeal. Proceedings are cumbrous and attitudes are hierarchical, all decisions being referred from the periphery to the centre and then from the bottom to the top. 'If death came from Madrid,' said sixteenth-century Spaniards, 'we should all live to a very great age.'

"Much the same comment must have been made about Babylon, Peking, Persepolis, Delhi, and London. Less frequently noticed are two other results of over-centralization. The first is that the normal processes of retirement and promotion will bring to the centre the people who have been robbed of all initiative while posted at the circumference. The second is that the capital city is now appallingly vulnerable to internal sedition or external assault. When all roads lead to Rome, all cables to London, the usual channels to Paris, the whole administrative machinery can be knocked out by a single rocket attack. There are no centres of authority outside the target area, no alternative capital city to which a government might move. With the capital city gone, there is nothing left."

Parkinson goes on to describe the second stage in the decline and fall of great states: the growth of taxation. But that is another vast subject—to which, conceivably, I may address my puny talents on some other occasion. Let me proceed, just now, to my peroration. The worst thing about excessive concentration of power, I believe, is that in the long run such Behemoth centralization fails; and then the whole social structure falls apart, as in the Soviet empire at this moment.

Reasons exist why a supplanting of the old constitutional order, if completed, would present most serious dangers to American order and justice and freedom. I will mention only four of these perils.

The first is the problem of efficiency. The general government is designed to carry out certain responsibilities, fairly well defined: most notably, the conduct of foreign relations, the defense of the country, and the management of undertakings too widespread for any one state in the Union to manage. But already the government at Washington is dismayingly oppressed by too much work and too many feeble servants. By endeavoring to do everything, the Washington government might end in doing nothing successfully.

The second difficulty is the problem of scale. Measures which the provincial governors at Graz or Innsbruck would refuse to entrust to Vienna are proposed, in America, as if the governing of two hundred and fifty million people were little more difficult than the conduct of a town meeting—and quite as democratic, so long as President and Congress still are elected. I have heard American advocates of social-welfare measures, for instance, seriously advance the example of social-democratic legislation in Denmark as precedent for American policy—though some American counties, not to mention states, are larger than Denmark, and other counties have more people than there are Danes.

Appeals against imprudent or unjust administration become immensely difficult when they are only the faint voices of individuals or local groups, opposed to the prestige and influence of administrators at the capital; indeed, the chief administrators themselves cannot possibly look deeply into such complaints. Detailed administration on such a scale would require from civil servants a wisdom and a goodness never experienced in human history. "Well, appeal to your Congressman," the centralizers say, perhaps ingenuously. But Congressmen already do not have time enough to answer the mail from their more important constituents, let alone act as so many Don Quixotes of the mass state.

The third difficulty I raise here is the problem of leadership. Centralized political power functions smoothly only in nations accustomed to defer to the measures and opinions of a governing class—that is, in aristocratic or autocratic lands. Soviet centralization would have failed altogether, and almost at once, had it not been for the long-established powers of the Old Regime at Moscow and St. Petersburg. And such a body of decision-makers, of governors, of aristocrats, must possess a high degree of self-confidence and the habit of command. They must be accustomed to dealing with deferential populations.

But these United States, accustomed to territorial democracy, have no class of leaders and administrators competent to undertake the consolidated direction which the centralizers propose. I do not discern a class of men here competent to rule wisely this immense nation, once territorial democracy and the federal framework—both principal schools of national leadership—should be undone.

Fourth, even had we a class of Winchester old-school-tie administrators, I do not know how we could expect the most expert of statists to direct paternally and justly the concerns of this nation, once local volition and private self-reliance had been seriously weakened. A man has but twenty-four hours in his day, and can read only a limited number of papers. Such centralization defeats its own object, in persons as in departments. The man-killing job of the Presidency—to which the centralizers would add numerous fresh responsibilities—maybe sufficient illustration of my meaning.

To destroy territorial democracy and the federal system in America is quite possible—or to let them atrophy; but it is less easy to provide some alternative satisfactory scheme of politics. Once the principle of volition, with the sense of participation and local decision, vanishes from American life, Americans are liable to become an unmanageable people. On a grander and more catastrophic scale, we might see again the resistance to authority and resort to violence which were provoked by the Eighteenth Amendment and the Volstead Act. Both the Eighteenth Amendment and the Volstead Act were "democratically" adopted; but somehow national positive democracy is not the same thing as territorial prescriptive democracy. Indeed, already we see great American cities in anarchy, from time to time—the anarchists those people, black or white, who feel that they have been excluded from full participation in society. What would occur when the majority should feel excluded from decision-making?

Within a few years, if not immediately, any "guided democracy" or "plebiscitary democracy" would meet with evasion and hostility everywhere, and among the results of this could come a diminishing of the really effectual and popular authority of the general government. The energies and loyalties of volition would have been supplanted by the compulsions of a latter-day Jacobinism, or of the Directory. And a great big Federal Bureau of Investigation would not be able to enforce the decrees of such a regime; for though a new broom sweeps clean, and an elite federal detective force aiding the local police is one thing, a permanent national secret police would be quite another—and possibly disagreeable to some of the "liberal" advocates of centralization. For that matter, a garrison of federal troops in every city might not suffice to keep the public tranquillity.

Yet life still rises in the tree of American federalism, and territorial democracy's powers of resistance and reaction ought not to be disregarded. It is true, as Tocqueville remarked, that men in power generally feel impelled to augment central power, while the opponents of centralization are either stupid or powerless. Notwithstanding this, attachment to the doctrines of division of authority and of state and local powers remain so popular in the United States that an intelligent plan for preserving the old system would obtain a hearing, and stand some chance of enactment.

An enormous, unitary, omnicompetent nation-state cannot abide the American political tradition and cake of custom. If the federal system is obsolete, then we ought to prepare to train the leaders of a new order, and to define the character of that domination, novel to us. If territorial democracy deserves to live, and if the federal system has virtue still, then the constitutional structure ought to be buttressed and helped to function. At present, most of the Americans qualified to think about such matters decline to take either of these courses. They are willing to let the norms of politics shift for themselves—which is not in nature.

Such is another huge prospect for conservatives. Let us hope that the rising generation of conservatives may have the courage and the imagination required to avert the triumph of the triumph of the centralizers; for that triumph would be followed swiftly enough by the decay of the American Republic.

XVI

Cultivating Educational Wastelands

With some trepidation I set down on paper my sentiments on this large subject, the lot of educational reformers being hard. In 1953, Professor Arthur Bestor, of Indiana University, published his book *Educational Wastelands: the Retreat from Learning in Our Public Schools.* There survives a Jewish tradition that all the Prophets were stoned to death or otherwise slain by the People. From 1953 onward, the Educationists belabored Dr. Bestor with epithets, until he departed from Indiana to the uttermost fringe of the western world, the coast of Washington. As for me, though, I can flee to my native Michigan backwoods.

Elsewhere I have suggested the possibility of an Augustan age for the United States and for the twentieth-century world—supposing we Americans do not endeavor to impose our ways upon all the peoples of the earth. But in discussing American education, I cannot be so sanguine.

Marxist educational notions and methods have been exposed as grim fallacies—except in these United States, perhaps. Yet what are we to say of present American educational notions and methods? Ever since the publishing of the report of the National Commission on Excellence in Education, "A Nation at Risk", a decade ago, a great deal of talk about education, and scribbling about it, have occurred. As for any evidences of general improvement, however—why, one does not discover them easily.

The United States now is the great power in the world. Nevertheless, who can praise an educational system that turns out young people marvellously ignorant—except for a very small minority—of history, geography, and foreign languages, and so unfitted to have much of anything to do with concerns larger than those of their own neighborhood? Worse still, what future have a people whose schooling has enabled them, at best, to ascertain the price of everything—but the value of nothing? We Americans stand today politically dominant, intellectually enfeebled. Conservatives have before them a complex work of intellectual restoration.

Nowadays nearly everybody—except for the National Education Associations bosses and affiliates, and the professors at most schools of education—confesses that something is badly wrong with learning in America. While we linger in a mood of remorse and recrimination, opportunity exists for genuine reform. Therefore I venture to exhort you first, and basically, on the plight and possibilities of the higher learning.

For half a century, our higher education has been sinking lower. Nobody is more painfully aware of this decay than is the conscientious professor of some experience, and nobody suffers more from it than does the perceptive undergraduate. America's higher learning lies in a state of decadence. But eras of decadence sometimes are succeeded by eras of renewal. It is all a matter of will, reason, and imagination. As Samuel Johnson put it, "Why, sir, we *know* the will is free; and there's an end to it."

Conceivably we Americans, after decades of blundering and incertitude, may be entering upon an American Augustan age. For successful healing, candid diagnosis is required. The people of the United States now spend annually upon higher education more money, probably, than did all the nations of the world combined, from the foundation of the ancient universities down to the beginning of the Second World War. Yet there prevails a widespread discontent at the results produced by this costly endeavor. Surely it is time for us conservatives to examine afresh the mission of the higher education.

The primary end of the higher learning, in all lands and all times, has been what John Henry Newman called the training of the intellect to form a philosophical habit of mind. College and university were founded to develop right reason and imagination, for the sake of the person and of the republic. By its nature, the higher education is concerned with abstractions—rather difficult abstractions, both in the sciences and in humane studies. In any age, most people are not fond of abstractions. In this democratic milieu, therefore, higher education stands in danger everywhere from levelling pressures.

In Britain, a very few years ago, the member of the opposition party who had been designated minister of education in a prospective Labour government denounced Oxford and Cambridge universities as "cancers". Presumably he would have converted those ancient institutions, if given his way, into something like the Swedish "people's universities"—that is, lax institutions at which every lad and lass can succeed, because all standards for entrance or graduation have been swept away. Every man and woman an intellectual king or queen, with an Oxbridge degree! The trouble with this aspiration is that those kings and queens would be intellectually impoverished—and presumably Britain generally would be impoverished in more ways than one.

Recently we have heard similar voices in the graduate schools of Harvard. Why discriminate against indolence and stupidity? Why not let everybody graduate, regardless of performance in studies? Wouldn't that be the democratic way? If young people don't care for abstractions, and manifest a positive aversion to developing a philosophical habit of mind, why not give them what they think they would like: that is, the superficial counter-culture?

The educational degradation of the democratic dogma already has prevailed, with few exceptions, throughout the western world: it has gone far in France and Italy. In the United States, ever since the Second World War, the lowering of standards for admission and for graduation, the notorious disgrace of "grade inflation", and the loss of order and integration in curricula, are too widely known and regretted for me to need to labor these afflictions here. Some cold comfort may be found in the fact that we have not sinned more greatly than have other nations of the West—somewhat less, indeed.

Here and there, some signs of renewal in higher education maybe discerned; certainly we hear much pother about it. But it remains to be determined whether it is possible to restore or improve the true higher learning, what with powerful political and economic pressures against improvement. Being somewhat gloomy by conviction, yet sanguine by temperament, I may mutter to myself, "Say not the struggle naught availeth!"

Why are this lowering of standards and this loss of intellectual coherence ruinous to higher education? Because the higher learning is intended to develop, primarily, a philosophical habit of mind. The genuine higher education is not meant, really, to "create jobs" or to train technicians. Incidentally, the higher education does tend to have such results, too; but only as by-products. We stand in danger of forgetting, during our pursuit of the incidentals, the fundamental aims of learning.

Why were colleges and universities established, and what remains their most valuable function? To discipline the mind; to give men and women long views and to instill in them the virtue of prudence; to present a coherent body of ordered knowledge, in several great fields; to pursue that knowledge for its own sake; to help the rising generation to make its way toward wisdom and virtue. The college is an instrument to teach that truth is better than falsehood, and wisdom better than ignorance. Of course the college has done other things as well, some of them mildly baneful—such as serving as an instrument of social snobbery. But I am speaking still of the college's fundamental mission.

The college is intended to confer two sorts of benefits. The first sort of benefit is the improvement of the human person, for the individual's own sake: opening the way to some wisdom to young men and women, that there may be something in their lives besides getting and spending.

The second kind of benefit is the preservation and advancement of society, by developing a body or class of young people who will be leaders in many walks of life: scientists, clergymen, political officials or representatives, officers, physicians, lawyers, teachers, industrialists, managers, and all the rest. The college is a means to help to form intellects, to assure their competence, and (a point often forgotten today) to help to form their characters. Here I am not speaking of an elite, for I share T. S. Eliot's conviction that a deliberately-cultivated series of elites would tend toward narrowness and arrogance. Rather, I refer to a fairly broad and numerous class of tolerably educated men and women who would leaven the lump of society in a wide variety of ways.

Where is the knowledge we have lost in information, not to mention the wisdom? What college and university used to endeavor to impart was not miscellaneous information, a random accumulation of facts, but instead an integrated and ordered body of knowledge that would develop the philosophical habit of mind—from which cast of mind one might find the way to wisdom of many sorts.

Doubtless the prevalence of computers may confer upon us various material benefits. But so far as genuine education goes, the computer and its Informational Society may amount to a blight. They seem calculated to enfeeble the individual reason and to make most of us dependent upon an elite of computer programmers—at the higher level of the Informational Society, I mean; they may develop into vigorous enemies of the philosophical habit of mind.

One thing to remember, then, in discussing what higher education should do for people in the dawning years, is that waves of technological innovation commonly carry on their crests a mass of flotsam. Such a disagreeable mass was flung upon the beaches of Academe by the ideological tempests of the 1960s and 1970s. At university and college, we are only beginning to recover from the damage done to the philosophical habit of mind by that storm. Gentlefolk and scholars of the Academy would be highly imprudent if they should assist in fresh devastation by setting gadgetry above intellectual discipline.

I am arguing that educational neoterism does mischief often. Nor do I believe it to be the primary function of university and college to create a kind of tapioca-pudding society in which everybody would be just like everybody else—every young man and woman, ideally, possessed of a doctoral degree, if innocent of philosophy.

Instead, the primary mission of university and college is to point the way toward some measure of wisdom and virtue, through developing the philosophical habit of mind. I am saying that universities and colleges were founded in the hope that those institutions might help the rising generation toward two forms of order: one, order in the soul of the person, the direction of will and appetite by reason; the other, order in the commonwealth, through the understanding of justice and freedom and the public good. I am arguing that our basic reform of the higher learning must be the restoration of these venerable aims—at ask for conservatives.

Is it absurd to imagine that our vast factory-like campuses might be humanized? Is it ridiculous to argue that the American obsession with getting and spending could be chastened sufficiently to permit American higher learning to be sought for its own sake? Perhaps; but perhaps not, too.

I lack time to offer you a detailed program of educational reformation. But I venture now to suggest the essential measure that must be undertaken if we are to move from intellectual decadence toward intellectual renewal.

First, the quality of American primary and secondary schooling must be mightily improved before there can be any very marked increase of intelligence and imagination among college and university students. This improvement must have two aspects: the teaching of true intellectual disciplines, and the rousing of the moral imagination. Despite endeavors of the federal Department of Education to entice schools into improving themselves, little has occurred as yet in the way of practical reform.

I find it highly doubtful that any marked reformation of the public schools can occur until the several states, and perhaps the federal government too, adopt some form of the "voucher plan", which would provide for much greater diversity and choice in schooling. Here I commend to you, ladies and gentlemen, the recent book by John E. Chubb and Terry M. Moe, *Politics, Markets, and America's Schools* (Brookings Institution). As Mr. Chubb puts it, "The public education system functions naturally and routinely, despite everybody's best intentions, to burden schools with excessive bureaucracy, to discourage effective school organization, and to stifle student achievement."

Second, the American appetite for requiring vocational certification must be curbed. A very great part of the student body on nearly all campuses is enrolled mostly because "you have to get a degree to get a job." Thus universities and colleges are crowded with young people who would prefer to be somewhere else, earning money or at least active and emancipated from abstractions. It needs to be remembered that university and college are centers for the study of abstractions; and most people's interest in abstractions is distinctly limited. Many of the skills in business, industry, technology, and governmental service are best acquired by internship or apprenticeship; being compelled to linger in college is little better than marking time for many undergraduates. Were university and college relieved of the responsibility for turning out half-finished candidates for routine employment, they could undertake their primary duties so much the better; and the whole atmosphere of the typical campus would grow far more cheerful.

Third, the humane scale in learning should be regained by creating no more mass campuses with many thousands of undergraduates in a lonely crowd, and decentralizing so far as possible the existing Behemoth campuses. The old collegiate structure of the academic community should become the model once more. Institutes for technical training, as distinct from the abstractions with which higher education is supposed to be concerned, should be situated elsewhere than on the same campus with college or university.

Fourth, curricula at nearly all universities and colleges should be greatly revised, rigorously, so as to provide students with a genuine intellectual discipline, purged of the intellectual boondoggles that have disgraced college programs to some extent ever since the beginning of this century, but especially since the late 'Sixties. At the majority of American establishments of a learning allegedly higher, theoretical sciences and imaginative humane studies have been pushed into a dusty corner of the curriculum; that folly must be undone. Reading through directories of colleges recently, with a view to finding a good college for a fourth daughter, I discovered that at the typical college nowadays only some five per cent of the undergraduates are enrolled in "letters", which once upon a time was the American college's principal discipline! If the rising generation's more intelligent members have acquired little knowledge of great literature, history, languages, and the natural sciences—why, the person and the republic will fall into disorder, soon or late.

Fifth, we must emphasize through the whole of higher education the ancient principle that the ends of all education are wisdom and virtue. I do *not* mean that the purpose of the higher learning is to "impart values". The whole notion of teaching "values" is mistaken, although held often by sincere people who mean well.

For what true education attempts to impart is *meaning*, not value. This sly employment of the word *value* as a substitute for such words as "norm", "standard", "principle", and "truth" is the deliberate work of the doctrinaire positivists, who deny that there exists any moral significance of a transcendent or an abiding character. In America, the notion of educational "values" has been advanced by sociologists and educationists of the Instrumentalist school: it is intended as a substitute for the religious assumptions about human existence that formerly were taken for granted in schools. A "value", as educationists employ the word, is a personal preference, gratifying perhaps to the person who holds it, but of no binding moral effect upon others. "Other things being equal, pushpin is as good as poetry," in Bentham's famous phrase. Choose what values you will, or ignore them all: it's a matter of what gives you, the individual, the most pleasure and the least pain.

Etienne Gilson points out that positivists deliberately advance the concept of "values" because they deny that words, or the concepts represented by words, have real meaning. Thus the word "honor" may hold value for some, but may be repellent to other people: in the view of the positivist, the word "honor" is meaningless, for there is no honor, nor yet dishonor: all really is physical sensation, pleasurable or painful. But if "honor" has an illusory value for you, employ it; if you dislike "honor", discard it.

Time was when every schoolchild used to be familiar with the catalogue of the seven cardinal virtues and the seven deadly sins. The positivists and a good many other folk today deny the existence of those seven deadly sins, or of any other sin. As for the virtues—why, they would like to convert those back into "value preferences", with no moral imperative to back them. But justice, fortitude, prudence, and temperance are not "values" merely; nor are faith, hope, and charity. It is not for the individual, bound up in self-conceit, to determine whether he prefers justice or injustice; it is not for him to decide whether prudence or imprudence suits him better. True, the individual may so decide and act, to others' harm or his own. But it is the function of education to impart a moral heritage: to teach that the virtues and the vices are real, and that the individual is not free to toy with the sins as he may choose.

What true education transmits is not values, but instead a body of truth: that is, a pattern of meanings, perceived through certain disciplines of the intellect. The sort of education that prevailed in Europe and America until about 1930, say, was an endeavor to instruct the rising generation in the nature of reality. It traced a pattern of order: order in the soul, order in the commonwealth. That old system of education began with information; it passed from information to knowledge; it moved from knowledge to wisdom. Its aim, I repeat, was not value, but truth.

The Benthamite and Deweyite educational structure of our day, little concerned with meaning, aims confusedly at personal advancement, technical training, sociability, socialization, custodial functions, and certification—not to mention fun and

games. The very possibility of ascertaining the meaning of anything is denied by many a department of philosophy. What
does this twentieth-century educational system transmit to the
rising generation? Chiefly certain technical and commercial
skills, together with that training in the learned professions
which is indispensable to our civilization. Modern schooling,
at any level, offers little toward the ordering of the soul and the
ordering of the commonwealth.

The education of yesteryear was founded upon certain postulates. One of these was that much truth is ascertainable; another, that religious truth is the source of all good; a third, that
we may profit by the wisdom of our ancestors; a fourth, that
the individual is foolish, but the species is wise; a fifth, that
wisdom is sought for its own sake; a sixth, that for the sake of
the commonwealth, schooling should quicken the moral
imagination.

These postulates have not ceased to be true; it is only that
they have been forgotten in our century's obsession with power
and money, and our century's illusion that ideology is a ready
and satisfactory substitute for thought. Some eyes have been
opened to the mischief done by that obsession and that illusion.
Here and there, some attempts at recovery of the true ends of
education are being made.

Many in America and throughout the world have been dis-
inherited of their cultural patrimony. Yet they may win back
that inheritance, if they have fortitude and tenacity sufficient.
"The dead alone give us energy," we are told by Gustave Le Bon.
In the long run, the man and the state that have rejected the

legacy from many centuries will be found nerveless. And the man or woman who has excavated that intellectual legacy will be emboldened to defend the Permanent Things against Chaos and Old Night.

My old comrade in arms Arthur Bestor found the schools of America in 1953 educational wastelands; they are no less arid today: elementary school, intermediate, high school, college. Conservative irrigation may cause the desert to bloom. If nothing is done—why, hand in hand with the Hollow Men, we go round the prickly pear at five o'clock in the morning, in the cactus land of Educationism. Renewal failing, by the conclusion of the twentieth century America may have achieved complete equality in education: everybody compulsorily schooled, and everybody equally ignorant.

XVII

Prospects for the Proletariat

F rom time to time, I am asked what I believe to be the greatest difficulty the American Republic confronts nowadays. I reply that our most puzzling and distressing social misfortune is the growth of a proletariat.

Let us define our terms. The words *proletariat* and *proletarian* come down to us from Roman times. In the Roman signification of the term, a proletarian is a man who gives nothing to the commonwealth but his progeny. Such a being pays no taxes, subsists at public expense, fulfills no civic duties, performs no work worth mentioning, and knows not the meaning of piety. As a mass, the collective proletarians, the proletariat, are formidable; they demand entitlements—principally, in antique times, bread and circuses; in our day, much larger entitlements, which are granted to them lest they turn collectively violent. To the state, I repeat, the proletarian contributes only his offspring—who in their turn, ordinarily, become proletarians. Idle, ignorant, and often criminal, the proletariat can ruin a great city—and a nation. What Arnold Toynbee calls "the internal proletariat" so dragged down the Roman civilization; the barbarian invaders, the "external proletariat", burst through the fragile shell of a culture already bled to death.

Karl Marx, that hard hater of the patrimony of modern civilization, called upon the modern proletariat to arise and shed blood on a grand scale. Triumphant in the Russian empire after the First World War, and in eastern Europe and many other regions of the world not long after the Second World War, Marx's ideological disciples installed brutal proletarians in power, at least on the local level, where they were as merciless as they were stupid. The proletarian cannot build; but he is able to destroy.

The United States of America, during the eighteenth and nineteenth centuries and the early decades of the twentieth, was not afflicted by a proletariat on any large national scale—though Jefferson feared the coming of such a class when cities should grow, and Macaulay in 1857 foretold a "downward progress" in America, at the end of which "Either some Caesar or Napoleon will seize the reins of government with a strong hand, or your republic will be as fearfully plundered and laid waste by barbarians in the twentieth century as the Roman Empire was in the fifth . . ."

As Macaulay pointed out with some force, in the United States the proletariat would be possessed not merely of the power of intimidation through violence, but of the yet more effective power of the ballot-box. "Your Huns and Vandals," he went on, "will have been engendered within your own country by your own institutions."

Now in America today, whom do we specify when we talk of a proletariat, a rootless and discontented class that is a burden upon the commonwealth? It is necessary first to specify groups that we do *not* have in mind.

The proletariat is not identical with "the poor". Although most proletarians are poor, a man may be rich and yet a proletarian, if he is nothing better than a vexation to the commonwealth, and has the mind of a proletarian. Also there are many people of very modest income who nevertheless are people of commendable character and good citizens. Incidentally, I am given to quoting an aside by Robert Frost when he was conversing with liberal friends: "For Christ's sake, don't talk about the poor all the time!" The poor we have always with us, as Jesus of Nazareth instructs us.

The proletarian is not identical with "the working-man"—indeed, it is characteristic of the proletarian that he does *not* work voluntarily. I was reared almost literally in the Pere Marquette railway yards outside Detroit, my father a locomotive engineman and fireman; we were not proletarians, nor were my schoolmates and their parents.

The proletarian is not identical with the "welfare recipient", even though the vast majority of proletarians are on the welfare rolls. For of course among the recipients of local, state, and federal relief and entitlements are many elderly, infirm, or otherwise distressed people who are not so unfortunate as to share the proletarian mentality and morality.

The proletarian is not identical with the black city-dweller. It appears that about half of America's proletarians are white, and the other half people of color, blacks especially—although this means, obviously, that the proportion of proletarians among America's black population is considerably higher than the proportion of proletarians among America's white population.

The proletarian population is not an urban population only. Increasingly, the proletarian condition of life spreads even into remote rural districts. In my backwoods or backwater Michigan village, a dismal rookery of decaying trailers, immobilized "mobile homes", hems in my tall archaic house; the sale of narcotics proceeds in our village's public park; and the rate of crimes, especially offenses against women, rises annually. The village's only church has been converted into an antique shop.

The proletariat, in short, is a mass of people who have lost—if ever they possessed—community, hope of betterment, moral convictions, habits of work, sense of personal responsibility, intellectual curiosity, membership in a healthy family, property, active participation in public concerns, religious associations, and awareness of ends or objects in human existence. Most proletarians live, as dogs do, from day to day, unreflective. The *lazzaroni* of Naples, I suppose, for centuries have existed in such a proletarian condition; but the *lazzaroni* of American cities and countryside, proliferating in recent years, are more aggressive than their Neapolitan counterparts.

The cores of many American cities now are dominated by the proletariat; or if not the core in some cities, then a grim and dangerous urban ring encircling the core. Some thirty years ago, dining with the economist Colin Clark at an Oxford inn, I remarked that I didn't know what would become of American cities. Professor Clark replied, "*I* know; they will cease to exist." He went on to suggest that suburbs beyond a city's political boundaries would survive, surrounding a devastated and demolished and depopulated accumulation of ruins, the former urban area looking much as if it had been showered with gel bombs, after the fashion employed against Dresden at the end of the Second World War. Just that has been coming to pass with dismaying speed.

Permit me to turn to striking instances. I have known the city of Detroit ever since I was a small boy—that is, for more than half a century, during which the "arsenal of democracy" has been quite thoroughly proletarianized. When I was a college student, and wandered the streets of Detroit every week-end, the city had a population of two million; now it has one million, at best, nine-tenths of the white folk having fled away. The art institute, the public library, the Detroit historical museum, and Wayne State University survive, for the present, along with some tall stone churches, in the midst of an overwhelming decadence. On the campus of the University, telephone kiosks have been erected at short intervals. In these structures, the telephone is installed at ground level, so that persons wounded or violated conceivably may crawl to the kiosk and pull the phone off its hook; even if no words are spoken, a police patrol is supposed to investigate. Such is the intellectual life of Detroit in the year of our Lord one thousand nine hundred and ninety-two.

Tempting although it might be to offer to you vignettes of existence in proletarian Detroit, I have not world enough and time. Some who take up this volume may have read the very recent book by Zeʹev Chafets, *Devil's Night and Other True Tales of Detroit*; or have seen my own article on Detroit's Devil's Night, published in *Newsday* during 1986; or have seen the television program in 1990 which infuriated the foul-mouthed demagogue who is mayor of Detroit; or have been somewhat startled by a piece in *The New Yorker* revealing the miserable and depraved proletarian condition in which that mayor deliberately keeps the rising generation, virtual prisoners in a black ghetto, of which the immense sculptured black fist of Joe Louis is a sufficient symbol. In any event, I do not suppose that any person present today is quite uninformed concerning the degradation of what once was a booming and hopeful city, with some culture of its own.

What worked the ruin of Detroit, proletarianizing the place? The complex causes of this decay have been at work in most other American cities, too; but they were especially acute in Detroit. I venture to list some of the principal afflictions.

First, the automobile, which brought a great deal of money into the city, and much increased its population, nevertheless did mischief to what had been a rather pleasant and peaceful big town on a principal inland waterway. Ford and the other automobile manufacturers recruited labor wherever they could find it, especially from central and eastern Europe and from the Southern states; the masses of semi-skilled or unskilled men who came to the automobile factories were uprooted, cut off often from some traditional rural culture. With American thought, politics, and manners they never obtained much acquaintance, most of them. They became deculturized, rather than acculturated, and demagogues found them easy prey. So late as 1932, by the way, the most conservative "minority" or ethnic group in the city were the negroes of the Paradise Valley wards, stout Republicans who stood by Herbert Hoover. They were also very nearly the poorest bloc in Detroit.

Second, the triumphant automobile made it possible for the more affluent Detroiters to build houses in the suburbs, particularly in the Grosse Pointes, abandoning their mansions near the heart of the city—the beginning of what later would be called "white flight". With the coming of the New Deal, this outflow of ability and wealth from the old city was much accelerated by the Home Owners' Loan Corporation and later programs of low-interest loans, federally backed, available to people who were good credit-risks; thus increasingly the old city was drained of the classes, from rich merchants, manufacturers, professional people, and bankers to skilled craftsmen—leaving a vacuum to be filled successively by ethnic and economic groups of decreasing means and talent for leadership. The shifting of Henry Ford from a little house on Bagley Avenue, near the city's heart, to a great rustic estate near Dearborn, is sufficient illustration of this. The same flitting occurred in most other American cities, of course—New York and San Francisco being the chief, if partial, exceptions.

Third, military production in "the arsenal of democracy" during the Second World War attracted to Detroit great numbers of industrial workers, chiefly Appalachian whites ("hillbillies" to natives of Michigan) and Southern blacks; to the number of the latter were added, soon, more Southern blacks left technologically unemployed by the perfection of the mechanical cotton-picker and other alterations of the economic patterns of Dixie. People whose ancestors had been settled for several generations in place and in customs, south of the Mason-Dixon Line, found themselves bewildered, often resentful, and shaken in their beliefs and habits, up in Detroit of the barbecued ribs.

Fourth, soon, with the ending of war production, these people were short of work and moneys—and often in social or moral confusion. Divorce, and desertion of wives and children, became common in Detroit and other cities; out of this arose the successive programs for Aid to Dependent Children, federally financed, and well-intentioned. But out of this humanitarian scheme came the one-parent family, the welfare household on a huge scale, the street-corner gangs of bored and idle black youths who looked up to the brothel-keeper, the numbers racketeer, and presently the drug-pusher, those ingenious successful men. And presently the first generation of such dependent children fathered a second dependent generation; and then the second generation fathered a third—these true proletarians giving nothing to the commonwealth but their progeny—which progeny would emulate their fathers and mothers in turn.

Much of the old city grew shabby, and some of it dangerous, in consequence of the changes I suggested just now, yet still, in the 'Forties, I walked mean streets unarmed, at all hours. By the early 'Fifties, I adopted the precaution of wearing a sheath-knife when I walked those mean streets, Michigan

Avenue included, nocturnally; later, I carried a pistol. By the 'Sixties, it was well not to walk those streets except under necessity. Incidentally, it became necessary for the most part either to drive a car or to walk, public transportation dwindling: the city never had built a subway, which might have been done readily during the Depression years; and gradually the streetcar system withered on the vine. If one were earless, old, infirm, or timid—well, one could stay home, vegetating—though corner groceries were vanishing, too.

The city's decay having become physically obvious, why not knock much of it down and start all over again? So argued the enthusiasts for the "urban renewal" of the administration of President Johnson. What resulted were urban deserts and urban jungles, not renewal; great profits, though, were made by eminent developers and contractors. Here was a fifth cause of Detroit's collapse: the deliberate destruction of the neighborhoods of people of modest incomes, together with many small businesses. The newcomers to Detroit had only begun to settle into tolerable community, to find a church to attend, to obtain fairly regular employment, to come to understand the city—when down the street came the federal bulldozer. Where to flee now? Why, to newish, ugly, often dangerous public-housing projects—of which there were not enough to go round; or else to double up in some surviving low-rent district, which in consequence would become a slum.

Permit me to digress, so as to offer you a graphic example. Detroit's Corktown, a century ago crowded with newly-arrived Irishmen, is a district little more than a mile distant from the old handsome City Hall (itself demolished, wantonly, as part and parcel of that wondrous Urban Renewal). In the late 'Forties and early 'Fifties, Corktown was rather a pleasant quarter of well-built old houses, near Briggs Stadium and the boozing-kens that lined Michigan Avenue, Detroit's Skid Row. The people who lived in Corktown were a rather elderly generation of Irish—old women, chiefly; and also men employed in the printing trades at the nearby plants of the Detroit News and the Detroit Free Press, earners of high wages; and a great many Maltese, family people, Catholics, one of Detroit's many "minorities". An old Catholic church, Most Holy Trinity, was the center of Corktown's identity.

At the beginning of massive federal-financed "renewal", zealous civic planners noticed on their maps that apparently Corktown suffered from a high rate of robbery—and of disorderly conduct, too. Had they scrutinized their map more closely, they might have discerned that the crime—chiefly mugging of intoxicated men—occurred almost entirely along Michigan Avenue, the alcoholic paradise of the lowly in Detroit—and distinctly not in the residential streets of Corktown itself; it merely happened that Michigan Avenue formed the boundary of part of Corktown. But the city planners drew no such fine distinctions; according to the statistics available, crimes occurred in a quarter called Corktown. What to do? Why, renew Corktown by pulling it down and later building factories there. How does one get rid of rats? Why, by burning down the barn, of course. To get rid of old Corktown would be to get rid of crime. On this first grand project of urban renewal, the federal

bulldozers went to work, clearing away many interesting houses, clearing out a great many families long settled there; eventually they demolished the last place of public resort in Corktown,
a modest restaurant; they did spare a large second-hand bookshop lodged in an old house—but spared no other business.

I came to know Corktown well while this mischief was in
progress. Did crime cease? Why, there had been little or no
crime to abolish, in Corktown's residential streets. But now
crimes commenced in the rubble-strewn vacant lots, and the
surviving dwellings stood always in danger of invasion. Left
with no place to resort, gangs of boys—this was an all-white
quarter, by the way, unless one excepts a few American
redskins—began to fight among themselves and to snatch
women's purses. Presently the gangs took up profitable rackets,
and gang murders occurred. This was one means of obtaining
relief from boredom, in a district made grittily hideous—even
the trees having been cut down—by the civic improvers. I knew
one of the lads indicted for murder, an amiable young man with
some taste in architecture, a Maltese door-to-door salesman in
negro neighborhoods. He had been forced into a gang for survival; he hated what was being done to Corktown by the civic
renewers.

At that time I was courting a redheaded girl who was engaged in charitable work, unpaid, in connection with the parish
of Most Holy Trinity. She lived near the church in an apartment
house that had seen better days, and was then inhabited by
elderly Irishwomen who dared not go out of doors for dread of
having their purses snatched and themselves perhaps beaten. I

offered Mary the loan of a pistol of mine, that apartment house being a chancy place; but she declined the weapon, saying that if the boys should learn she possessed anything of the sort, they would break in to snatch the gun.

But I must not prolong this digression. My immediate point is that the very process of public policy, the misguided urban-renewal fiasco, did much to turn the remaining inhabitants of Corktown into proletarians. Now that most of Corktown's old population has been expelled, has died, or has fled, some gestures toward architectural restoration and even repopulation have been made in Corktown: gentrification may come to pass. That is pleasant news, but there linger in my memory the faces of certain honest ungenteel Corktowners who were reduced to poverty and indeed to a proletarian state by Lyndon Johnson's "war on poverty", more accurately described as war upon the poor.

When the tremendous Detroit riot of 1967 occurred, some of the rioters, as they threw bottles of gasoline to burn down the shops of Chaldeans (whom the blacks called Jews), cried mockingly, "Instant urban renewal!" They were not grateful for the ministrations of the Department of Housing and Urban Development. Governor George Romney, in his last public address before leaving Michigan to take a cabinet post in Washington, declared that the riot—almost an insurrection—had been caused by resentment against urban renewal and federal highway-building. Too true!

The Kerner Report (the author of which, you may recall, presently was sent to prison) declared that the fierce disorder had been a race riot, provoked by "white racism". (Presumably these white racists were the Chaldean and Jewish grocers and other small shopkeepers.) In fact, blacks and whites were nearly equal in numbers among the looters and arsonists; of those arrested on suspicion of sniping, all were white. The Great Riot was a proletarian stroke that Jack London would have relished, and not an organized black protest against "racism".

A sixth cause of the reduction of Detroit to a generally proletarian state has been the construction of gigantic freeways that destroyed established neighborhoods—as Governor Romney pointed out. It became nearly impossible to get from one old quarter of the city to another district, without an automobile and various detours. Thousands of decent homes, many family-owned, were swept away in the remorseless progress of the freeway system. The new freeways sometimes became impassible barriers against access to a church or to shops. Forgetting that cities are places for people to live, the highway builders thought of Detroit as a massive inconvenience to be got into and got out of so swiftly as possible. Presently violent crimes against people whose cars happened to stall on a freeway became almost commonplace.

The seventh, and most catastrophic, cause of the reduction of Detroit to a warren for unhappy proletarians was "white flight" on a tremendous scale, after the Great Proletarian Riot of 1967. The police had lost effective control of the sprawling city. Virtually all white families who could find money enough to buy a house and a lot in the outer suburbs scurried out of old Detroit. A single district, Indian Village, remains predominantly white in population—and now is turning somewhat scruffy. Most former Detroiters have retreated beyond Eight Mile Road, Detroit's northern political boundary. From the Detroit River to Eight Mile Road, Detroit's principal thoroughfare, Woodward Avenue, is almost all ghastly dereliction, except for public buildings and churches. A Detroiter remarked to me recently that it is no longer possible to buy a shirt in downtown Detroit. The great elegant department stores were abandoned or demolished years ago. The "black power" mayor speaks contemptuously of the "hostile suburbs"; he rules over a gigantic black ghetto.

Eighth among the causes of the forming of a classless society in Detroit—that is, a society consisting of a single class, the proletariat—has been the crumbling of the public-school system. Compulsory integration and busing greatly accelerated white flight beyond Eight Mile Road; compulsory congregation, where accomplished, turned out to be worse schooling for both blacks and whites, not better; the abandonment of neighborhood schools alienated both parents and pupils; the tax-basis for the school system dwindled. Schools became unpleasant and dangerous places where teachers' energies were spent mostly in maintaining some semblance of physical order. Public-opinion polls showed that both white and black parents strongly objected to massive busing—but their mere opinion did them no good, decisions being in the hands of omniscient judges, those infallible educators.

The causes of Detroit's social sickness are complex indeed: it is almost as if some evil genius had plotted intricately the undoing of a great metropolis. Woe unto the city!

Yet let me name a ninth major cause of Detroit's undoing: the frightful curse of the narcotics traffic and of widespread narcotics addiction. Possibly the city of Washington is worse off in this malady than is Detroit—but I doubt it. (True, Washington during the past several years has deprived Detroit of its former proud distinction as "Murder Capital of the United States".)

In 1990-91, a scientific and confidential study prepared for General Motors Corporation, Detroit, revealed that thirty-one per cent of General Motors' "blue-collar" employees in the city were seriously impaired by, or dangerously under the influence of, narcotics or alcohol—while at work. This was true also of twenty per cent of the corporation's "white collar" employees. An automobile worker may spend six hundred dollars a week on cocaine, marijuana, and distilled liquor—and yet stay employed.

It is unnecessary for me to describe here the fatal consequences, personal and social, of addiction to narcotics. The proletarian seeks hallucinatory drugs or the stupefaction of too much strong drink, because he retains no end or object in life. Narcotics addiction will convert people of good prospects into empty proletarians. When nearly a third of a city's industrial laborers—remember, General Motors is very much the biggest employer in Detroit, and the plague of drugs and drink appears quite the same in Detroit's other factories—are so addicted, how long can an urban society continue to cohere?

And yet life goes on amidst the ruin, the hideousness, the depravity, the dangers of Detroit. What is it that still keeps Detroit half alive, and functioning after a fashion?

Why, it is the Christian churches. (Synagogues are found only in the Detroit suburbs now.) Those churches staunchly resist proletarian despair. Along Woodward Avenue, the huge Gothic or Romanesque churches of a century gone have black congregations now, for the most part. It is said that within the boundaries of Detroit stand some two thousand, five hundred church buildings, from cathedrals to scruffy store-front bethels. Some of the black temples and tabernacles maybe remarkably eccentric varieties of the religious experience; but even the wildest of them offers some sort of hope and consolation beyond the decayed City of This Earth; even the smallest of these churches or quasi-churches is a surviving anchor of community. Fervent Christian profession still breathes into wrecked Detroit some life of the spirit.

The influence of the black preachers is undiminished. In 1973, at the climax of a bitter political contest over abortion, I gave the chief address to Michigan's principal pro-life organization, meeting in a big hall on the riverfront. Behind me on the platform, as moral and physical reinforcement, sat three or four ebony monoliths, huge black Baptist preachers. A white Protestant clergyman was there, too, and one public man—Mr. William Ryan, then Speaker of the Michigan House of Representatives. (No Catholic priests ventured to take a visible stand on the platform.) The presence of those ebony ministers signified that we pro-life partisans had won the day in Detroit. For when the statewide initiative for abortion-on-demand appeared on the ballot in November, the pro-abortion people were defeated nearly two to one. Every black ward in Detroit voted against abortion by large majorities; in one ward, the ration of ballots was sixteen to one against abortion. The proletarian, Marxist model, has cast off the fetters of religion. Clearly there remains in Detroit one strong influence that impedes total proletarianization.

I have offered you the spectacle of Detroit in the year 1992, ladies and gentlemen, because probably Detroit illustrates better than any other city the concurrent and converging causes of the reduction of a city's population to a miserable proletarian state. Some people tell me that Newark is worse stricken than Detroit; Washington might be worse off, were it not for the restraining power, and the resources, of the federal government. The cities of America have become what Jefferson called them about the end of the eighteenth century, the social equivalents of sores upon a human body.

This tendency of the American people toward a proletarian condition—often a drift more subtle than the processes I have mentioned today—ought to be the urgent concern of all genuine conservatives. The devising of any remedies or palliatives will require high power of imagination. Something is being done already—for instance, the federal programs for encouraging "minority" businesses. A number of economic innovations and reforms, to such ends, have been put forward in recent years by the Heritage Foundation.

The main work of redemption and reconstruction, however, must come from conservatively-minded people who at present suffer under the dreary domination of demagogues and charlatans—self-styled "leaders" leading their dupes only to the proletarian condition. I have known some such restorers of responsibility and community who have brightened the corner where they were—among them, Elmo and Mattie Coney, of Indianapolis. I take it that some residents of Washington, Mayor Barry having been unseated, are taking arms against a sea of troubles. Courageous volunteers, not "welfare professionals", may yet preserve their neighbors from being converted into proletarians.

The recovery of a schooling that has wisdom and virtue for its ends, and which is moved by the moral imagination, could teach the rising generation to look for something in life beyond violent sensation; and could incline them toward a society of the common good, rather than a defiance of all authority. A voucher-system for choice of schools might achieve much good within a few years. I think of an occasion on which some New York newspaper reporters visited a Catholic school in the South Bronx. Accustomed to the barbarous manners and sneering attitudes of New York's public schools, these journalists were astounded when a little black girl, appointed their hostess, came gently up to them, introduced herself, kissed them all round, and intelligently led them from classroom to classroom. The public schools with which they had been familiar were turning out young proletarians, with few exceptions; the Catholic grade-school in the South Bronx—it was the only undamaged structure left standing for a substantial distance round about—was turning out the heirs of a cultural patrimony, obstacles notwithstanding.

No effort at all is required to become a proletarian: one needs merely to submit to the dehumanizing and deculturizing currents of the hour, and worship the idols of the crowd. Much effort is required to conserve the legacy of order, freedom, and justice, of learning and art and imagination, that ought to be ours. Some malign spirits, in the name of equality, would have us all be proletarians together: the doctrine of equal misery. The conservative impulse, *au contraire*, is to rescue so many men and women as possible from that submerged lot in life, without object and without cheer, which is the proletarian condition.

XVIII

Popular Government and Intemperate Minds

At the beginning of the twentieth century, few states in the world could be called democratic. Yet much personal and local freedom existed, under the reign of law.

Near the close of the twentieth century, nearly every political regime, throughout the world, professes to be democratic. Yet in many lands personal and local freedom have been extirpated.

On the face of things, it appears that the triumph of democracy, far from preserving or enlarging freedom, has brought to power a host of squalid oligarchs.

How is it that we find ourselves in this bent world of *anno Domini* 1992—all the evangels of Progress having been refuted by circumstances? T. S. Eliot, in 1939, on the eve of the Second World War, stated better than I can today the hard truth about our political condition.

"For a long enough time we have believed in nothing but the values arising in a mechanized, commercialized, urbanized way of life: it would be as well for us to face the permanent conditions upon which God allows us to live upon this planet," Eliot wrote in his little book *The Idea of a Christian Society*. He went on to decry the Benthamism and secularism which continue to oppress us half a century later:

> Unless we can find a pattern in which all problems of life can have their place, we are only likely to go on complicating chaos. So long, for instance, as we consider finance, industry, trade, agriculture merely as competing interests to be reconciled from time to time as best they may, so long as we consider 'education a good in itself of which everyone has a right to the utmost, without an ideal of the good life for society or for the individual, we shall move from one uneasy compromise to another. To the quick and simple organization of society for ends which, being only material and worldly, must be as ephemeral as worldly success, there is only one alternative. As political philosophy derives its sanction from ethics, and ethics from the truth of religion, it is only by returning to the eternal source of truth that we can hope for any social organization which will not, to its ultimate destruction, ignore some essential aspect of reality.

Amen to that. "Democracy", as an abstraction, cannot be substituted satisfactorily for the authority of God. The modern mind has fallen into the heresy of democracy—that is, the ruinous error of *vox populi vox dei*, that an abstract People are divine, and that truth issues from the ballot-box. When Tocqueville travelled through the United States, society was sufficiently democratic in America—more so, really, than today—but Americans had not yet succumbed to the heresy that the people's will is the divine will. Nor have all Americans, even today, embraced that error; but general resistance to Rousseau's notion of democracy has been weakened, the old "territorial democracy" of the early United States is much decayed, and more and more is rendered unto Caesar: that is, to a Caesar now styled Plebiscitary Democracy.

. . .

Some years ago I lectured at the University of Oklahoma on the prescribed subject, "What Is the Best Form of Government for the Happiness of Mankind?" This annual lectureship, always on the same subject, was endowed; and in every previous year, the chosen lecturer had declared that Democracy was the best form of government for the happiness of mankind; the previous lecturers doubtless assumed that such a profession of faith was expected of them, as loyal subjects of King Demos, the most praise-hungry of sovereigns.

But for my part, I heretically denied that dogma of ideological Democratism, out in Oklahoma, asserting to the contrary that there exists no single best form of government for the happiness of all mankind. The most suitable form of government necessarily depends upon the historic experience, the customs, the beliefs, the state of culture, the ancient laws, and the material circumstances of a people, and all these things vary from land to land and age to age. Monarchy may defend the highest possible degree of order, justice, and freedom for a people—as, despite shortcomings, the Abyssinian monarchy did in Ethiopia, until the Marxist revolution there. Aristocracy, under other circumstances, may be found most advantageous for the general welfare. The Swiss form of democracy may work very well in twentieth century Switzerland; yet it does not follow that the Swiss pattern, imposed abruptly upon Brazil, say, would function at all.

Nor would the American pattern of politics, developed through an intricate process extending over several centuries, be readily transplanted to Uganda or Indonesia. Attempts by Latin American states to emulate the North American democratic pattern have failed. The simple formula of "one man, one vote" will not cure all the ills to which flesh is heir.

For democracy is neither a political philosophy nor a plan of political organization: rather, it is a social condition that may have political consequences. Two centuries ago, not one of the framers of the Constitution of the United States employed "democracy" as a term of approbation. To the Framers, "democracy" signified the rule of the crowd; and of such politics, they had beheld sufficient in Shays' Rebellion. The Constitution of 1787 established not a democracy, but a federal republic.

A measure of democracy did develop in America with the electoral triumphs of Jefferson and Jackson. Yet that was what Orestes Brownson called "territorial democracy", rooted in township or county, hostile to political centralization, suspicious of executive power, bound up with the rural interest. It did not resemble in the least the "plebiscitary democracies" and "people's democracies" of our era.

The American democracy, Tocqueville perceived, was distinguished from the unstable and often bloody democracies of Europe, moreover, by the restraining power of Christian mores upon American politics. "While the law allows the American people to do everything," Tocqueville wrote, "there are things which religion prevents them from imagining and forbids them to dare. . . . For the Americans the ideas of Christianity and liberty are so completely mingled that it is almost impossible to get them to conceive of the one without the other; it is not a question with them of sterile beliefs bequeathed by the past and vegetating rather than living in the depths of the soul."

Throughout the nineteenth century, then, the American democracy did not try to do duty for religion or to assert claims to total loyalty: it was no ideology, in short; it did not culminate in what Tocqueville called "democratic despotism." The general understanding of the word "democracy" among Americans was sufficiently expressed by this definition in the ten-volume Century Dictionary of 1904: "Political and social equality in general; a state of society in which no hereditary differences of rank or privilege are recognized; opposed to aristocracy." The Dictionary's editors quoted a couplet of John Greenleaf Whittier's poem "The Grave by the Lake" as illustrative of this meaning:

> *Rank nor name nor pomp has he*
> *In the grave's democracy.*

This analogy to the grave, nevertheless, was somewhat ominous; one thinks of Bulwer Lytton's exclamation, in 1859, "Democracy is like the grave—it perpetually cries, 'give, give,' and, like the grave, it never returns what is has once taken. . . . Do not surrender to democracy that which is not yet ripe for the grave."

Even the American democracy was voracious. Only two decades after publication of the 1904 edition of the *Century Dictionary*, the ideas of John Dewey and his educationist colleagues were at work upon American minds; by the 1930s, those Instrumentalist concepts were triumphing in America's public schools. To Christian doctrine the Deweyites were systematically hostile, eager to separate the political order from religious dogmata. "Democracy" was a word exalted by Dewey's school—but not the territorial democracy of yesteryear, nor the democracy interwoven with Christian mores that Tocqueville had praised. To Dewey and his friends, "democracy" signified equality of condition, a social and intellectual tableland, closely resembling Tocqueville's "democratic despotism". The Dewey pragmatists, holding the past in contempt, looked forward to a universal democracy on utilitarian lines.

This belligerent ideological democracy is sufficiently idealized in Carl Sandburg's poem "The People, Yes!" Instrumentalist educationists proceeded to propagandize for such "democratic values" through the apparatus of the public schools. (It is worth noting that Sandburg became the poet laureate of twentieth-century democracy in the new school textbooks, with Walt Whitman as his nineteenth-century forerunner.) From textbooks in social studies (a discipline which had commenced to supplant history), the phrases "representative government", "constitutional government", "American republic", and the like began to vanish: in their place appeared the word "democracy"—monolithic democracy, apparently, with no distinctions as to different types of democracy. Democracy was good, virtually flawless; all other forms of government, past or present, were bad. Thus the study of politics for the young was reduced to cant phrases and genuflections before King Demos.

I am not suggesting that the influence of the Deweyites alone changed the American understanding of "democracy". An ideological signification of the word is sufficiently evident in Woodrow Wilson's declaration that American troops would "make the world safe for democracy" in 1917. But the educationists' systematic propaganda for an absolute and abstract democracy, purged of religious notions, gradually did much to break down the old constitutional and moral restraints upon the momentary popular will. In the Supreme Court of the United States, during the Warren years, the Benthamite doctrine of "one man, one vote" triumphed because public schooling had opened the way for submission to judicial intervention in the name of an absolute democracy. Courts' interference in the apportionment of legislative districts, federal or state, ever since then has damaged practical representative democracy, an ideological abstraction preferred over the practical functioning of representative government.

By subtle processes, the idea of democracy, once intimately associated with concepts of personal liberty, and with Christian teachings, was transformed into an ideology or quasi-ideology, even in the United States. This word *democracy* tends to signify nowadays something rather different from the institutions of the democratic Republic of the United States, as those political institutions used to be described in high-school courses about American government when I was a student. "Democracy" now means to American liberals—and to a good many folk who might be surprised to be called liberals—substantially the notion of one man, one vote, as an inviolable principle; a political order totally secularized, disavowing any transcendent authority over society, a presumption that one person's judgement is as good as any other person's (aside, perhaps, from the accumulation of university degrees); a hankering after perfect equality of condition, although that may not be attainable immediately; and a confidence that the American pattern of democratic institutions could and should be imposed upon all the world.

Such is the ideology of Democratism: examination of social-studies textbooks and manuals in history, of the sort exhibited in the famous "textbook trial" in a federal court at Mobile early in 1987, should sufficiently confirm this chapter's hasty analysis of what the word *democracy* implies two centuries after the Constitutional Convention. All ideologies, that of Democratism included, lead their dupes into intemperance—and presently into servitude. What the master-ideologue seeks is power, not freedom. In the words of Edmund Burke, "Men of intemperate mind never can be free; their passions forge their fetters." Ideology is political fanaticism and unreality. Far from preserving our freedom, the ideology of Democratism already has weakened the American constitutional structure, and will do greater mischief to the cause of ordered freedom unless we Americans recognize that peril and renew the old restraints upon the levelling impulse.

. . .

One hears on every hand such phrases as "That's the democratic way of doing things," or "Elitism can't be tolerated in our democracy." But can't aside, what advantages do certain factions or interests in the American Republic find in the existing American democracy?

For no inconsiderable number of our citizens, democracy seems to mean opportunity to indulge one's appetites, unrestrained. Isn't one man's preference as good as another man's? (Plato discerned that the fundamental impulse within democracies was for every man to do as he might arbitrarily choose to do, without regard for others.) Having cast aside those Christian mores of which Tocqueville wrote, they find in the ideology of Democratism warrant for every excess. If one man's values, or absence of values, is as good as any other man's—well,

why not gratify every craving? When Democratism of this description has corrupted society for a few decades, at most—why,
it is terminated by force and a master, out of the human instinct
for the preservation of some sort of tolerable society.

For another faction of Americans—although of course
these categories overlap—the ideology of Democratism serves
to justify grandiose designs for the alleged attainment of "eq-
uity" through "entitlements"—that is, employment of the political power to tax, for the especial benefit of particular interests
or classes. The tremendous "Welfare Lobby" immediately
comes to mind when such concerns are discussed; champions
of the Welfare Lobby went so far as to approve in print the attempt to murder President Reagan—on the ground that the
undemocratic Mr. Reagan had endeavored to reduce expen-
ditures approved by them, and so richly deserved to die. But
many other organizations besides the Welfare Lobby are of
the opinion that Democracy amounts to the opportunity to
plunder other people—that is, the general public; for hasn't
the American democracy a limitless supply of money and
goods, the products of exploitation, the rightful spoil of enterprising egalitarians? Doesn't everybody deserve more of
everything, and isn't the apparatus of taxation well designed
to secure that more for tolerably-organized factions? The
National Education Association, with the most powerful of
lobbies at Washington, finds itself especially deserving of public benefaction, and the NEA never ceases to cry up the merits
of democracy. The postal workers' unions, and the Concrete
Lobby, and all manner of energetic—that is, energetic at

lobbying—groups and factions demand their democratic share. A good many years may elapse before the essential functions of government are so reduced by these democratic exactions that something desperate must be done.

In the realm of education, the ideology of Democratism leads before long to general lowering of the standards of scholarship. For aren't all of us born equal? It's elitism, isn't it, to reward some young persons merely because they study harder or are unfairly endowed with better brains? Or because their parents have reared them intelligently? Anyone familiar with the requirements of American or British or European universities four decades ago, and the reduced standards prevalent at the same institutions in 1992, knows the consequences of the academic democratism that won its victories in the 'Sixties and 'Seventies. The decay of primary and secondary schooling, which commenced earlier, is yet more striking. All this abandoning of the works of the mind has been justified by the argument that "everybody deserves an equal chance" and the theory that "after all, it's socialization that's important in schools." Scientific and technical skills already have suffered gravely from this aspect of Democratism; but what matters more, the intellectual and moral education of the natural leaders in society is so dismayingly neglected that one must ask where competent servants of the democracy are to be discovered, half a century from now.

These phenomena of Democratism have been tripled and quadrupled in their corrosive power by the ascendancy of television, films, radio, and other means of swift communication that can form public opinion almost worldwide with a few hours. The demands of doctrinaire egalitarians are easily publicized by the mass media, and awake ready sympathies; while the case for restraint or for prudent alternatives to proposed egalitarian measures are less attractive to the people who profit by the mass media, and are less easily apprehended by the viewing or listening multitudes. One marvels, indeed, that the prejudices and habits and inherited opinions of a good many Americans remain strong enough, even today, to resist the tearful or mocking egalitarianism of the mass media.

The more dramatic and perilous consequences of the ideology of Democratism, nevertheless, occur in the conduct of foreign affairs, rather than in the internal concerns of this Republic. On one occasion, Democratism enfeebles the diplomacy of the United States, subordinating practicality to sentiments; on another occasion, Democratism propels America into rashness abroad, all the way to large-scale war. We suffer from the notion that Democracy must be instituted throughout all the world, at whatever cost; and that every democracy must be cloned or reconstructed in the image of the perfect American Democracy.

I have been arguing somewhat hurriedly that an ideology called Democratism afflicts often both domestic and foreign policies of the United States. Servitude to ideology—that is, to irrational political dogmatism—leads to intemperance of thought, discourse, and action. Russia and her satellite states now are disillusioned with Marxist ideology, but many Americans cling fondly to their own Democratist ideology.

Democratism in action, far from preserving American freedom, may reduce American liberties in more ways than one.

. . .

If the twentieth-century god called Demos has feet of clay,
whatever shall we do? Away back in 1918 we were promised that
glorious democracy would prevail universally; but nothing of
the sort has come to pass. The word "democracy" is everywhere
venerated and employed; but the reality of that concept, or what
we expected to become the reality, the brotherhood of man and
the federation of the world, is not to be found, seven decades
later.

Yet we need not despair. The first thing for us Americans
to do is to recall the admonition of Eliot that "It is only by re-
turning to the eternal source of truth that we can hope for any
social organization which will not, to its ultimate destruction,
ignore some essential aspect of reality." We must remind ourselves that politics is no more than the art of the possible; it is
no source of eternal truth. The ideology of Democratism, like
all other ideologies, is a pseudo-religion, "immanentizing the
eschaton", as Eric Voegelin wrote of political heresies. The cure
for ideology is a recovery of religious understanding of the
human condition.

Then let us not worship an abstraction called Democracy.
Let us come to understand that democracy is a condition of
society, not a moral ideal. The democratic political forms are
one means for attaining a tolerable civil social order; but those

forms are not the only means for enabling human beings to live together in peace. In some ages and some circumstances, democratic forms may be suitable means for social organization; in other times and conditions, democratic forms may not function at all.

It must be emphasized that the ends of a tolerable human community are order, and justice, and freedom. Democracy, per se, is not the end or object of human existence; it is a possible means, rather, toward those three real ends of the civil social order. Great mischief may result from confounding means with ends. So let us set our faces against those American neoterists who would have us establish a civil religion worshipping the great god Demos. The prevalence of Christian mores among the American people was the cause of the success of the American democracy, Tocqueville discerned nearly a century and a half ago. Only the renewal of those religious norms can reinvigorate the American Republic. Those who prostrate themselves before the graven image of the divine Demos cannot, in their heart of hearts, have faith in their own creation. Render unto Caesar only the things that are Caesar's.

A great many Americans have not become ideologues who mistake an abstraction called Democracy for the complex living continuity of human existence. A good number of Americans still are aware that there exists an authority higher than the dominant political regime of the hour. Not a few Americans remain aware that it is they who must guard their nation's order and justice and freedom, vigilantly, that Democracy is not a mystical presence competent to supplant Providence.

I venture to suggest to such Americans that we ought to discourse more of constitutional government, the rule of law, prescriptive rights and duties, and other long-established benefits of the civil social order. We might benefit substantially from widespread intelligent discussion of the distinction between a legislative representative and a legislative delegate; for our legislatures decay. But we ought to discourse less, in a vague ideological fashion, about some fancied future perfection of society: some sprawling "global village", perfectly democratic, in which everybody will be precisely like everybody else. In such a utopia no freedom at all would survive; and humanity would expire of boredom and license.

In the twenty-first century, doubtless the word "Democracy!", shouted as an ideological slogan, will continue to echo through the world; but anything much resembling genuine democracy as a political form will be difficult then to discover, perhaps even in Europe. In one form or another, nevertheless, the American democracy probably will endure. Whether it survives as a polity of friendship, or as a pseudo-religion masking decadent appetites, must depend upon the moral convictions of the American people.

"Politics is the preoccupation of the quarter-educated," George Gissing wrote near the end of the nineteenth century. To that aphorism we may add, near the end of the twentieth century, "Democracy is the preoccupation of the half-aware." What our age desperately requires is not more mediocrity, but more elevation of spirit, awareness of the eternal source of truth. That failing, order and freedom and justice fall into ruin.

It was said of the Romans that they created in northern Europe a wilderness, and called it peace. Let it not be said of the Americans that they created in the world one enormous boredom, and called it democracy. Even though American aircraft have saturation-bombed Mesopotamia, the cradle of civilization, it is not yet too late to return from political hubris to political prudence.

May the Rising Generation Redeem the Time?

Spiritually and politically, the twentieth century has been a time of decadence. Yet as this century draws to its close, we may remind ourselves that ages of decadence sometimes have been followed by ages of renewal.

What can *you* do, young men and women of the rising generation of the 1990's, to raise up the human condition to a level less unworthy of what Pico della Mirandola called "the dignity of man"? Why, begin by brightening the corner where you are; by improving one human unit, yourself, and by helping your neighbor.

You will not need to be rich or famous to take your part in redeeming the time: what you require for that task is moral imagination joined to right reason. It is not by wealth or fame that you will be rewarded, probably, but by eternal moments: those occurrences in one's existence during which, as T. S. Eliot puts it, time and the timeless intersect. In such moments, you may discover the answer to that immemorial question that now and again enters the head of any reflective person, "What *is* all this? What is this world that surrounds us, and why are we here?"

You and I are put into this present realm of being as into a testing-ground—into an arena, if you will. As Stefan Andres expresses it, "We are God's Utopia". You and I are moral beings meant to accomplish something good, in a small way or a big, in this temporal world.

The Roman Stoics taught that some things in life are good, and some are evil; yet that the great majority of life's happenings are neither good nor evil, but in different merely. Wealth is a thing indifferent, and so is poverty; fame is a thing indifferent, and so is obscurity. Shrug your shoulders at things indifferent; set your face against things evil; and by doing God's will, said the Stoics, find that peace which passeth all understanding.

Such counsels, classical and Christian, will not guarantee your winning any of the glittering prizes of modern society: for those too are among the things indifferent, and some of them among the things evil. Why should we be guided by such counsels? Because they are derived from true authority, the common sense and ancient assent of mankind, what G. K. Chesterton called "the democracy of the dead". As John Henry Newman wrote in 1846 concerning Authority, "Conscience is an authority; the Bible is an Authority; such is the Church; such is antiquity; such are the words of the wise; such are hereditary lessons; such are ethical truths; such are historical memories; such are legal saws and state maxims; such are proverbs; such are sentiments, presages, and prepossessions." Believe what wise men and women, over the ages, have believed in faith and morals, and you will find a firm footing on which to stand while the winds of doctrine howl about you.

What *is* all this—this confused world of glittering material things and of appalling personal and social decay? I have found it to be a real world, its vices notwithstanding: a real world in which one still may develop and exercise one's potential virtues of courage, prudence, temperance, and justice; one's faith, hope, and charity. You will take your tumbles in this world, Lord knows; but also you may enjoy your triumphs. It is a world in which so much needs to be done that nobody ought to be bored.

All this creation about us is the garden that we erring humans were appointed to tend. Plant some flowers or trees in it, if you can, and pull some weeds. Do not fancy that a sorry policy of Looking Out for Number One will lead you to Heaven's gate. Do not fail to remind yourselves that consciousness is a perpetual adventure. Do not ignore the wisdom of the ages, the democracy of the dead.

Those of us who aspire to conserve our inherited order and justice and freedom, our patrimony of wisdom and beauty and lovingkindness, have a hard row to hoe nowadays—that I confess. Many voices have declared that life is not worth living. A multitude of writers and publicists and members of the class of persons commonly styled "intellectuals" gloomily inform us that we human beings are no better than naked apes, and that consciousness itself is an illusion. Such persons insist that life has no purpose but sensual gratification; that the brief span of one's physical existence is the be-all and end-all. Such twentieth-century sophists have created in the murky caves of the intellect an Underworld; and they endeavor to convince us all that there exists no sun—that the world of wonder and of hope exists nowhere, and never did exist. Plato knew just such sophists in his day.

These doctrines of despair, you of the rising generation must confront and refute. Redeem the time, redeem the dream—in ways mundane as well as ways spiritual. Let me turn to the art of worldly wisdom.

What of practical politics? How does one who hopes to conduct a conservative defense of the Permanent Things contrive to forge ahead, politically, in the sprawling American democracy?

Why, ordinarily it is simple to make one's way in the American political structure. American political parties could not function without volunteers. Offer your help, and you will find it gladly accepted, such as you being needed urgently, you may find, indeed, that a number of your fellow-volunteers are rather peculiar people, almost Outcasts of Poker Flat, but welcome in a local political organization (if not welcome in a great many other circles) because, whatever their peculiarities, they are willing to work for a common cause.

If you become an intelligent and adept volunteer, you will be made much of by the party leaders and faithful, and will be advanced in your responsibilities. You may be asked to become a delegate, whether elected or appointed. If chosen delegate, arrive early at caucus or convention. When the meeting commences, endeavor to sit at the chairman's right hand; then others may take you for his right-hand man. There flourish many little arts by which one may gain ascendancy over the minds of one's political colleagues. But the great necessity is to have acquired previously a fund of knowledge and some mastery of rhetoric—and honest principles. That is why I sometimes advise undergraduates not to expend their time in street demonstrations, but instead to *study*. If Karl Marx, instead of reading books within the British Museum, had spent his days parading round and round the exterior of that building, a placard "Down with the bourgeoise!" tacked to a sandwich-board over his shoulders—why, had he been so foolish, the world would be better off today.

Practical politics aside, if you should resolve to take a vigorous part in restoring the American Republic, choose your vocation accordingly, so that the work by which you gain your livelihood, and the work by which you help to redeem the time, may coincide. Take to the law, if you can endure the boredom of our law schools nowadays. Or take to serious journalism—or, for broader and more immediate influence, to television and radio. You may accomplish some reform of the American mind through book-publishing. Supposing you possess fortitude sufficient to fight your way through our graduate schools, aspire after a college professorship that might enable you to counteract the professors of the Academy of Lagado. Or take to pedagogy, if you can surmount the dull obstacles to certification as a teacher. If you feel a religious calling—why, in no way might you accomplish more to restore meaning to lives in the twenty-first century. The best way to rear up a new generation of friends of the Permanent Things is to beget children, and read to them o' evenings, and teach them what is worthy of praise: the wise parent is the conservator of ancient truths. As Edmund Burke put it, "We learn to love the little platoon we belong to in society." The institution most essential to conserve is the family.

If we aspire to redeem this age of ours, so far gone in decadence—well, we have no time to lose before commencing our endeavors. Fixed to the walls of the entrance-hall of my Italianate house, called Piety Hill, are masks of the archaic god Cronos, in his role of Time the Devourer; his half-leonine, half-human countenance bares his fangs, so dreaded by the old Greeks. Those grim masks serve to remind me daily that the night cometh when no man shall work.

Yet Time is not a devourer only. With proper use of the life-span allotted to us, we may do much to redeem modernity from vices, terrors, and catastrophic errors. With Demosthenes, I beg you of the rising generation to take thought. This point was well put by Orestes Brownson, in 1843, speaking at Dartmouth College on "The Scholar's Mission".

"Ask not what your age wants," Brownson said, "but what it needs; not what it will reward, but what, without which, it cannot be saved; and that go and do; and find your reward in the consciousness of having done your duty, and above all in the reflection that you have been accounted to suffer somewhat for mankind."

Many among the rising generation have not known a tranquil and confident America. They scarcely can imagine a time, not many decades past, when it was the diversion of families or couples to stroll in an evening in New York's Central Park or Detroit's Belle Isle Park or Los Angeles' MacArthur Park. Families and couples do not venture to stroll there now. Most of the rising generation have experienced little of continuity and stability; the expectation of distressing change has been greater far. Yet many of them sense that much remains to conserve, and that much ought to be restored.

In the later 'Sixties, some of the rising generation fancied it amusing to pull down what earlier generations patiently had built up. In the early 'Nineties, I trust, many of the rising generation will find it satisfying to restore and redeem their patrimony—so to save the world from suicide.

Index

307